The Worldwide Legacy of FRANK BUCHMAN

Compiled by Archie Mackenzie
& David Young

CAUX BOOKS
INITIATIVES OF CHANGE

First published 2008
by Caux Books
rue de Panorama, 1824, Caux, Switzerland; www.caux.ch
and Initiatives of Change
24 Greencoat Place, London SW1P 1RD; www.iofc.org

ISBN 2-88037-517-7
978-2-88037-517-1

Cover design by John Munro
Typesetting and text design in 10.5 Sabon by Blair Cummock

Printed by Biddles, King's Lynn, Norfolk

Contents

Foreword

The year 2008 is a significant one for Moral Re-Armament, now Initiatives of Change. It marks the 100th anniversary of Frank Buchman's formative spiritual experience at Keswick in northern England; the 70th anniversary of the public launching of MRA in London and the holding of an important gathering at Visby in Sweden which marked a changing of gears in Buchman's work prior to the outbreak of World War 2; and the 40th anniversary of the opening of the Asian conference centre at Panchgani in western India.

Each of these events will doubtless be suitably remembered by different groups of people: but 2008 also seems an appropriate moment to attempt a general re-appraisal of Buchman's life and work as seen from the perspective of the 21st century.

Hopefully this will be of interest to the younger generation who are now assuming positions of responsibility in Initiatives of Change but who never knew Frank Buchman. And hopefully also, it will recall to some of the older generation adventurous chapters in their earlier lives. What follows, however, is written no less for those who may be learning about Frank Buchman for the first time.

Archie Mackenzie & David Young

Introduction

by Archie Mackenzie

NOT long ago someone in his twenties asked me: 'Why is Frank Buchman important?' It was not a sceptical question. Yet it betrayed a puzzlement that was not wholly surprising given that Frank Buchman died nearly fifty years ago and would be 130 if he were still alive today.

I then recalled that by a curious coincidence I had been asked exactly the same question 50 years ago in London when I was working in the British Foreign Office. I also recalled that I had given a three-part answer and I now suddenly realised that I could – and would – give the same answer today.

I said: first, because he diagnosed the real roots of the world's current problems years before most other public figures; second, because he faced the consequences in his own life; and third, because he built up a world network of people just as committed as he was to living out an answer as he saw it.

What was he really like?

This can be analysed in detail. But my young interlocutor might have interrupted to say: 'But what was Frank Buchman really like?' In this case I would have replied on the following lines.

Frank Buchman's chief characteristic was his spontaneity and warmth. He loved company and he regularly moved around with a team of people. He was no lone-ranger: nor a *monstre sacré*, as the French call celebrities who hog the limelight. There was a sparkle about him. It came from the way he lived. There was no bluffing.

He would laugh uproariously when something amused him: but he would also keep silent for long periods as if listening to music of which other people were scarcely aware. He was skilled at reading people, discerning motives. He told one politician: 'Mr Prime Minister, you need to learn to read people like a page of print.' Later events proved that Buchman's advice was well-grounded when the PM was ousted by a military coup.

He had an enormous range of friendships – from royalty to radicals, young and old, people of all colours. And he kept his friendships despite the attempts of ill-wishers to dislodge them.

He showed himself extremely sensitive to the well-being and needs of his co-workers. He loved to include them at the best seats at notable public events. Yet he was never lavish with money. His traditional birthday gift, both to women and men, was one quality handkerchief, and he used to buy them by the score, often in Switzerland.

He could be a stern boss, because of his high standards, but he was also a forgiving one. One of his assistants said: 'Life around here is like a mixture of Christmas morning and Judgement Day.'

He was a man of faith who deeply believed that God would guide people who listened and were ready to obey. But his faith was not exclusive or combative. He would have endorsed what Mother Teresa said: 'What we are all trying to do by our work is to come closer to God. We become a better Hindu, a better Muslim, a better Catholic, a better whatever we are, and by being better we become closer and closer to Him. What approach would I use? For me naturally it would be a Catholic. For you it might be Hindu, for someone else Buddhist, according to one's conscience. But I cannot prevent myself from giving what I have.'

If he were still alive today, Buchman would doubtless have moved with the times; but he would not have been shaken from his own roots.

One could dissect Buchman's character, hunting for flaws. But it would seem more profitable to look at him objectively to find things we might learn for the difficulties we face today.

The fact is that most of us who are associated with Initiatives of Change today would not be where we are but for Frank Buchman.

* * * * *

THE world of the 1950s, when I was first questioned about Frank Buchman, was, of course, different in countless ways from our 21st century world with its screaming headlines on Darfur, suicide bombings, Guantanamo Bay, etc. Yet a moment's reflection reveals that at rock-bottom there are many similarities and Frank Buchman specialised in dealing with rock-bottom problems. He used to say, 'Never forget: you can plan a new world on paper, but you have got to build it out of people.' He realised that in the 20th century perhaps more than ever before experts of all kinds were concocting paper plans for reforming society: global plans like the United Nations;

regional plans like the European Union; and national governmental plans to deal with economic and social problems in every independent country. But the one common factor of all these plans was the human factor. They all depended on the response of people and their motives, individually and in groups. And yet all too often the human factor was the forgotten factor.

Frank Buchman did not discover the human factor, but he zeroed in on it. He did not suggest that the human factor was the only issue that had to be dealt with. For example, he was present in San Francisco in 1945 throughout the conference which drafted the United Nations Charter and followed its proceedings with interest. But neither then, nor later when I was working at the UN in New York, do I ever recall him dismissing or deriding the organisation as a mere paper plan.

He was always interested in my accounts of the latest developments in the organisation – in the ups and downs in the Security Council, in the endless speechifying in the General Assembly, and in the delays and compromises in the decision-making process. But I could see that he maintained considerable doubts about the organisation's prospects unless there was a much more conscious recognition of the complications caused throughout the edifice by the human factor and a much more committed effort by member countries, even at the cost of national pride, to deal with that factor. And history has proved him right.

But Buchman's interest did not stop there. He had committed himself totally at the age of 30, from the time of his decisive spiritual experience, to doing something about the human factor, starting in his own life. The moment of change for him came in 1908, a hundred years ago, and he often recounted the story in detail. He had been working as superintendent of a poor boys' hospice in one of the toughest areas of Philadelphia. He quarrelled with his board of directors over the running of the place and particularly over what he saw as their stingy budget policy. He had walked out so angry and depressed that his doctor told him to take a trip to Europe to get over the aggravation.

Crisis at Keswick

However, he soon recognised that this European 'change' was only external and that his resentments against the board had gone with him. It was when he was attending a religious conference at Keswick in northern England as part of his tour that his inner crisis came to a head. It occurred at a Sunday afternoon meeting conducted by a relatively unknown woman speaker. However, what she said on the significance of Jesus Christ's sacrifice on the Cross brought home to Buchman with great intensity the cost of his own pride and self-centredness in the way he had submitted his resignation in Philadelphia.

He went straight back to his lodging house and wrote six letters of apology to the directors of the hospice. At once, as he often recounted later, he felt such a strong sense of release that he told the other delegates in the hotel of his experience. This in turn so deeply affected one of his listeners, a student at Cambridge University that he asked if he could talk privately to Buchman. The outcome was that before the day ended this student also made a life-changing decision comparable to Buchman's.

This Keswick experience had a permanent effect on Buchman's whole outlook on life. One could almost say that it was like St Paul's Damascus Road experience. He saw the cost of his own pride, i.e. the human factor. He faced the consequences by taking remedial action. And he saw the results in another person's life.

Buchman's experience was not a discovery of his own. Thousands of philosophers and theologians have written about the problems of the human factor and about redemption. But not so many of them moved on to the second phase of recognising and repenting for their own failings and doing something concrete about them.

Nor did Buchman stop there. In the years after 1908 he moved to a third phase, seeking a deeper understanding of the implications of his discoveries at Keswick. He turned down lucrative offers because he felt he should concentrate on this further phase of building a closely-knit network of people who would follow his example, going through the same experience of change and then committing themselves to living out the implications of their spiritual discoveries in their different walks of life.

This expanding group of people became known publicly first as the Oxford Group (simply because many of the earliest members were students at Oxford University), then as Moral Re-Armament, and today as Initiatives of Change.

Thus Buchman deserves to be remembered not so much as a philosopher or as an ecclesiastic, but rather as someone who tried to embody, as best he knew how, 'the full dimension of change'. And he himself described this as 'economic change, social change, national change and international change, all based on personal change'.

There have been innumerable attempts to encapsulate his life and work in a single phrase or sentence. Many have compared him to St Francis of Assisi or other revolutionary figures. Recently, speaking from an entirely different background, a retired general in the US Air

Force, who had never met Buchman personally, said that his work 'underscored the exceptional power of a constructive idea, along with faith, to attract the right volunteers at the right time to move mountains'. Every phrase in this description fits. So would Mahatma Gandhi's dictum: 'A small body of determined spirits fired by an unquenchable faith in their mission can alter the course of history.'

A turnaround in campus living

There was little in Buchman's ancestry or upbringing that would have led one to expect him to become a significant figure in world affairs. He came from Swiss-German stock like thousands of others who migrated to America in the 18th and 19th centuries. He was reared in a small town in Pennsylvania and went to a local school and a local college, not to a prestigious university. His first job in Philadelphia, after he graduated as a Lutheran pastor, could hardly be described as a springboard onto the career ladder. But something quite new clearly came into his life as a result of his experience in Keswick. He returned to the United States and took up a post as the YMCA representative in Penn State College and almost immediately surprising things began to happen around him.

The college was at a low ebb. Indiscipline was rife. Drinking was at an all-time high. Both scholastic results and sporting achievements were deplorable. Yet Buchman's arrival on the scene seems to have started an extraordinary turnaround in campus living. Dealing with students individually rather than en masse, and using his Keswick experience to the full, he brought about a transformation in the college's fortunes. Key students began to respond to his creative friendship and quite soon the intellectual and moral atmosphere changed. Buchman remained there for seven years and it was at Penn State that he hammered out the basic techniques of life-changing that became central to his subsequent life work.

Eventually, in 1915 he accepted a suggestion from John Mott, world head of the YMCA, to leave Penn State and move to Asia as part of a team preparing for a world evangelical mission being planned by Mott. So Buchman spent nearly two years, 1915-17, travelling through India and China. They were years of widening experience and intellectual stimulation and were a preparation – unknown then to Buchman – for the historic mission he was to undertake in Asia in very different circumstances forty years later. Students at Penn State later recalled that even there Buchman had urged them to 'think for continents', but this was his first chance to absorb Asian culture and meet personally with leaders like Mahatma Gandhi, Rabindranath Tagore and Sun Yat-Sen. Buchman was a globalist from his youth.

However, the journey was not free from friction, and friction that erupted not with Asians but with Westerners, including some of Buchman's fellow countrymen. Although he was taking part in preparations for a major evangelical campaign, Buchman found amongst the missionaries, who should have been his allies, disturbing signs of a cushioned Christianity which was deemed to be compatible with private indulgences of which he deeply disapproved.

So Buchman returned to America disturbed both by his findings and by alarming trends in the world. In fact, looking back from the 21st century, we can see that the tectonic plates beneath 19th century Christendom were moving. On the one hand, Christian leaders were speaking of 'the evangelisation of the world in one generation' and a highly impressive World Missionary Conference had taken place in Edinburgh in 1910, bubbling with optimism.

'World-changing through life-changing'

Yet only four years later the leading Western nations became engulfed in a catastrophic world war. It was so devastating that when peace was finally attained in 1918 both victors and vanquished found themselves facing not the prospect of world evangelisation in one generation, but a new era of moral relativism, cynicism and materialism in which the doctrines of Freudianism and Leninism were spreading fast. It became abundantly clear that the 19th century concepts of evangelisation and progress would have to be radically rethought.

Faced by this scene of ideological confusion, Buchman came down firmly on the side of 'world-changing through life-changing'. The priority for him was going to be not new structures or treaties but new people. 'The most necessary work in the world today,' he said, 'is the work from heart to heart. We must be in daily and God-filled touch with people, or we shall not touch the fringe of the problems facing us.'

In this situation Buchman felt he was being called on to undertake new and larger tasks. When he returned to the US he turned down an offer from the Rockefeller family to head up a wide-ranging and generously endowed programme, provisionally called 'The Inter-Church World Movement', because he considered the conditions would be too confining. In 1921 he resigned his teaching post at Hartford Theological Seminary and he never again took on a paid job. Instead, he returned to England to follow up contacts with students in Cambridge and Oxford Universities, and it was in Cambridge while riding his bicycle through its narrow lanes that the wholly unbidden thought flashed into his mind: 'You will be used to remake the world.' He said that, not surprisingly, his bicycle wobbled at this point, and of course, the phrase can be subjected to scores of interpretations, but in Buchman's career it marked another milestone. He was 42 and in the light of his past experiences, at Keswick, Penn State, India and China, he pondered what his exact role should be.

He decided to focus first on students, the potential leaders of tomorrow, and principally at Oxford, Cambridge and Princeton Universities. Many of these students in 1921 were returning soldiers, hardened by years in the trenches during World War 1, and one of his first recruits (who incidentally remained at his side until his death) was a Scotsman, Loudon Hamilton, who was a veteran of the battles of the Somme and of Passchendaele. Buchman's residence mainly in Britain and the United States in the 1920s also helps to explain why many of his earliest full-time co-workers were of British or American origin.

Towards a colour-blind South Africa

One of the first international initiatives taken by these men was a visit to South Africa in the summer of 1928. Buchman did not accompany them (though he followed them there in the following year) but the effect of the group's fresh Christian experience was felt in all sections of South African society, white, black and coloured. One of the earliest recruits was a Springbok rugby star, George Daneel, then in training to become a minister of the

Dutch Reformed Church. The commitment he undertook then to work for a colour-blind South Africa continued until full interracial independence was achieved in 1991. Daneel died aged 100 in 2000. The South African prime minister Johannes Vorster later acknowledged that Daneel had been right all along. (*See chapter* 6)

Impact on Norway

Another early international initiative was Buchman's acceptance of an invitation from Carl Hambro, President of the Norwegian Parliament (whom he had met at the League of Nations in Geneva) to visit Norway in 1934. He took with him a party of 80, mainly from Britain, and their impact on all strata of Norwegian life was instantaneous and lasting. Church leaders, politicians, authors and editors all responded. In fact, his initiative not only immediately affected national life but in due course provided resistance leaders in Norway's struggle against Nazism in the 1940s. The editor, Fredrik Ramm, nationally known because of his vigorous campaign against Denmark over a sovereignty dispute concerning Greenland, made a public apology in Copenhagen as a result of Buchman's impact on his life. He also became prominent in the resistance movement and died in 1945 on his way back to Norway from a German prison camp.

Another prominent Norwegian who responded was the well-known author Ronald Fangen and an essay which he then wrote about Buchman has recently resurfaced. In it he gave a vivid picture of Buchman's daily work-schedule and of his relations with his growing team of supporters. Fangen wrote: 'His work capacity was phenomenal. I have often thought: from where does he get his strength? On major days I have seen him lead a group meeting of 300 people, then prepare and participate in as many as five meetings, and at the same time have talks with individual people, taking care of correspondence and seeing to all manner of things... Far into the night he gets into bed and the next morning at nine o'clock he is again in the midst of a meeting, radiating morning freshness, good humour and fighting spirit... By then he has already had his private quiet-time, said his prayers, received guidance and read his Bible.'

Fangen's description of the people surrounding Buchman is also interesting: 'Frank Buchman and his team meet resistance. It takes different shapes, from underground gossip to solemn bulls of excommunication. None of these manages to stop the men and women of the movement. There is an irresistible secret in them; they have fully and totally surrendered their lives to God. There is no need to idealise them: they are people, they have their faults, they can admit their faults, they can ask forgiveness. But they are the most liberated and luminous bunch of people you could possibly meet.'

The developments in Scandinavia attracted wide international attention and Buchman's work expanded rapidly, especially in Britain and the Netherlands, but it was not until five years later that the full implications of this work were realised. 1938 was a decisive year for Buchman and for Europe.

The call for Moral Re-Armament in 1938

By then the dangers of world war were all too clear. The voices of totalitarianism were becoming ever more strident. The western democracies were awakening all too slowly. The League of Nations had been exposed as impotent. And in this situation Buchman was again ahead of his time. He publicly proclaimed the need for world-wide 'moral and spiritual re-armament' as the top priority – necessary if war were to be avoided (as alas proved impossible), and no less necessary for the survival of freedom if war happened. His call for Moral Re-Armament, issued from London in May 1938, produced positive responses around the world and, as we shall see, shaped Buchman's work for the next decade and beyond.

But he also saw that the changing world situation had implications for his own undertaking. In August 1938 he delivered one of the most confrontational speeches of his career to an international gathering at Visby in Sweden. He had no prepared text and it was obviously a speech he would have preferred not to make. He contrasted 'religious revival' (or 'armchair Christianity') with 'moral and spiritual revolution', and went on: 'I know revolution makes people uncomfortable. I am not here to make you comfortable. I am not here to make you like me... I am not going back, no matter who does, no matter what it is going to cost.' Urging people to bypass the scheduled afternoon meetings, he suggested they ponder the issues privately and continued, 'The thing you have got to decide is between you and God. You turn over your life to God for full and complete direction as a fellow revolutionary.'

He had deliberately drawn a line. Some people did not respond, but most did.

* * * * *

By now Buchman was becoming a focus of hope for millions and was exerting influence on governments in many countries. However, his peace-making efforts were unavailing and the march towards war continued until its fateful outbreak in September 1939.

Buchman was then in the United States, accompanied by a large international force, campaigning by every possible means to awaken America to the dangers facing her as well as the rest of the world. Some of his co-workers naturally had to return to their countries after the outbreak of war, but in the summer of 1940 – when France had been overrun and the blitz on London was starting – Buchman drew off 200 of his colleagues to a simple campsite at Lake Tahoe, on the borders of Nevada and California. There they remained for over three months, locked in serious discussion. It proved to be a decisive and deepening experience for many. In fact it marked another milestone in the development of Buchman's own life and thought.

The group lived simply, preparing their own meals, and met daily to think through the implications of the struggle which was by then threatening the very roots of civilisation. And out of this heart-searching grew a much more disciplined and committed force which soon demonstrated its value, both in its wartime efforts to strengthen America's morale and also in launching MRA's post-war work in many countries. There was pain and sacrifice involved in the generation of this force of people, and its creation was undoubtedly part of Buchman's enduring legacy.

On to the stage & screen

The Tahoe experience was also significant in that it marked the launching of the first dramatic and musical expressions of Buchman's message, productions which were to play such a prominent role in MRA's efforts during and after World War 2. Buchman had few artistic talents himself, but he sensed the need to find arresting new ways to express old truths, and so initiated a wave of productions, via stage and screen, that went round the world.

Many of the productions became internationally celebrated. *The Forgotten Factor* skilfully illustrated how industrial disputes and family problems were often interrelated and how an ignored spiritual factor could help to resolve both. President Truman, when chairman of the Senate War Investigating Committee, called it 'the most important play produced by the war' and after the war it was used in translation in Germany and many other countries. *Jotham Valley* was a musical drama based on a true story of two brothers farming in Nevada who found an answer to a bitter dispute over water rights. It turned out to have a no less powerful message for Asian countries facing water shortages.

The Good Road was a musical production which had a powerful effect in key areas of post-war Europe. *Freedom* was a play written by Africans out of their own experience (as will be explained later) which was turned into a successful film. It had its première at the United Nations in New York and was then used on every continent. For example, President Jomo Kenyatta of Kenya showed it in Nairobi at a state banquet in honour of President Nkrumah of Ghana. *The Vanishing Island* was a musical drama, with strong ideological overtones, which went around the world at the height of the Cold War shedding light on the need for both sides to change. *The Crowning Experience*, another powerful stage and screen production, concerned itself with the race conflict in the United States, being based on the life of Mary McLeod Bethune, a pioneer of black education in America.

These and numerous other plays and musical productions were made possible because of the many highly talented figures from the theatrical, musical and film worlds who rallied to Buchman's call. Some of them were first produced at the MRA training centre on Mackinac Island, Michigan, or at the Westminster Theatre in London which was bought in 1945 by British supporters as a memorial to British and Commonwealth service personnel who had given their lives in World War 2. For two decades prior to the arrival of mass television they proved to be successful instruments for reaching millions of people living outside normal religious frameworks.

In the same way MRA's international conference and training centres – notably at Mackinac Island, Caux in Switzerland, Panchgani in India and Armagh in Australia – provided facilities for the people touched by MRA's plays and films to reflect on both global and personal problems and on the links between them.

Illness strikes

Meantime in January 1942, when he was 64, there occurred another decisive moment in Buchman's life-story. While visiting upper New York State he suffered a severe stroke from which it took him many months to recover. Thereafter he walked with a stick or used a wheelchair. His convalescence was a period of considerable difficulty for him and those closest to him, as he and they adjusted to his new limitations. Fortunately his mental powers and creativity were unimpaired, but he had to rely more on others to implement his insights. The value of his trained force of co-workers was being increasingly demonstrated.

Although they were not destined to meet for three

more years because of war conditions, Buchman – with his diminished strength – began to turn more and more to the talented Peter Howard as a potential future leader. Howard had had a meteoric rise as a hard-hitting journalist on Lord Beaverbrook's newspapers and his decision to throw in his lot with Buchman and MRA in 1942 – at the expense of his job – had shocked Fleet Street. Buchman immediately recognised his gifts of leadership but did not spare him in any way because of his glamorous if stormy reputation. Howard for his part accepted the disciplinary treatment and remained loyal to Buchman till his death. It was a great loss to Buchman's work that Howard, a gifted author and playwright, himself died suddenly only four years later.

Buchman remained in America until the end of the war and over this period he and his co-workers laid the foundations for the continent-wide operations that were to develop after the war affecting American and Canadian life at many key points, especially in the fields of industrial and race relations. (*See chapter 11*)

Post-war reconciliation a priority

Even before World War 2 ended Buchman's thoughts were turning to the vast tasks of reconstruction and reconciliation that lay ahead, especially in Europe. In April 1946 he sailed from New York to Britain with a team of over a hundred and then moved to Switzerland in July to open the first conference held at the new MRA centre at Caux. During the war some of Buchman's Swiss friends had spotted, high in the Alps above the Lake of Geneva, a large and picturesque building which had originally been one of Europe's top hotels but which had fallen on hard times and was being used as a war-refugee detention centre.

After consulting Buchman in America, about ninety Swiss families dug into their pockets and purchased it as a base for stimulating the reconciliation process so obviously needed after World War 2. Restored to its former splendour, it still functions as a proven centre for reconciliation in the 21st century. (*See chapter 1*)

The story of the impact that Buchman and MRA made on France and Germany after the war, much of it emanating from Caux, has been told many times and recognised by historians. It filled an ideological gap which was never bridged after the first World War and which is again painfully evident in the Middle East today. Paul Hoffman, administrator of the Marshall Plan, put the point succinctly: 'You are giving the world the ideological counterpart of the Marshall Plan.'

It is also striking to note how top European leaders like Chancellor Adenauer of Germany and Foreign Minister Robert Schuman of France responded to the relatively unknown figure, lacking any governmental status, and almost immediately gave him their personal friendship and support. It almost seemed as if they sensed that they shared with Buchman a common spiritual quest, or a common spiritual gene. (These quickly established, instinctive bonds of friendship also characterised Buchman's relations with certain other public figures, people as radically different as Prime Minister U Nu of Burma; Foreign Minister Mohammed Fadhel Jamali of Iraq; Orthodox Patriarch Athenagoras in Istanbul; King Michael of Romania; Mrs John Henry Hammond of New York, a member of the Vanderbilt family; Phra Bimaladhamma, a senior member of the Buddhist hierarchy in Thailand; and Chief Walking Buffalo of the Stoney Indian tribe in Canada.)

Building bridges over the Rhine

The ideological vacuum in the Ruhr, which Marxist forces had immediately spotted, was an obvious threat to Allied planners. However, Buchman had also recognised this and poured in MRA workers equipped with plays like *The Good Road* and *The Forgotten Factor* which helped to fill the gap and win the support of men like Herman Kost, head of the German Coal Board, and Hans Boeckler, president of the German Trade Union Federation. An MRA pamphlet entitled *Es muss alles anders werden* (Everything must be different) filled the ideological vacuum and was distributed by the million throughout Germany.

Aid also came from France in the form of Irène Laure, resistance leader in the Marseilles region and post-war leader of the French Socialist Women's Organisation. At Caux she had found dramatic release from her hatred of Germany caused by her wartime suffering. She thereafter played a prominent part, along with her husband, in MRA's reconciling efforts across Germany. In fact, Robert Schuman said later that she had done more than any other person to 'build bridges over the Rhine'.

The cumulative efforts of these initiatives in Germany and France in the early post-war years undoubtedly helped to provide a moral infrastructure for the later governmental agreements which were to change the history of Europe. (*See chapters 2 & 3*)

Reaching out to the humiliated

After the war's end Buchman's mind had also turned immediately towards Japan where he already had established many friendships from his pre-war visits. He did not go there immediately in person but he sent senior representatives from the teams who had been seasoned by the training at Lake Tahoe in 1940.

Buchman's gesture roused a widespread response in the humiliated country and delegations of Japanese leaders began to visit Caux from 1948 onwards. These initiatives had the approval of both General MacArthur (Supreme Commander, Allied Forces in the Far East) and the Japanese Prime Minister Shigeru Yoshida who said they were 'opening a new page in our history'. When the conference to sign a peace treaty with Japan eventually assembled at San Francisco in 1951 Buchman was again present and Robert Schuman, head of the French delegation, said to him: 'Of course, the truth is that you made peace with Japan years before we signed it.' (*See chapters 4 & 5; also Basil Entwistle's book* Japan's Decisive Decade, *Grosvenor Books, 1985*)

By 1952 Buchman's mind was turning to another even larger initiative. Despite the physical limitations resulting from his stroke, he personally led a group of 200 people (including the casts of five plays) on a seven-month tour of South East Asia. The timing was remarkable. Some would call it serendipitous. Buchman insisted that it was the result of divine guidance. Coming so soon after the gaining of independence by India, Pakistan and Sri Lanka, with all the turmoil and bloodshed that this had involved, the response to Buchman's initiative was extraordinary.

Although he had been invited by a distinguished group of Asian leaders, his arrival was greeted by initial opposition from Marxist quarters, orchestrated by a series of hostile radio programmes from Tashkent and Moscow; but this was quickly counterbalanced by a tidal wave of support from Bombay to Calcutta and Kashmir to Kerala.

The ideological significance of Buchman's move was dramatised early on at a diplomatic reception in Delhi where the Chargé d'Affaires of the West German Embassy – with the French Ambassador standing at his side – presented Buchman with the German Order of Merit in recognition of his contribution to rapprochement between the two countries over the previous five years. The significance of this event was not lost on the Indian and Pakistani governments, nor on the members of the Delhi diplomatic corps who witnessed the ceremony.

Enough for everyone's need...

Buchman's vision for India had been stirred originally by his visit in 1915, plus eight subsequent visits, and was now vindicated by the response his efforts elicited at all levels of society. Especially significant was the enlistment at his side of many young educated Indians, including Rajmohan Gandhi, a grandson of the Mahatma, who renounced career plans and some of whom remain leaders in Buchman's ongoing work today.

Such support also led directly to the creation in 1968 of a large conference and training centre at Panchgani in western India which is still in full use for a wide range of activities today.

In 1952 Buchman and his party also spent time in Pakistan and Sri Lanka and it was in a rice paddy field near Colombo that Buchman articulated his basic economic philosophy in terms that found echoes fifty years later in the pronouncements of G8 world leaders at the Gleneagles Summit on poverty in 2005: 'There's enough in the world for everyone's need, but not for everyone's greed. If everyone cares enough and shares enough, everyone will have enough.' (*See chapters 9, 15 & 16*)

To Africa, and the filming of Freedom

Meantime African countries in the 1950s were following in the footsteps of South-East Asia towards independence. And simultaneously Buchman was inviting large numbers of Africans to conferences in Europe and America. He himself only made one post-war trip to Africa and that was to Morocco in 1954 at the specific request of his friend Robert Schuman. He spent several months there with a small group, working quietly amongst both Moroccan and French leaders, and his efforts brought about several key reconciliations between prominent personalities which helped Morocco – and also Tunisia – to move towards independence without bloodshed.

In sub-Saharan Africa Nigeria is a key country from every point of view and Nnamdi Azikiwe, a father figure in her struggle for independence, had gone to Caux in 1949 while en route to a Communist-inspired gathering in Prague. As a result of the influence Caux had on his thinking, Azikiwe abandoned Prague and returned to Nigeria where he became one of the early voices advocating MRA.

In 1955 a large group of Africans attending a Caux conference were preparing to leave when Buchman intercepted them and explained that during the night he had had the unexpected but insistent thought that the Africans should stay longer at Caux and write a play, based on their own experience, that would illustrate a new path to independence based on change not conflict. The Africans were so arrested by this proposal that they changed their plans and in a remarkably short time produced the outline of a play called *Freedom*. It was presented in Caux by its authors within a few days and then taken in succeeding weeks to several European capital cities. It was eventually brought back to Nigeria where it was turned into the first full-length colour film to be produced entirely on African soil. Except in some colonial enclaves, it roused widespread support and is still being used as an instrument of peace-building.

The film was also used in harness with the efforts of the Colwell brothers, three talented young American singers, who had renounced promising careers in Hollywood to devote themselves to Buchman's work. They criss-crossed Africa for years, often in circumstances of great danger, to carry their meaningful songs – in numerous African languages – to different war-torn nations. A Catholic bishop in the Congo said at the time that they were 'the one voice of sanity' in his devastated country.

Buchman's work also spread rapidly through southern Africa, including Rhodesia during its years of civil strife prior to independence. The dramatic change in the life of Alec Smith, son of Ian Smith, the white Rhodesian leader, triggered off changes also in the lives of African leaders, and the unobtrusive work of an MRA-inspired black/white body known as the 'cabinet of conscience' in Harare helped to pave the way for the eventual independence of Zimbabwe. (*See chapter 6*)

Outreach into Australia & New Zealand . . .

Frank Buchman often had Australia and New Zealand in his thoughts. He had a high expectancy of what both countries could achieve, not only for their own citizens but for the outside world. He spent three months in Australia as early as 1924 and described enthusiastically the positive response he had received from people in different walks of life, and he returned there for an extended stay in 1956. The life story of Kim Beazley senior, later Minister for Education, who first visited Caux in 1953 on his way back from Queen Elizabeth's coronation in London, and who subsequently became a model – on a Wilberforce scale – of what a modern politician can achieve when committed to the highest moral standards, has gone around the world. And so has the outreach of Buchman's work on the Australian waterfront and in carrying forward the efforts for racial harmony inside Australia. (*See chapter 8*)

. . . and Latin America

Buchman never spent much time personally in Latin America but he sent some of his best-trained people to work there and welcomed large numbers of Latin Americans at conferences in the United States and Caux. The dramatic story of the transformation in conditions in the docks of Rio de Janeiro also went around the world in a film entitled *Men of Brazil*. (*See chapter 10*)

Depth of spiritual commitment

In the post-war period Buchman was not able to spend time in either the Soviet Union or China because of cold-war conditions. Nor did he travel much in the Arab world, nor in the Israeli-Palestinian complex. Yet his sense of concern stretched to all these areas, as his collected speeches reveal, and the seeds that he planted in these territories began to bear fruit in the years after his death. (*See chapter 12*)

However, while the 16 years from the end of World War 2 till his death in 1961 saw a spectacular expansion of his work around the world, it seems clear that his primary concern throughout was not with the scale of this expansion but with the depth of spiritual commitment in those who brought it about.

Robert Schuman was in fact one of the first observers to spot the historic significance of what Buchman was doing. In his preface to the French edition of Buchman's collected speeches (written before he knew Buchman really well and before his visit to Caux) Schuman said: 'To provide teams of trained people, ready for the service of the state, apostles of reconciliation and builders of a new world, that is the beginning of a far-reaching transformation of human society in which, during fifteen war-ravaged years, the first steps have already been taken.' These trained teams were, in fact, the essence of Buchman's legacy. (*See chapter* 2)

* * * * *

Conclusions

To restore a commonplace truth to its first uncommon lustre, you need only translate it into action.

Samuel Taylor Coleridge

If a man does not keep pace with his companions, perhaps it is because he hears a different drummer. Let him step to the music which he hears, however measured or far away.

Henry Thoreau

The world has changed radically since Frank Buchman's day. Indeed he might not even recognise some of the problems that now dominate our headlines: the dangers of climate change, atmospheric pollution and fuel shortages. Yet it is important to note that scientists increasingly assure us that they can save humanity from such disasters if only there is the right spirit of co-operation from governments and ourselves. So these so-called scientific crises turn out, in fact, to be a race against time for moral enlightenment, for what Buchman would have called moral re-armament. Therefore, instead of consigning Buchman to the historical archives, it becomes clear that we would do well to look again at his life and doctrine and see what we can learn that will help us in our present predicaments.

Buchman was certainly a transcendentalist, not a humanist. He spoke constantly of the importance of finding God's plan for humanity. His doctrine, when stripped down to essentials, could be summarised in these concepts which recur regularly in his speeches – faith in God; belief in two-way prayer; absolute moral standards; discipline; total commitment; a quality of life; inner freedom; life-changing; and a world view.

The practice of listening was central to Buchman's faith. He said: 'When I first began I'd listen ten and talk five.' And he added: 'So live that God can talk to you at any hour of the day or night.' He was an intuitive, rather than a logical, thinker. After his disabling stroke, when he had to face long periods of wakefulness at night, he would even call a secretary to write down immediately some important thought that had come to him.

Coupled to his belief in divine guidance was his unshakeable attachment to absolute moral standards, particularly to the four absolute standards he took over from his early mentor Henry Wright of Yale University: absolute honesty, absolute purity, absolute unselfishness and absolute love. Of course, he recognised that there are many other values that are inseparable from the Christian life: humility, compassion, patience, courage, etc. But he considered that these four absolute standards had a special centrality in relation to right living.

He would have agreed with the philosopher William Hocking at Harvard who said: 'It is a mark of the shallowness of Western life that it should be thought a conceit to recognise an absolute and a humility to consider all standards relative, when it is precisely the opposite. It is only the absolute which rebukes our pride.'

Yet his belief in absolute standards was linked to an earthy recognition of the difficulty of attaining them. There was no exclusiveness about his concept of Moral Re-Armament. He used to say: 'MRA is like a lake where an elephant can swim and a lamb can wade.' It was this sort of catholicity coupled to his personal warmth that drew people to him instead of rebuffing them. He may well have had an autocratic streak in him, like so many other leaders; yet he inspired in his closest associates a level of loyalty and sacrifice that went well beyond the call of duty.

He never shrank from personal confrontations: but his incisiveness, and readiness to strike a deep note even with new acquaintances, was balanced by his injunction to his friends to preserve 'an intelligent restraint and a nonchalant reserve', when this was appropriate.

His intuitiveness also helped him to spot hidden potential in the most ordinary people. 'The ordinary person under God can do extraordinary things' was one of his maxims, and he once added: 'Half my time has been taken in pulling the cork from bottled-up people.' He certainly put the art of individual life-changing at the heart of his message and method. He staked everything on it. To him changed human lives were the raw material for a new world order. 'Do you expect total commitment to be the result of your work with people?' he asked. 'Then you are doing the most necessary work in the world today.'

In 1931 a young Canadian woman in her twenties approached him tentatively with a suggestion that the time might be ripe to launch a campaign in Canada. His response was instant and characteristic: 'Fine; you do it.' The startled Canadian rose to the challenge and three years later the Prime Minister of Canada said that her initiatives had 'made the task of government easier'.

Achieving unity between thought and action was his constant quest. The French philosopher Gabriel Marcel was quick to spot the significance of the linkage between what he called 'the intimate and the global' which characterised Buchman's work. His normal approach to even the most complicated situations was to focus on change in a key individual. When he found himself confronted at Penn State College with the problem of heavy drinking throughout the campus – 'binge drinking' we would call it today – his strategy was to win the one man, the unlikely Bill Pickle, who was supplying the campus with its liquor.

This same technique can be spotted throughout Buchman's career. During the Norwegian-Danish dispute over Greenland he focussed on Fredrik Ramm. During the French-German animosity after World War 2 he focussed on Irène Laure. In apartheid-dominated South Africa he focussed on George Daneel. In the Alabama race riots he focussed on Daisy Bates and Mary McLeod Bethune. And with corruption in Ghana he focussed on the Tolon Na.

He never oversimplified things by suggesting that change in an individual was enough. His point was that unless you dealt with the human factor, you are hemmed in from the start. And conversely, when you do bring change to a key person, it is like reconnecting a severed electrical wire. And he was very clear that, as well as creating well-meaning institutions, it is necessary to continue the moral battle inside the institutions if lasting results are to be obtained from them.

It is relatively easy with a wave of optimism to launch a new organisation designed to do some specific good in the world. But when the wave expends itself, you find yourself getting bogged down by vested interests, including the jobs and privileges of the very people who were part of such well-intentioned schemes. Without reactivating the original creative spirit, you will find yourself part of the status quo.

When I worked with the Brandt Commission, which was designed by the World Bank to find ways of bridging the menacing gulfs between the rich and poor worlds, I read scores of papers by eminent experts which all seemed to end with almost the same sentence: 'Therefore X or Y is the answer to the problem, provided the necessary political will exists.' And there apparently the experts closed shop and moved on to their next project. But, of course, they were leaving the most crucial question unanswered: 'how to create that necessary political will?' That was the point at which Frank Buchman started. He focussed on the human factor as the key to creating 'the necessary political will'.

Yet probably the most important characteristic of Buchman's style of leadership was his emphasis on working through teams of trained and committed people. This was the significance of his three-month retreat at Lake Tahoe in 1940 and this technique was to be a regular feature of his work. In fact, he had already sounded a warning note at the gathering at Visby in Sweden in 1938 between those who were content with 'armchair Christianity' and those ready for revolutionary change. He shared the belief of the celebrated British historian Arnold Toynbee in the special role of 'creative minorities' in bringing about civilisation's advances.

There exists an interesting account of a private discussion between Buchman and a few friends in Germany in 1949 when he was obviously in reflective and even speculative mood. From the informal record it seems that he was keen to dispel any impression that Moral Re-Armament was a closed intellectual box or a tablet written in stone. Rather, it was a living organism which involves 'a definiteness of experience directly observable by someone else but not easily describable to someone else'. It is characterised, he suggested, by 'a peace, a confidence, a recovery of freedom and a spontaneity of thought, will and nerve'. It is 'something directly discernible but not joinable. You have to experience it for yourself.' In other words, the further vistas to which Buchman was alluding would not necessarily become clear to the brightest intellectuals but rather to those who were practicing MRA's God-centred message to the full. As he said on another occasion, 'No one can be wholly God-controlled who works alone. It is to a willing group of men and women that God speaks most clearly.'

Thus there is plenty of scope for spin-offs from Buchman's work. The first such spin-off was Alcoholics Anonymous in the USA in the 1930s, and in recent years there have been many more such initiatives focussing on specific social problems. However, the most vital need will be the continuance, and the reproduction, of a core of fully committed people at the heart of all such manifestations. Buchman said more than once that he wanted 'all my fine horses to run all-out together, neck and neck'.

One of Buchman's early recruits in the East End of London was an unlikely character called Tod Sloan, a gnarled street-fighter who had often seen trouble with the police and who described himself as 'a watchmaker by trade and an agitator by nature'. Tod Sloan described Buchman's work as 'a laughing, living, loving, obedient willingness to restore God to leadership'.

That was an early definition. Yet it still has validity. It is a vivid reminder of what Frank Buchman's work was all about. That work has already become part of history. It could also become a flightpath to the future.

* * * * *

Apart from the chapters that follow, our primary source in preparing this introduction has been Garth Lean's authoritative biography ***Frank Buchman: a Life*** *(Constable, 1985). We have also benefited from the outstanding study on* ***Religion, the Missing Dimension of Statecraft****, edited by Douglas Johnston (OUP, 1984) and have been grateful to consult an as-yet unpublished manuscript of 234 pages, entitled 'My Friend Frank Buchman' by Ray Foote Purdy.*

Many of the events recorded here were dramatised in the film, ***Cross Road****, an hour-long documentary on Frank Buchman made in 1974. DVD copies are obtainable from 24 Greencoat Place, London SWIP IRD, UK, or email: info@FLTfilms.org.uk. In North America from MRA Productions, 14831 57B Avenue, Surrey, British Columbia V3S 8W5, Canada, or email: mraproductions@ca.iofc.org*

1

How Caux began

by Pierre Spoerri

Pierre Spoerri is from Zurich where his father was Professor of Romansh Language and Literature and later University Vice-Chancellor. He worked with the world-wide programme of Moral Re-Armament, as well as reporting for European newspapers and radio. He has been one of those responsible for the Centre at Caux and is author of several books, notably *Rediscovering Freedom* with Dr J S Lester.

WHEN Frank Buchman, in the middle of July of 1946, stepped through the doors of Mountain House, the newly created conference-centre of Moral Re-Armament (in Caux-sur-Montreux, Switzerland), he looked more towards the future than back to the past. So he enquired about all the people coming to attend the planned conference, and in the weeks that followed, 3,000 men and women from 34 nations arrived in Caux to participate in this first international gathering of Moral Re-Armament since the end of the war. Even Japanese, Chinese and Indians made the then long trip to Switzerland and expressed their vision for the future. The first deep conversations between the Germans and their former enemies took place. My parents were both there and I joined them in uniform during a week-end leave from my military service.

Few of the guests and participants knew that the decision to buy the former Caux Palace and to transform it into Mountain House had only been taken four months before and that those responsible for this initiative had only just taken possession of the building on June 1. For Buchman – in 1946 68 years-old – and for some of the Swiss, however, the former Caux Palace was not an unknown place. Buchman had visited it as a tourist in August 1903 during its heydays. And in the spring of 1942, just before entering the Foreign Office, Philippe Mottu had expressed to his friends the following thought: 'If the Swiss were to escape from getting involved in the war, our task will be to put at the disposal of Frank Buchman a place where the Europeans, torn apart by hate, suffering and resentment, can find each other again. Caux is the place.'[1]

Mottu repeated this conviction again in 1944, still in the middle of the war, when he was able to join Frank Buchman for a few weeks in the States. Then in the summer of 1945, he joined Buchman again at a conference on Mackinac Island (USA) together with his friend Robert Hahnloser and several other Swiss, British and Dutch friends. One day, Buchman took Mottu and Hahnloser aside and asked them to organise a first international post-war conference in Switzerland.

About to be sold

Looking for an adequate place for the gathering, Mottu again thought of Caux and visited the building one sunny March day in 1946. They found the old caretaker and discovered that the building was going to be sold to a French company. The banks had taken back the derelict hotel after it had been run by the Swiss Army as a refugee camp, first for Allied officers who had escaped from prison-camps in Germany and Italy, then for several hundred Jewish refugees who had been able during the last weeks of the war to flee from Budapest and who arrived at the Swiss border after a short stay in the concentration camp of Bergen-Belsen. The caretaker had been able to hide the hotel china and silver and hoped against hope that the building would be restored to its ancient glory.

Then things moved very quickly. At Easter 1946, several hundred Swiss and a few friends from outside gathered in Interlaken, and in the middle of the conference a group of them – including the three couples, Philippe and Helene Mottu, Robert and Dorli Hahnloser, Erich and Emmy Peyer – made the journey to Caux to look at the building and decide whether to take it or not.

It was a cold and unfriendly day, and the house received them in a similar way with empty rooms, destroyed furniture and endless dirty corridors. Still, Robert Hahnloser, a qualified engineer, saw immediately the potential of this building. He envisaged what could be done to transform the big hall into a meeting-room, the ballroom into a theatre, and to make the kitchens which were described by one as similar to 'the black hole of Calcutta' into a workable place for potential cooks.

When the group met after a visit of two hours in the building, they all agreed, well realizing the gigantic effort that would be needed, that they should go ahead. From London, Frank Buchman gave his agreement and asked: 'Can you find the needed money in Switzerland?' Mottu answered with a clear 'Yes', knowing – or not fully knowing – what he was letting himself in for.

Neglected, battered, filthy

On May 25 1946, the contract was signed with the Banque Populaire Suisse in Montreux by Mottu and Hahnloser who took on to find within a few months the more than one million Francs needed to pay for the hotel and the whole land surrounding it. On June 1, Robert Hahnloser took possession of the building. Also on June 1, a group of 25 Swiss, British, Scandinavians, French and Dutch arrived knowing that they had just six weeks to transform this half-ruin into a home ready to receive up to six hundred guests from all over the world.

Four of them wrote a letter describing the experience: 'When we arrived the building was for us a symbol of what Europe is today. Neglected, battered, filthy, upside down, cold and empty. It waited for a new era to dawn. Coming into the vast and desolate-looking hall that first evening we were gripped by the fear of the huge task before us. We had six weeks . . .'[2]

At the same time, the needed money was coming in big and small sums. Hahnloser answered the question where the money was coming from with the following words: 'Some gave from their income, others from their capital; again others gave everything they possessed. Some sold their life-insurance, others shares or their houses. One of the first gifts received in 1946 came from an important Swiss trade union. One of my best friends had put 10,000 Francs aside to build a ski-chalet for his children, but he came to the conclusion that for the future of his children Mountain House would be the best place to invest this money.'[3]

The first payment of 450,000 Swiss Francs was paid on time on July 1 to the bank. It was all money coming from Switzerland, from sacrificial giving by 95 Swiss families.

How did all these elements come together in time? One moment of decision had clearly been the 1946 Easter Conference in Interlaken. Besides the Swiss, there were also three hundred friends from neighbouring countries who took part. Probably the most unexpected group were four from Germany. The first contact between some of Buchman's friends from Germany under occupation was made thanks to a Swiss industrialist, Paul Suter, who worked on the German side of the border and continued during the war to live in a village on the Swiss side. He 'smuggled into Germany' some invitations to the Interlaken conference.

The four candidates received their exit permits thanks to the chaplain to the French Forces in Germany who had known the Oxford Group[4] before the war. For them, participating in this gathering was a rather shattering but unforgettable experience. The Germans who could go to Caux in 1946, in the spring and in the autumn, were all from the French Zone only.[5]

It is a fascinating exercise to read the names of the people who took part in the Interlaken Conference, many of whom then decided to 'buy Caux' and were ready to come and clean up the rooms and prepare the building. Many of them also made the financial sacrifices needed to buy the building and to support the group which had decided to give its whole time to this enterprise. When one looks at all these names, one makes an amazing discovery: practically all these people had found a new direction for their lives and a deepening of their faith in the early Thirties during Buchman's first visits to Switzerland.

'Why not prepare to live?'

The first of these visits happened through an extraordinary set of circumstances. Buchman was having dinner in the spring of 1931 with Mrs Alexander Whyte, the elderly widow of a once-famous Scottish theologian. He asked her what was her greatest concern. 'I'm preparing to die,' she replied. Buchman responded, 'Why not prepare to live?' Mrs Whyte then spoke of her hopes for the League of Nations where her son was working at that moment. Some months later she suggested to Buchman that he take a team to Geneva, and in true Buchman fashion he answered by saying, 'You do it.' So, in January 1932, she booked a hundred rooms in Geneva. Buchman prepared an adequate group to go with him and stayed there for ten days.[6]

In the summer of 1931, a young Swiss student, Walther Staub, had participated in Oxford at one of the house parties organised by Frank Buchman. When he returned to Zurich, he found that his professor, Theophil Spoerri, was in profound spiritual need. Staub had the extraordinary courage to suggest to his professor in January 1932 a visit to Geneva where, as he had heard, Buchman was holding a series of meetings. As a cautious Swiss, my father did not announce his coming but arrived anonymously in the hall where the meeting took place. He was staying with his sister, a deaconess, in order not to seem to be too keen.

He was not too impressed by what he heard but was struck by the fact that all of those who spoke or whom he met knew where they were going and were obviously enjoying life. When he asked one of them how he could find the same sense of direction he was told that he had to be ready to make a simple experiment: he would need to take the principles of the Sermon of the Mount – absolute honesty, purity, unselfishness and love – and compare them to his present life. Then he would just need to take time in silence to let God – or his conscience – talk to him.

Much too simple

After returning to Zurich, with the impression that all this was much too simple, he one day took time to be silent in his study on the second floor of our house. He expected to get some 'moral' thoughts, for instance to be more patient with his wife or to clean up a bit of his thought-life. But what he got was of a totally different nature: 'Come down from your second floor!' Till then he had fled upstairs whenever there was a need on the ground-floor – where my mother ruled – and had in more ways than one avoided getting involved in any unpleasant things of any kind. 'Coming down into the street' meant a profound change of motive. When my father accepted the truth of this call, the whole atmosphere in our family changed. I was six years old when all this happened, but I definitely noticed the difference. My room had been next to my parents' bedroom. So I had heard them argue at night. I had not understood the words but the music was unmistakable!

It was natural that such a deep change would affect very quickly several of father's friends. One of them was the well-known professor of theology, Emil Brunner. Another was the Genevese doctor Paul Tournier. The latter met the ideas of the Oxford Group[4] through an extraordinary set of circumstances in which he could not help but see later the hand of God. Tournier used to replace a colleague of his during the summer holidays.

The colleague, Henri Mentha, had one very difficult patient, an Austrian Baroness, Connie von Hahn. And in the first summer, Tournier found the lady very difficult. Then Mentha told him one day: 'You remember the Austrian Baroness?' 'Indeed,' was Tournier's reply. Mentha: 'Well, she's changed.' The two doctors were determined to get behind the secret of this change. One of their friends made this possible and so Tournier found himself meeting with two Zurich professors, Spoerri and Brunner, and another impressive visitor from Zurich – the psychiatrist Alphonse Maeder – and a senior official of the League of Nations, Jan de Bordes. Tournier described that evening as 'the great turning point in my life'.[7] When he then met Buchman in Oxford the following summer, the latter told him: 'Now you must apply what you have found here in your profession.' He wrote later: 'So I decided to devote my life to reflection about the influence of the spiritual life on personal health.'

In August 1932 Buchman returned to Switzerland for a first major conference on Swiss soil at Ermatingen on Lake Constance. My father and Emil Brunner were the main initiators of this gathering for which they had chosen a place half-way between Munich and Zurich, as there was a growing interest in Germany now for the Oxford Group ideas. One family that was to play an important role in the creation of the conference centre of Caux took a prominent part in Ermatingen, the de Trey family. Mrs Lydi de Trey was the sister of Emil Brunner, and Emmanuel was a very successful inventor and businessman. They addressed the gathering together with their eldest daughter Helen, who was to become in 1939 the wife of Philippe Mottu.

Riches as goods loaned to him by God

Mrs de Trey said that her deepest wish had been fulfilled – to see the family united with the same purpose. Helen spoke about a new relationship with her brothers. But the most spectacular changes seem to have happened to Emmanuel de Trey, who spoke after a former communist lady about the 'sins of a capitalist'. He spoke about 'the misery in a man who is the slave of Mammon.... The only salvation for a capitalist is... to use his riches as goods loaned to him by God, goods that do not belong to him but whose administrator he is, in order to serve his neighbour in a better way.'[8]

In 1946 Emmanuel de Trey bought the Hotel Maria, across the road from Mountain House, to be an integral part of the conference centre. It is still used for seminars and conferences outside the summer months. He also gave major sums for the work of Caux in Asia and Africa.

After Ermatingen, dozens of meetings, house-parties and gatherings took place all over Switzerland. My father wrote: 'From Geneva it swept across the country like a hurricane. There were mass meetings in the major cities. In Zurich not only was the great Börsensaal packed out but an overflow meeting had to be arranged. It was a keen, invigorating, uncomfortable time. It went beyond all expectations.'[9]

To a friend he wrote: 'We had to cancel the open evenings in Zurich as too many people came and the halls became too small. All the groups in private homes are overflowing. We do not make any propaganda, but rather discourage people from coming. But we still do not have enough time to receive all the hungry souls. Last time when I had a group-meeting in our house, I had to open the side-room as well and people had to sit on the floor. I guess we were about sixty...'[10]

In his biography of Frank Buchman, Theophil Spoerri describes the effects of this awakening on Swiss national life: 'It is difficult to measure all the results of these great meetings and of the countless personal contacts. There is no doubt that for many it was the turning point of their lives. It could also be described as a change of climate. It was almost as if something new was penetrating between the chinks in the shutters. A businessman, alone in his office, would feel a faint sense of unease if he was planning to cheat his fellow citizens. The public conscience became more sensitive. The Director of Finance in one canton reported that after the national day of thanksgiving and repentance, 6,000 tax payments were recorded, something that had never occurred before in the financial history of the Republic.[11]

Switzerland a prophet among the nations

'This breaking out of the religious sphere into public life took place in every imaginable way. A reception was given by the Swiss President and other government representatives in the Federal Assembly. The following week a large number of Members of Parliament met with Frank Buchman and his colleagues in one of the main committee rooms. News of this appeared in the daily press. *Der Bund* spoke with some astonishment about an 'hour of frankness in Parliament'.'

The closing event of the campaign was Buchman's speech in Zurich. After quoting the President of the Swiss Confederation, Rudolf Minger's words of welcome some days earlier, he went on to outline his vision of Switzerland's role in world affairs. 'I can see Switzerland a prophet among the nations, and a peacemaker in the international family... I can see Swiss businessmen showing the leaders of the world's commerce how faith in God is the only security. I can see Swiss statesmen demonstrating that divine guidance is the only practical politics.'

Besides the influence on the politicians and on thousands of individual lives, the wave of these new ideas also affected the economic life. Another good friend of my father and of Robert Hahnloser was Professor Alfred Carrard of the Federal Institute of Technology in Zurich.[12] He developed a new thinking about the relationships in industrial enterprises and through his work developed a warm friendship with the leaders of the Swiss machine- and watch-making industry and of the trade union leadership in the same industry. He had a part in making possible a remarkable peace agreement[13] in this industrial field which was quite revolutionary at that time and which is still lasting at the beginning of the second millennium.

The teamwork of Emil Brunner and my father reached its high-point at Easter-time 1937 in a national gathering attended by 10,000 people from all over the country in Lausanne. In 1938, again at Easter, several hundred Swiss met for four days in Caux in the hotel that they were going to develop into a world centre ten years later.

When the war broke out, the contact with Buchman who was in the United States at that time and until 1946, was interrupted. Most Swiss men were mobilised in September 1939 and spent many months in uniform guarding the frontiers. A small group of women decided to keep a contact-office open in Berne, in the Hotel Bristol. Their main mission was to ensure liaison between Buchman's friends who had been called up in their various countries, and to supply them with news and literature.

My father writes. 'The many letters they received showed how the seed sown by Buchman bore fruit in the most hopeless situations. A young man who had been at the Interlaken Conference in 1938, in a letter to his father just before he was killed, wrote: 'Looking back I am grateful for my life because God has guided it wonderfully... I pray for you to be able to accept my death so that it brings neither rebellion nor sorrow, but spurs you on to fight all the more for the common cause to which God has called us in different ways.' From a concentration camp another wrote: 'Even in a concentration camp where everyone is fighting for sheer survival, often at the expense of others, it is possible to be completely happy when you forget yourself. That is very hard to do, especially here, and I often fail. But I know that if every day I start by thinking of others, I can do something for them.' This group in Berne built a bridge leading to the post-war years.'[14]

We are back in 1946. It was as if the country and many of its citizens had been kept in reserve. When the call came, they were ready. The doors then were opened to the world, especially to the nations that had fought against each other to the bitter end. And they came by the hundreds and thousands.

Notes:

1) Philippe Mottu, *Caux – De la Belle Epoque au Rearmament Moral* (A la Baconniere, Neuchatel 1969). p.54. Translation by the author. Many facts in the following paras also emanate from this book.

2) Letter signed by Philippe and Helen Mottu, Elspeth Spoerry, Kärstin Rääf, Theo Metcalfe (Archives cantonales vaudoises)

3) Le Monde Ouvrier et Caux (Editions de Caux 1949) p.79.

4) *Oxford Group, Groupes d'Oxford, Oxford-Gruppe, Gruppenbewegung* – These were the names used in the thirties to describe the work of Buchman and his team in English-speaking, French-speaking and German-speaking countries worldwide. In 1938, Buchman launched the name *Moral Re-Armament*. It was replaced by *Initiatives of Change* in 2002.

5) Dr Siegfried Ernst, *Mit Gott im Rückspiegel* (Gerhard Hess Verlag, Ulm 1998) p.280/1.

6) Garth Lean, *Frank Buchman – a Life* (Collins Fount Paperbacks, London 1988), p.215/6.

7) Paul Tournier, in a letter written on the occasion of my parents' golden wedding anniversary 1965.

8) Quotes from the *Ermatinger Tagebuch* (Leopold Klotz Verlag Gotha und Wander Verlag Zürich 1932) (in the Archives cantonales vaudoises).

9) Theophil Spoerri, *Dynamic out of Silence* (Grosvenor Books, London 1976) p.90.

10) Pierre Spoerri, *Mein Vater und sein Jüngster* (Th. Gut Verlag, Stäfa 2002), p.30.

11) Theophil Spoerri, ibid. pp.94-6.

12) More about the thinking of Alfred Carrard in Jean Carrard, *Pionier der Wirtschaftsethik* (Paul Haupt Verlag, Bern 1990).

13) *Friedensabkommen in der Schweizerischen Metall- und Uhrenindustrie*, signed on 19th July 1937.

(4) Theophil Spoerri, ibid. pp.156, 158.

2

France and the Expansion of Buchman's Faith

by Michel Sentis

Born in 1925, Michel Sentis graduated in engineering at Ecole Polytechnique in Paris. After attending a session dealing with industrial tension in 1949 at Caux, he joined the young European team assembled around Buchman.

He was involved in relations between the French statesman Robert Schuman and Buchman, in the contact with the Catholic authorities in the Vatican, and with situations of tension in several countries (Vietnam, Tunisia, Algeria, and Quebec). Married with three sons and seven grandchildren, he lives with his wife Micheline in Burgundy near Taizé. He has written or participated in several books.

MANY religious leaders have marked their century by a spiritual radiance which enabled them to leave behind a large number of followers who in their turn became guides to the future; but at the same time they left men and women who were committed to secular activities which led their contemporaries to make social choices that enriched succeeding generations.

Someone like St Francis of Assisi left the long line of

Franciscans and Capuchins, and his spiritual influence is indisputable. And a Don Bosco, dedicated to providing education for poor children, inspired in the Salesian Order teachers who committed themselves to this pioneering work – his mark on history is equally indisputable.

So if I attempt to focus here on the practical outreach of Frank Buchman's life, I have no intention of neglecting his remarkable spiritual influence – from which I personally benefited enormously. One cannot live close to a man conscious of God's presence, not only in his own life but in the lives of those around him, without being powerfully marked oneself. Our different religious backgrounds could not block such a transfer from him to me ('his effect on me') precisely because the divine presence overarched us both. A lot could be said on this subject but I want to move on.

For me he was a teacher quite out of the ordinary. 'Michel,' he said one day, 'You need activities to keep you happy. You must learn to be happy doing nothing.' On one occasion, when I wanted to speak to him about something at Caux, I found him in his room watching the sun setting over the Jura mountains, with its beams reflected on the surface of the Lake of Geneva. He signalled to me to take a chair beside him. As he said nothing to interrupt his contemplation, I was obliged to follow suit. As the sun's last rays disappeared, Buchman turned towards me and said, 'Wasn't that nice? Goodbye.' Contemplation was not my strong point, I had to admit.

Another time Buchman invited me to accompany him on a car trip leaving at 3 pm. I arrived three minutes late. Buchman had left but there was a message for me with a 20 Swiss franc note for my rail ticket, saying 'We shall meet you off the train.' That particular lesson cost Buchman the 20 franc rail ticket, but it remained with me for life.

On yet another occasion when he was sending me on a mission of three or four days to another country, he asked me how much money I would need. Without much reflection I mentioned a sum, which he gave me. Twenty-four hours later I realised my mistake and my purse was nearly empty. A call came from Buchman: 'Michel, how are you off financially?' 'I'm very short, Frank,' I replied. 'Yes, that's what I thought; so I have wired some money to you. You will get it tomorrow morning.' Once more I was learning something – and he was paying.

He never set himself up to be a spiritual director, and yet he was often a valued counsellor. He never hesitated to make a transatlantic or a transpacific telephone call to help me when I was facing a delicate situation. When his perspective seemed to be different from what my conscience was telling me, he would give way, saying, 'You know better than I do. I trust you.' And that, of course, forced me to take real responsibility as I was not just following his advice.

I shall mention one other lesson I learned a few days before his death. I was returning to Caux from a Muslim country where the Head of State had received me as Buchman's envoy. I felt I must see Buchman immediately, even although he was already in bed, to convey the presidential greetings. The next day, hearing my voice amongst a group of people around him, Buchman called me. He said, 'Michel, last night you came to see me. After you left, I tried to remember what you had said, but my only thought was: 'Michel is full of himself.' These were the last words he ever spoke to me as he died three weeks later. And he was right. I *was* full of myself.

What a friend he was – even though we were separated by fifty years.

A message well beyond the limits of his own culture

Having made these points to illustrate Buchman's spiritual influence, I should like to focus on the more practical legacy he left. The brief period that Buchman spent in Grenoble as a young man was hardly enough to enable him to speak French, let alone absorb the Latin mode of thought. When someone has spent his whole life in what we French call 'the Anglo-Saxon world' – i.e. essentially in America and Britain, plus the countries in Europe, Asia and Africa which have taken these two countries as development models – it is not easy to adapt to the Latin mind. Yet Buchman's contribution to the Latin world shows clearly that his message went well beyond the limits of his own culture. But many of his colleagues, coming from the same cultural background, had difficulty in the post-war years in allowing his message to expand beyond that culture and take wings into a universal dimension.

Having worked with Buchman from 1950 till his death in 1961, I can attest that, even if he was not always fully conscious of this need, he was still driven by a natural impulse springing from his own spiritual life, which led him to welcome all those who could help him to accomplish this wider mission.

A brewer like Louis Bouquet; the Cardinal Achille Liénart, Bishop of Lille; the trade unionist Maurice Mercier; the Socialist militant Irène Laure; the statesman Robert Schuman; the representative of the employers' organisation in Northern France, Robert Tilge; young men from the French Resistance like Maurice Nosley and Armand de Malherbe (and I am only giving a small sample of

French men and women) enabled Buchman's message to penetrate into the Latin world.

This was not an easy task. The activities of the Oxford Group and of Moral Re-Armament had spread from one country to another in a continuing stream of acquired experience. When it launched into Europe in 1946, the team which Buchman had built up on the American continent found itself confronted by historical realities which reshaped it profoundly. It became aware of the diversity of European culture.

Robert Schuman wrote a preface to *Remaking the World*, the book containing the principal speeches of Frank Buchman, with the aim of making his message understood throughout France. But the poor quality of the translation of the speeches, in frenchified English, undercut the objective. Another team (of which I was a part) had to immerse themselves in Buchman's way of thinking, not just his words, to express it in French. Buchman gave it his approval and in this way the French vocabulary of his message came into being. Schuman's clarity and precision of language was preserved: 'To provide teams of trained people, ready for the service of the state, apostles of reconciliation and builders of a new world'. Nothing else has better described Buchman's goals.

As he acknowledged, Schuman took advantage of an enforced convalescence, brought on by his heavy work schedule, to read Buchman's complete texts and immerse himself in them. When one re-reads his preface carefully, one is struck by the way the text clearly draws out the universal significance of Buchman's message. This message, reflecting Buchman's religious roots, is closely bound up in the text with his own spirituality. This typically Latin distinction between the spiritual and temporal spheres acquired growing importance as one got involved, first in Catholic countries, then in the Muslim, Buddhist and Indian worlds and also in the spiritual life of aboriginal peoples.

Spiritual insight

Schuman wrote as a statesman concerned about world problems. Buchman identified himself completely with his text because he totally shared Schuman's perspective. When European statesmen set out to describe the society they have to build, Buchman finds himself completely at one with them. The temporal challenges which unite them are clarified by the spiritual factors which might seem divisive at one level but which converge when it comes to state-management.

Such a claim is being vindicated in the 21st century, for all religious leaders now endorse it, or at least do not dare to contest it. In 1946 the spiritual insight of Buchman was needed to drive home this point. One has to acknowledge that the spiritual convergence of the three Catholic statesmen – Schuman, Adenauer and De Gasperi – helped him to launch out. The global dimension of his message began to get recognised. But his task was not made easier by those who deliberately put obstacles in his path.

The end of the Second World War left the world polarised between the United States and the Soviet Union. The latter was counting sooner or later on tipping the peoples of Europe one after another into its camp. It deliberately focused on that end. Though it was able fairly easily to draw into its orbit its neighbouring countries or those occupied by its armies, it had more difficulty when it tried by every device to achieve its goals in France and Italy. For Moscow the dividing line between the Anglo-Saxon and Latin worlds appeared to be an exploitable fault-line which could turn the Mediterranean into a new '*mare nostrum*'. But Buchman's penetration of the Latin world might undermine that plan. So to accuse him of belonging to the Protestant American camp might be a way of blocking his access to the Catholic Mediterranean countries.

Baseless reports appeared portraying Buchman and his co-workers as an American sect threatening Catholicism and they were taken seriously in certain authoritative quarters in Rome. As a result Moral Re-Armament was banned from the diocese of Milan, then in Belgium, and was tainted with suspicion in a number of other countries.

However, Buchman's work was ultimately judged not by these tendentious stories but by its fruits. That is where all the work done by Moral Re-Armament to improve industrial relations in Northern France became so important. This work, which had been watched and encouraged by Cardinal Liénart, who went to Caux himself in 1947, grew into a real social transformation involving factory owners and trade unionists. There is not space here to go into all the details of the profound changes of attitude that affected not only the textile industry of Northern France but several other economic sectors of the country (the coal mines, the chemical industry, railways, etc). (*See chapter 15*)

The Holy See's representative in France, Monsignor Guiseppe Roncalli, took a special interest in various spiritual initiatives going on in the country (the Taizé community, the protestant-catholic dialogue at the Trappist monastery of Les Dombes, the prayer week on Christian Unity initiated by Abbot Couturier), and so he did not fail to appreciate what was happening between bosses and workers in France. When he was appointed Pope as John XXIII, he had no hesitation in distancing himself from these baseless rumours.

Nor can one separate what happened in Italy from the French experience in this field, for the same sequence of events occurred. Buchman's efforts to help Italy when she was threatened by communistic pressure were hampered by opposition from the same quarters. When Monsignor Giovanni-Battista Montini (the future Pope Paul VI) was appointed Archbishop of Milan, he received Buchman in the chair of his cathedral for the solemn New Year Mass of 1956 to show his respect for the work done in the communistic suburbs of Milan. By this gesture he dispelled the warnings left by his predecessor.

It should be remembered that a similar attempt was made in the Anglican Church by certain individuals with dubious motives to put a brake on the work of Buchman in Britain.

'Overcoming the prejudices which separate classes, races and nations'

If I have featured Buchman's efforts on the French industrial scene, it is because it seems to me that they had the widest repercussions in facilitating the global outreach of Buchman and his co-workers. It was not a question of the personal influence of an eminent preacher in the spiritual domain but of the initiative of someone concerned about contemporary problems who was seeking how to influence things in the secular and spiritual world. In the precise wording of Schuman: 'What we need is a school where by a process of mutual teaching we can work out our practical behaviour towards others; a school where

Christian principles are not only applied and proven in personal relationships but succeed in overcoming the prejudices and enmities which separate classes, races and nations.' What better definition could there be of the relationship between spiritual and secular from the standpoint of a statesman like Schuman?

Having got rid of the Protestant American label, which some people wanted to hang on him, Buchman's work could be adapted to the Muslim and Buddhist worlds and to the peoples who have preserved their own original spiritual values – a work that continued after Buchman's death and continues today.

But there is another no less important contribution which Buchman made to Europe: with the support of the three Catholic heads of state already mentioned, he took up the great task of European reconciliation to which the name of one French woman, Irène Laure, is forever attached. Many books have been written about her and we shall not go into them here. But we have to recognise that Franco-German reconciliation, to which Caux contributed so much, has become today a source of hope to millions around the world. 'If the Germans and French can do it, why can't we?' That is the thought stamped on millions of human hearts which undercuts the arguments of those who champion division by exploiting ethnic and racial hatred. Even if Franco-German relations are not always what they should be, that page of world history will stand as a reference point for generations to come. In saying so, I have a picture in my mind of the Mufti of Zagreb speaking in the great hall of his mosque, which was full of Christians and Muslims, and inviting Irène Laure's daughter to relive that page of history for them.

The impact of Buchman's message on the Latin world

However, we have so far hardly scratched the surface of the theme raised at the outset: the impact of Buchman's message on the Latin world. The arrival at Caux of the French philosopher Gabriel Marcel, a Catholic existentialist, intrigued Buchman. At the outset he was surprised by Marcel's long preface, entitled *Letter to three anxious friends*, which became a classic in philosophical writing and appeared as the introduction to *Un Changement d'Espérance*, a book collecting many instances of change brought about by Buchman's work. The subtle nuances of the French philosopher were not characteristic of his style of thought, but he trusted Marcel and the preface contributed greatly to the Latinising of Buchman's work in many countries.

Thanks to Gabriel Marcel, Edmond Michelet, Minister of Justice and Garde des Sceaux in General de Gaulle's government, went to Caux in person, hoping to make contact with the head of the provisional government of Algeria who had himself previously turned up there. Even though this gesture had no concrete result, it was significant that in the midst of the Algerian war Caux should be thought of as a meeting place between the Northern and Southern shores of the Mediterranean. (Let me say in passing that Michelet and Robert Schuman are two statesmen whom the Catholic Church is considering as candidates for Beatification, the first step toward sainthood.)

I would offer another illustration. Central to Buchman's message was the practice of silent listening to one's inner voice and then of sharing or exchanging the intimate thoughts that came in the silence. These habits, in a Latinised form, became part of the regular practice of thousands of families around the world, thanks to Abbé Cafarel who went to Caux along with two couples who had adopted this discipline. They stimulated a movement of Christian couples known as Foyers Notre-Dame who practise what they call 'the duty to sit down', time which couples set aside for listening and sharing. The thousands of homes which adopted this discipline in Latin America and Europe did not even realise that they were indirect beneficiaries of the spiritual life of Frank Buchman.

An Italian Jesuit, Father Franco Lombardi, impressed by the spirit of Caux, even tried to copy Buchman's initiative by creating near Rome his own centre called 'Il Mondo migliore' (The Better World). He invited Buchman to the launching of his project. After attending, Buchman expressed doubts to me as to whether the initiative would prosper but it is interesting that his dynamic example made its mark in Rome.

Another young priest went to Caux in the 1950s and celebrated one of his first masses in the Caux chapel. A few years later he told me of the deep impression that his conversation with Buchman left on him. Today he is a cardinal.

It was not easy for Buchman to feel that in Rome he was regarded with suspicion by certain individuals simply because the opening to ecumenism had not yet happened. Nevertheless Eugene Tisserand, dean of the Sacred College of Cardinals and Prefect of the Congregation for the Eastern Church (and in this capacity worried about the injustice done to the Syriac Catholic Church in Kerala) appreciated Buchman's constructive efforts to restore religious tolerance there. Tisserand always gave Buchman a warm welcome.

Buchman's determination to come to grips with world

problems made him undertake a trip through the Far East in 1956, to Japan, Taiwan, Philippines, Vietnam and Thailand. He was received in Saigon by President Ngo Dinh Diem, a Catholic who was then head of the South Vietnamese government. Buchman, after sending me a short note with the President's greetings (as a group of us including Irène Laure and her husband had visited him earlier in 1956) made sure that I would receive a full report of the visit. The fact that a Catholic head of state would lean on Buchman's experience to find how to deal with a population composed of many different religious communities made its mark on my contact in the Holy Office in Rome, the very body which had harboured most reservations about Buchman's initiatives.

A different mentality began to operate

Sadly it was only after Buchman's death that certain personalities who had displayed most hostility acknowledged to those who were carrying on his work that they had been victims of a grave 'misunderstanding'. From talking with some of the pioneers of ecumenism, Brother Roger of Taizé in particular, I came to understand that the reservations encountered by Buchman were largely due to the fact that he was ahead of his time and in a way the victim of the slow pace at which that venerable body, the Catholic Church, was ready to value his pioneering spirit.

In the year after Buchman's death, Pope John XXIII opened the Second Vatican Council. A different mentality began to operate. Cardinal Franz König, Archbishop of Vienna, became a regular visitor to Caux and organised there one of the first colloquies between scientists and political and religious leaders on the future of the planet. He was coming to grips with the problems of the world exactly as Buchman would have done!

That having been said, I have no wish to hide the fact that certain leaders of the Catholic Church would have liked to help Buchman to understand better the role of spiritual authority which they wished to preserve and which they were not ready to hand over to him. Working among Christians of all denominations, Buchman – without wishing to – had been led by his co-workers to assume some of that authority. Monsignor François Chauvin, Bishop of Fribourg, Lausanne and Geneva, the diocese in which Caux is situated, assured Buchman of his unqualified paternal support but sought at the same time to pass on this Church's message – which Buchman was disposed to accept, as I can testify. One can legitimately ask whether this issue of spiritual authority was not more a problem for Buchman's entourage than for Buchman himself. The older he got, the more other people took over an authority which they should not have had.

I cannot finish this study of Buchman's influence in the Latin world without mentioning Maurice Mercier. Shaped in the doctrines of trade unionism from a young age by the French Communist Party, and having helped to create the great French trade union movement, Force Ouvrière, Mercier became one of the pioneers of '*paritarism*', i.e. the spirit, in his case inherited from Buchman, which enabled managerial and trade union movements to co-operate in running the great social organisms of France. Fifty years on, one realises that, even if that spirit has sadly disappeared, these institutions still shape French social life. Mercier – who remained outside all religious bodies until his death – seemed to me to be a symbol of Buchman's extraordinary outreach. What did they have in common? Remove from Buchman his religious side, his beliefs, his faith, his spirituality, and what remains? Mercier found even then in Buchman someone who understood him, who shared his vision of a more humane and just world, a lover of truth, someone with faith in mankind.

For those of us who since 1989 have seen so many Soviet citizens, steeped in eighty years of atheism and lacking any spiritual background, find at Caux something they have been seeking for years, it is like finding more Merciers, as millions of them do exist in the world.

Buchman's great merit is to have shown the way by which such atheists could find access to a faith which they discovered through silence at the very roots of their being.

So let us learn to be silent.

3

A German Veteran remembers

Extracts from a biography* by Hansjörg Gareis

Hansjörg Gareis, born in 1926 in Germany, served in the German Navy during World War 2, studied electrical engineering in Stuttgart and volunteered, in 1948, for full-time service in Moral Re-Armament. In 1968 he started a career in industry, was a director of personnel and finally founded and managed a firm providing jobs for long-term unemployed.

At the opening of Mountain House, Caux in 1946, Frank Buchman's opening words – it is said – were 'Where are the Germans? You will never rebuild Europe without the Germans.'

So it was that masses of Germans, like myself, were given a chance to enter into a dialogue with the outside world, seeing in Germans not outcasts but fellow human beings who were needed to pursue a common objective. They were people who came to us with no pointed finger. We stepped onto new ground every day. It was perfect timing, therefore, when we were introduced to an idea that might help us get on our feet again.

But there was no easy way around it. We Germans

*Stepping Stones 2001, ISBN: 3-00-008306-5

must first of all face the depth of our guilt, humbly ask God's forgiveness, and then courageously go on from there. We were given the grace of rebirth. It was like a life-belt for a drowning nation. Countless ordinary men and women, like me, all over the country were reaching out for it, testing it, trying it out.

No person alive could have dreamt, planned or even hoped for the evolution of the following years when a new nation rose like a Phoenix from the ashes. None of us will ever forget the, journey through Switzerland (for myself in 1949). It was not the institutionalised strength of an organisation but the contagious effectiveness of individuals who simply lived in accordance with their deepest beliefs.

The first thing I had to learn was that MRA's absolute moral standards meant not only that a person must not lie, steal, fornicate, murder, nor live a totally selfish life – it meant that in every detail of day-to-day affairs a standard of perfection must be aspired to.

I remember staying in an extremely old factory worker's two-room flat sharing the settee with Stan. He was a few years older than I, a red-headed, quiet and taciturn Australian. Stan told me about his wartime Air Force service as a bomber pilot when they hunted German submarines in the Atlantic. I shared with him how both my brother Claus and my brother-in-law had been killed from such attacks. We compared times. It could have been Stan who dropped one of the fatal bombs. During the night we prayed together and committed to God whatever we felt. Our host was deeply moved when we told him of our experience that night.

By summer 1950 it had become almost fashionable for German leaders to travel to Caux. It was still one of the few, if not the only place, outside our national borders where we could 'meet the world'. At Caux for the first time I rebelled against my friends. I had entered the inner circle of those who made the decisions about how the assembly was run. Nobody asked me to do so. But I felt terribly important attending all the planning strategy sessions, even the early morning ones in Frank Buchman's room. I always tried to be first in the room so that I could sit out of sight of the old gentleman lest he might ask me, 'Well, general's son, what do you think?'

It was just not right!

One day a number of dock-workers from the British Clyde shipbuilding industry were announced. At the chorus rehearsal, sheets with the music of a song were handed out which had been written during the war aiming to boost the patriotic spirit of the shipyard workers. The refrain was, 'It's the Clyde-built ships that win the war.' When I read these words I got up and declared that I was unable to sing them. It was just not right! Praising the British ships meant at the same time to condemn our Navy in which I had served and in which my brother and brother-in-law had been killed. This was applying two different sets of standards and I was not going to take sides against my own. Ursula, a girl from Hamburg (who was later to marry my friend Fromund) and I left the rehearsal in protest. The rest of the chorus did nothing to stop us.

Hours later, Ursula and I were summoned to Dr Buchman's room. We expected harsh accusations about still being Nazis at heart and so forth. Nothing of the sort happened. Frank, as he was called by everybody, heard us out and then suggested we listen to God together. I forget what thoughts were shared. Of course, we two ruefully accepted that we had behaved foolishly, that we must 'change' on the spot and do everything to make the British workers feel welcome. But Frank said something else. He suggested that my parents should be specially invited to attend a September session on the theme, 'The Role of the Armed Forces in the Age of Ideologies'. I had severe doubts that my parents would accept an invitation. So far they had declined any such attempt. Beyond that it would create an impossible open conflict situation when Allied army leaders would be compelled to meet their former German adversaries. The time was not yet ripe for such confrontation, I thought.

Still, I wrote to my mother and father and pleaded with them that here in Caux they would be able as in no other place in the world to voice all their feelings and fears, that they would find only open ears and hearts. No answer came from them. I had known it would not work. My sister Annemie had told me that our parents had been able for the first time to visit our relatives in Sweden. My father's only sister had married a Swedish pastor and had borne him five children, my cousins. They were our best loved relatives. Naturally, my parents would prefer to spend their summer holidays with them rather than being drawn into a mass of strangers and a cataclysm of feelings.

So the news, 'the Germans are coming and your parents are among them', was a complete surprise. Unknown to me, Peter, another German full-time worker of my age, had been sent with a large American car to Lennep and advised not to come back without them.

It never failed to move our compatriots deeply when they saw, above the driveway at the main entrance of

Mountain House, the German flag hoisted among those of many other nations. It is normal today. But at that time we knew of no other place where it would be thus demonstrated that we were accepted as equals. Inside, in the lovely entrance hall, our chorus was lined up. We had no German anthem then, so a hymn-like song had been composed, 'Deutschland, land loved by God'. When I saw my parents and the other Army men and their wives come in I was so excited and caught up in emotions that my voice failed me. But all the others sang fervently. Then somebody spoke a few words of welcome and the newcomers were led to their rooms. They had been given all the best apartments on the fourth floor, each with a balcony from where one had the most breathtaking view of Lake Geneva.

For the first plenary session next morning the large assembly hall was packed to capacity. An unusual tension had gripped everybody, it was almost tangible. From my place with the chorus behind the speakers' platform, facing the audience, I could see the frozen, suspicious faces of the Germans. They sat together in a tight group as if they wanted to protect each other. On the rostrum were a French retired general – one of the great figures during the war, a Swedish and a Swiss general, and one or two others. I guess many of us prayed that someone would find the right words to break down the invisible wall.

But it was not until the last speaker that it happened. Retired Rear-Admiral Owen Phillips of the Royal Navy mounted the podium. He was a jolly, heavy-set man with a round face and a booming bass voice. He wore big horn-rimmed glasses, and a navy-blue blazer with a colourful crest – he could have been nothing but a retired

British navy man. He spoke simply and to the point with a clear, manly voice. He addressed the Germans who were present in the audience.

We remained aloof, self-righteous and indifferent

Bill Phillips went back to the years between the two great wars when Germany suffered from the plight of the Versailles Treaty and its consequences. 'We British watched your predicament from our island, and we remained aloof, self-righteous and indifferent. I have always felt deeply ashamed about this attitude, and I am convinced that our lack of human greatness has contributed to creating the causes for yet another war. We must stand to our part of the blame.' The Admiral said he wanted to take this first chance of meeting responsible Germans to ask them to accept his sincere apologies for his own and his country's failures. Stepping down from the platform, he walked up to my parents and the other Germans and shook hands with them. It was a genuine gesture. We all knew he meant what he said.

Hours later, I looked for my father and mother and found that they had silently retreated to their room, unable to talk to anybody. They both embraced me, a show of affection my father had always avoided. During the following days I watched with wonder the transformation taking place in them. The reason for their coming – to get me down from the mountain – was never again mentioned: no, now they were able to understand what kept all of us so involved. Their bitterness melted away like ice under the sun, and that made free the way to clear their own consciences. It was natural for another German, General Hossbach, and my father to speak to the assembly, in the name of their comrades, about their resolve to use what strength they had to work for a Germany the world could trust and respect again. A door had been pushed open to a road that allowed those who chose to travel on it to deal with the past instead of repressing it.

On 1 May 1951 my father and mother received a longish telegram which was signed by the chairmen of both the Senate and House Foreign Affairs Committees of the United States of America, along with other Senators. It read:

> *As members of the Foreign Relations and Foreign Affairs Committee of the United States Senate and House of Representatives, we wish to add our support to the invitation extended to you to attend the World Assembly for Moral Re-Armament of the nations at Mackinac Island, Michigan, June 1 to 12, and to the welcome already issued by our Michigan colleagues in Congress.*
>
> *Your presence in the United States, together with other distinguished leaders from Europe and Asia, can do much to focus the attention of the American people at this time on the positive steps that can be taken everywhere to answer the ideological threat of world Communism. We need such a demonstration of united strength in the field of inspired moral leadership, without which our common military, political and economic efforts to save the free world will certainly be less effective.*
>
> *We are impressed with the practical evidence of what such active moral leadership has accomplished to establish democracy as a working force in danger areas that affect the future of your country and ours. We recognize the opportunity this assembly offers to proclaim*

to the world an inspired experience of democracy based on moral standards and the guidance of God, which is the greatest bulwark of freedom.

We look forward to welcoming you on the occasion of your visit.

Since my parents' return from Caux a year earlier, their lives had been filled with a new purpose. They had opened their home to the host of friends they had found and, whenever possible, the three of us together went to attend meetings all over the country. We shared with each other a harmony we had not known before. For me, it was a miracle to watch their joy in having found what my father called 'the right road'.

Rapprochement with their hated neighbour

It was, for instance, but one of countless small mosaic stones that were beginning to form the picture of a new Europe, when my father was asked, with other Germans, to attend a large assembly in Lille, the industrial centre in northern France. Driving there in a car through countryside where he had fought in two world wars, he recognised the area so well that, when the driver lost his way, the general was able to guide him with unerring certainty. Although on this occasion the Germans came by invitation, among the French people the memories of millions of war casualties, of atrocities and humiliations inflicted on them, were much alive still.

Only a few months before, French foreign minister Robert Schuman had caused a sensation with his suggestion of merging the European coal and steel industries, including those of West Germany, while at the same time the overwhelming majority of the French people refused any kind of rapprochement with their hated neighbour country.

When my father was introduced as a wartime Tank Corps commander, the audience was stunned. He reported about the change of heart he had experienced which enabled him to accept his personal responsibility for the wrongs done by his country. He begged the French to forgive him if they could, and to believe and trust him. The warm-hearted response to what he said was, in his own words, one of the most overwhelming experiences he had ever had.

Thus strengthened, my parents had written to Frank Buchman saying they were prepared, as their part towards a national atonement, to be of service to the movement wherever they might be needed. Buchman's reply went far beyond their expectations. He wrote from California, 'If you can make arrangements, we would welcome you and your son at the Assembly at Mackinac Island in June and I would like you to stay on in this country after the Assembly is concluded if that should be possible.' As if to confirm that this was not just a friendly encouragement the telegram from Washington, quoted above, had arrived.

They faced an extremely difficult decision. They were both over sixty; they had no savings; and pensions were under discussion in Parliament with no outcome in sight. To go travelling, even for a few months would mean giving up the security of my father's job and to close down their home because they could not afford to pay the rent while away. And what would their relatives think, and my mother had 'nothing to wear' and no money to buy anything suitable! I admired the courage they had in deciding to go, when we had a family caucus to consider this.

One enormous incomprehensible myth

Few of us had ever been on a long-distance flight before and in those days we had to refuel at Shannon, Ireland, and Gander, Newfoundland, before reaching New York. During the last lap one of the engines broke down and despite the pilot's comforting words, we were scared stiff. On arrival the immigration procedures seemed to take for ever, each person being interrogated separately for half an hour. So although we had landed early in the morning, it was lunch-time before we were taken to Manhattan in a fleet of super-buses. Everything seemed big, enormous, fast and frightening. For us Europeans we got the general impression that to be of any interest in the States, something had to be the longest or the smallest, the first or the last, the biggest or the tiniest of its kind in the world.

The Grand Hotel on Mackinac Island, Michigan, was the location of the Assembly. The hotel and the island presented breathtaking sights to us as we arrived. After twenty years of strict isolation for many of the German delegates the frank discussions with people from so many different countries and so many different parts of the United States were sometimes shockingly revealing. Underneath the general impression of bonhomie and neighbourliness we often felt we were regarded as creatures from another planet. Germany was equated with Nazism, and Nazism stood for many people as one enormous incomprehensible myth, as a phenomenon whereby in a mysterious way the evils of mankind had been concentrated in one particular people.

For my parents the question of guilt, of national and personal culpability, became central. It was heatedly discussed among the German delegation. Obviously, the assumption of a particularly evil German character was ridiculous, and the suggestion of collective guilt of all members of one iniquitous race preposterous. But the Alabama journalist had told our little group, 'It must be crucifying for you Germans to live with these unspeakable crimes on your conscience.' How should we, how should each one of us individually deal with this? The world was not interested whether any one of us had personally committed atrocities or not. The world held us all responsible, as debtors for capital that had been squandered. The world would not tolerate us trying to silently repress our most recent past, nor any attempt on the part of any one of us to declare himself free from blame.

The three of us were asked one day to address the Assembly. For my father and mother it was like a trial, but they were both ready to publicly reveal some of the issues deepest in the hearts. They expressed their gratitude to Frank Buchman for his efforts to make us welcome again in the family of nations, and to men like Admiral Phillips whose action had opened for them and many others the chance to actively participate in an atonement.

It cost my father dearly to talk about his shame about his country's and his people's deeds. At the end, they were both pale-faced and shaking. My father felt terribly humiliated when no one thanked him for what he had said; only one young American clapping him on the back and saying, 'Well done, general, carry on the good work!' My parents wanted to return home.

Later in the evening we were walking along the shore line of the island. It was a lovely summer evening with only a light breeze coming in from the lake, causing the same rustling sound in the trees that we had loved so in East Prussia. That seemed to have been in another life.

But the sounds and sights of nature again had their soothing effect. We calmed down.

'Of course, we do not know what your words caused in those who listened,' I said. 'Remember how deeply you were stirred in Caux, and that it took you quite a while to be able to respond.'

'There is something in that.' 'What is more,' I went on, 'If I say sorry to someone for something I have done, and if I say it just for the reason to coax him to admit his own faults, then that is not the right motive, it seems to me. Like making a gift to someone and expecting something in return is not really a gift. It is a deal.'

We have an obligation to carry on

For a while we walked in silence. Then my mother said softly, 'The Good Lord put us on this track through these people. They have done so much for us and for our country. We have an obligation to carry on. We must learn from our mistakes and try to pass on what we have learned.'

My parents had become friends with a Protestant bishop who was a member of the Swedish delegation. With him they had a long conversation. I never knew what they talked about. But obviously, they had made their peace with God. They accepted their part of the blame as far as they could see it, mainly the lack of enough courage and care, and their unconditional need to be forgiven.

Peter Howard told them that with the reality of their experience they could play an important part in the USA, not only in gradually removing traditional anti-German sentiments with origins reaching back long before the Hitler era. Moreover, he said, the moral defeatism that enabled Hitler to come to power in the first place was just as rampant at present in the western democracies as it had been in Germany and Europe in the thirties. Our common task was to fight materialism in all its forms, the militant materialism of Communism just as much as the subtle but no less dangerous selfishness of the Capitalist world.

For me, these issues did not carry so much weight, at least not at that time. What my parents went through on Mackinac Island was very much their own personal affair. Today it is easy to be derisive about our idealism, to call it naïve and unworldly. At the time, everything seemed so clear and simple, so near at hand. It was intoxicating to be able to add something constructive to the living flow of events, partake in the organic build-up of a philosophy which, if proved to be right and valid, would give meaning to everything one thought and did.

Schopenhauer, the German philosopher, was convinced that the character of man is unchangeable. He wrote, 'The nature of man will remain the same all through his life. The outer frame, the circumstances of life, the sum of his knowledge and his opinions – all that might change. But underneath it, like a crab in his shell, will remain the identical, actual individual, unchangeable and unmistakable, always the same.' We were out to prove Schopenhauer wrong.

One day, my parents and I stood at the New York Embankment facing the Statue of Liberty and regarded the memorial with the thousands of names of Americans who had lost their lives in the war. 'People in this country do not realise how privileged and fortunate they are,' said my father. 'For them it is a birthright to honour their heroes. We Germans are not allowed to mourn our dead.'

I thought that was a rather profound remark. I did not realise it until much later – and I guess the outside world never comprehended the significance of the fact – that most Germans, eager to prove that they never had been and certainly were no longer Nazis, forcefully refused to deal, even less to come to terms, with our recent past. *Vergangenheitsbewaltigung* is not only one of those tape-worm words so loved in our language. It also signifies a trauma pursuing us to this very day.

In every Western country I visited one would find memorials, often decorated with national colours, fresh wreaths and flowers. In Germany most efforts to this end have been successfully prevented. The likelihood that among them those to be remembered had also been SS and other criminals contaminated the mass of innocents so much that we denied each other first the right and then the capacity to mourn. Such things leave indelible marks on a people.

Finally the time came for my parents to leave for home, while I stayed on in America. It had not been an altogether easy time for them in the States. However they had made a great contribution to the rebuilding of relations between Germany and the United States and in turn to the eventual creation of the new German Army. At the time of their departure, one newspaper called our family 'Ambassadors of a new Germany', which certainly described what they always hoped to be. Meanwhile I stayed on as a member of the cast of the musical show *Jotham Valley*, where I played the part of a cowboy. Often the showings of this play resulted in our being invited to visit people's homes or to parties by people who wanted to know more of what we were doing.

What on earth could I say?

One evening six of us young men from the cast were invited by a Rabbi to meet members of his Jewish community in California. I was not told beforehand and would have probably refused to go, if I had known. We found ourselves in a large room next to the local Synagogue with about forty or fifty men. So many things went through my mind. Had these people suffered from the Nazis? Had they perhaps survived a concentration camp? How would they receive me? What could I say to these Jews? I felt stigmatised and terror crept up in my body and I felt a nameless kind of anxiety. As my friends were speaking I was wondering what on earth I could say.

'Perfect love casts out all fear,' I jotted down in my notebook and, 'If you want to, you can open your heart and simply love them, each one of them. Have no fear and be honest. Tell them what you are going through and what you have decided to do with your life.'

When the Rabbi introduced me I was calm. He said that I had been a member of the Hitler Youth and later served in the German Navy. He told them my father had commanded a Tank Corps in the war and that my parents had been taking part in the campaign of Moral Re-Armament in America. You could feel a stone wall build up in the room. But I was not afraid any more.

Only a few clapped when I sat down again and the applause died down quickly. Nobody wanted to ask any questions. There was no discussion. The Rabbi closed the meeting and thanked us for coming. He told them that what I had said had made them thoughtful. We did not seem to have reached the hearts of our audience. It was sad.

As we left the hall a man stood in my way. He was

about fifty, an unobtrusive kind of person, whom one would not have noticed in a crowd. When I stopped, he hesitated for a moment and then, as if he had made up his mind, stretched out his hand and gripped mine. We stood there, hands locked for quite a while. Then he said, in German, 'In 1939 I swore a holy oath never again to defile my mouth with your language. I have been wrong. Don't answer me,' he went on, 'I have listened carefully to what you said. Would you give me the pleasure of coming to my home and meeting my family and having a meal with us?' He told me he would first ask his wife and call me to make a date.

He kept his word and a few days later picked me up in his car. His wife and son stood at the entrance of their house to receive me. She was an outgoing, happy lady with the gift of making one feel at home right away. Their son had had his Bar Mitzvah celebration recently and proudly showed me some of the gifts which relatives and friends had brought. His father told me their son had been just a small baby when they had been forced to flee from their German home. They were grateful that the boy knew nothing about the terrible circumstances into which he was born and that he was able to grow up in freedom. Before the meal, my host prayed in Hebrew. I felt that God was present and blessed this moment. Later I had the chance to meet many more Jews. For myself, the evening with that Jewish family is a priceless treasure that nobody can take away from me. It was a gift to realise that God can direct the hearts of men, to know that reconciliation is possible even between the hardest of adversaries.

4

The Hidden Ingredient of Japan's post-war Miracle

by Fujiko Hara, for Yukika Sohma

Born in 1912, founder of the Japan Association for Aid and Relief, and Japan's first English/Japanese simultaneous interpreter, Yukika Sohma is now in her mid-nineties. The mother of Fujiko Hara, she still travels around the world as vice-chair of the Ozaki Yukio Memorial Foundation and chair of the Japan-Korea Women's Friendship Association. She is the third daughter of Yukio Ozaki, a well-known liberal politician known as 'kensei no kami' or 'the god of constitutional government' in Japan.

Daughter Fujiko Hara has been an interpreter and teacher of interpreting for over twenty-five years. She is a member of AIIC (International Association of Conference Interpreters). Her work has included G7 Economic Summits, Interaction Council meetings of former heads of state and government, the World Economic Forum, and top-level conferences and negotiations worldwide in all major fields. She is a managing director of the Ozaki Yukio Memorial Foundation and the grand-daughter of Yukio Ozaki, who when Mayor of Tokyo presented the Japanese flowering cherry trees to Washington, DC.

SHINZO Abe, a grandson of Nobusuke Kishi, was the first prime minister of Japan to have been born after the Second World War. As there are fewer and fewer people who have lived through the war years and the challenging search for peace that has led to the world we know today, Yukika Sohma believes she has a responsibility to share her experience.

For Japan, finding a respectable place and playing a responsible role among the family of nations has been the most important item on the national agenda since the country's doors were opened after two hundred years of seclusion. The first stage of the new government's efforts was focused on developing a national industry and building the armed forces, emulating the post-industrial revolutionary marvels of the West, in order to be accepted as a 'modern nation' and defend the country from encroaching colonialism. After achieving these first objectives in an amazingly short span of time, the military soon invaded and defeated China (1894-5), Japan's erstwhile mentor, and thrust her presence upon a sceptical world by vanquishing Imperial Russia (1904-5). From that time onwards the triumphant militarists held the people and the nascent political system hostage and through reckless adventurism brought unprecedented defeat. In less than one hundred years after fumbling to find its place in the global community, Japanese militarists had brought misery and destruction on its people and those in the neighbouring countries.

Japan had to start all over again. The rebuilding of the war-torn nation could only come by finding a path to reconciliation. And rebuilding diplomatic relations was all about mending personal ties. In fact, Japan's successful economic rehabilitation began with a handful of citizens and politicians who were inspired to act as statesmen, apologising sincerely for their country's past. This time it was Frank Buchman, an American, who extended his hand to help the Japanese make amends for the past. For his creative initiative the Japanese government in 1955 presented Buchman with the Second Class Order of the Rising Sun. Of this same work the French statesman and former Prime Minister, the late Robert Schuman said to Buchman at the time of the Peace Treaty in San Francisco in September 1951, 'You made peace with Japan before we did.'

The Second World War, the costliest war in history, ended officially on 2 September 1945. In June 1948, nine Japanese civilians left Japan to attend an MRA meeting held in Los Angeles at the invitation of Dr Buchman. They were the first civilians to leave the country by special permission of the occupation forces. Among them were Takasumi and Hideko Mitsui, and Yukika and her husband Yasutane Sohma. They accepted the invitation, realising that while the New Constitution adopted in 1946 gave the Japanese a democratic system, the spirit was missing that would enable it to function. The San Francisco Peace Treaty that would bring Japan back into the family of nations was still years away.

Once the group from Japan was in the United States some Americans apologised for the atomic and hydrogen bombs dropped on Hiroshima and Nagasaki. Yukika was gratified to hear this. It was comforting to feel that one was a victim and others perpetrators. That year the Sohmas went on to Europe after the Mitsuis returned to Japan. There Yukika had a shock. She was told the British delegation had refused to be present at a meeting where she and Yasu were present. Yukika asked why and was told of the experiences the British prisoners of war had in Japanese camps in Burma. Governments often hide embarrassing truths from their citizens. This time it was Yukika's turn to face the truth and apologise. These were sobering but healing days.

Buchman generously invited seventy Japanese in 1949 and another seventy-five in 1950 to attend MRA meetings in the US and Europe, where he introduced them to members of his big world family.

Reconciliation – diplomacy of the humble heart

It was the autumn of 1957, and Mr Nobusuke Kishi, who had been sworn in as prime minister earlier in the year, was scheduled to go on a seven nation tour of Southeast Asia as well as Australia and New Zealand. Most of these countries had yet to make peace with Japan. As a maritime nation with few natural resources there was a pressing need for Japan to open trading relations with other countries to earn foreign exchange.

Two women, Shidzue Kato and Yukika Sohma, who had accepted Buchman's challenge to live by the principle of 'what is right' rather than 'who is right', felt strongly the need to atone for the wrongs committed by the Japanese military. Before trying to do business this stain on the country's honour had to be acknowledged and apologised for. Kato, a popular politician from the Japan Socialist Party who took up the issue in the House of Representatives inquired of Kishi, who was about to embark on his tour of the Asian countries, if he was prepared to do this, which drew a positive response from the premier.

The first port of call was the Philippines, where Mr Kishi's apology for the Japanese atrocities was received with positive surprise by the National Assembly. The late

ST. RICHARD'S PRAYER

THANKS BE TO THEE,
my Lord,
Jesus Christ,
For all the benefits which
Thou hast given me,
For all the pains and insults
which Thou hast borne for me,
O most merciful Redeemer,
Friend and Brother.
May I know Thee more clearly,
Love Thee more dearly,
And follow Thee more nearly.

Westbrook © P571 *Printed in England*

President Magsaysay, who had been killed in an air accident a few months before, had earlier invited the international delegation of MRA to visit his country. Yukika was part of the group and recalled how the delegation was warmly received, with a beautiful lei (garland) being offered to each visitor except the Japanese. She felt numbed by the bitterness and hatred in the cool stares of their hosts.

Mr Kishi's diplomacy of reconciliation proved successful in Australia as well. The prime minister had been invited to address the two houses of Parliament, but the Australian veterans' association was highly critical. Mr Kishi noted in his memoirs that he felt the cold and hostile atmosphere transform to one of acceptance and then to warm trust as his humble apology was interpreted. 'As Prime Minister,' he wrote, 'I intended to visit the United States. Before doing so, however, I felt I needed to visit Southeast Asia first so that I could negotiate on behalf of Japan speaking for Asia rather than as an isolated country... I made a point to apologise for Japan's wartime wrongs and urge my hosts to work hand in hand with us for peace and prosperity.' Mr Kishi also visited Burma and apologised there, too, in his capacity as prime minister. These bold initiatives were not well known in Japan but the media gave prominence to them wherever Mr Kishi visited. Yukika recalls how in this way he earned unwavering trust among the Asians.

In 1965, the Asian Pacific Parliamentarians Union (APPU) was established on the initiative of Mr Kishi and Mr Saburo Chiba, also a member of the House of Representatives. Japan by then had recovered to the extent that its government was able to offer official development assistance (ODA) to Asian countries. Mr Chiba had felt that relationships with these were still not quite right and that something was amiss. Dr Buchman learned about this and suggested creating an organisation of parliamentarians who would meet regularly to discuss how they could complement intergovernmental relations. Its five founding member nations were Korea, the Philippines, Thailand, Taiwan China and Japan. The organisation was renamed the Asia Pacific Parliamentarians Union in 1980 and draws its membership from twenty-three countries and regions. Yukika interpreted for the Union until 1975 when her daughter took over from her. Yukika recalls that there were many parliamentarians who were more concerned for their country's future than their personal ambitions.

5

Human Torpedo turns Creative Consultant

by Hideo Nakajima

Hideo Nakajima, one of a few selected Japanese who were trained as human torpedoes, survived the war because it ended before his first mission. Meeting Moral Re-Armament after demobilisation he found a purpose for his future and a training for life. He then began using this training in his work in business, where he became sought after as a 'trouble shooter' for companies in difficulty. Later he joined the Caux Round Table.

IT was a fine day, the sky was blue, and the trees were green and fresh – a typical beautiful early summer morning on Mackinac Island, Michigan. When I entered the meeting hall in the Grand Hotel, which in those days had the longest porch in the world, I found just a few people in the hall and no Japanese at all. Until the day before, a Japanese delegation of about fifty were there. I was shocked and I panicked. All the other Japanese were gone and I was left alone!

Peter Howard and Paul Campbell, two close colleagues of Frank Buchman, came to see me and told me that I was invited to go to Los Angeles on the same train with Buchman. When I got to my compartment I found I had an upper berth and Peter had the lower one. In the next compartment were Paul and John Wood, another colleague at the heart of the MRA international force. So during the course of those three nights and four days they helped me clean up all the dirt accumulated in my character and I felt completely washed. This experience has helped me throughout life more than I can say. I saw my true nature and became convinced of the reality of sin.

In spite the name having been altered from MRA to Initiatives for Change, I hope the same fundamental conviction still exists among young people deep in their hearts.

During the second evening on the train, Frank invited me to have lunch with him the following day. All next morning, I was thinking and writing down what I should say to him and how to make a good impression. Lunchtime came, and Frank and I ate alone. I was trying to tell him what I had written in the morning, while Frank was watching the beautiful scenery of the American West passing, just as in a Western movie. Obviously he was enjoying both the view and the lunch, but I can remember neither. At the end of the meal Frank stood up, and I did the same. Frank said to the waiter, 'Thank you. The lunch was delicious,' and walked back to his compartment.

I was thinking the whole afternoon and all next night. Early the following morning, a little voice in my heart came and said: 'NOT Frank, but God!' Later, when Frank walked by, I said to him, 'Not Frank, but God!' Frank stopped and looked at me with a twinkle in his eye and said, 'That's it, Deko, fine, fine, fine!'

This experience guided me throughout my life, for example when I served Prime Minister Nobusuke Kishi as secretary-general of the Asian Parliamentarians Union and afterwards as an Expert Committee member, and later still when I travelled with Prime Minister Takeo Fukuda. Both former prime ministers Kishi and Fukuda came to Caux in Switzerland with their wives, guided by Saburo Chiba, a leading member of the Diet, and Mrs Chiba, and did much to further rapprochement and normalisation of diplomatic relations after the Second World War.

Two by two

It was 1952 in Miami. We were preparing to go to Europe and Asia. Hisato Ichimada, Governor of the Bank of Japan, came to see Frank Buchman. Ichimada had come to the US with two purposes, first to secure money through the World Bank to build the Shinkansen (Bullet Train), and second to see Frank to talk over how to create an MRA Asian Centre. Frank and the cast of the musical *Jotham Valley* cared unstintingly for Ichimada. It so happened that when he was in Miami all the airlines were on strike, and he had seen how the struggle was settled in front of his eyes due to the efforts of MRA.

Ichimada, to whom Frank gave special care and attention, took his message deeply to heart. This clearly changed Japan. Ichimada approached top business people such as Keizo Shibusawa (grandson of Eiichi Shibusawa, founder of modern industrial Japan), Shinji Sogo who built the Japanese Bullet Train, Taizo Ishizaka who was chairman of the Federation of Japanese Economic Organizations (Keidanren), and Kichizaemon Sumitomo, head of the Sumitomo family. It was with their help that the MRA Asian Centre was built in Odawara.

It was due to Sogo's commitment, together with Ichimada's help in obtaining World Bank money, that the

Bullet Train was built in time for the Tokyo Olympics. I worked with Ichimada when he was chairman of the Japan-India Society. He often recalled those days when he visited Frank in Miami. He once said, 'That visit made my conviction clear. It was one of the turning points of my life.' On another occasion, we were gathered near the entrance of the hall in Caux, Switzerland, where we were holding the World MRA Conference. Kichizaemon Sumitomo and his wife were about to leave and Frank had come to see them off. 'If you want to save your country,' he told them, 'forget yourself and go all out.'

In the play *Road to Tomorrow* Sumitomo was cast as a tenant farmer who had stolen water. In the course of its tour of Japan it was performed at the birthplace and headquarters of the Sumitomo Corporation. All the top management were in the audience and everyone was shocked to see the 'head of the family' playing such a part. It was not only the Sumitomo people who were shocked but the whole city. And yet Sumitomo stood firm and spoke with deep conviction after the play.

Meanwhile, construction of the National Railways' Shinkansen was going quite well, and National Railways governor Sogo visited Buchman on Mackinac Island where an MRA world conference was being held. He expressed his gratitude to Frank for creating a really united spirit in the National Railways. After Sogo's speech, everyone marched from the conference hall to the dining room with Frank and Sogo walking in front to the musical accompaniment of 'Two by Two'.

Commitment to repent

There was a strange and awkward atmosphere at Manila airport. I had flown direct from the United States to

Manila, and was at the airport to meet an international delegation of politicians and businessmen, as well as the cast of an international musical. What I saw there shocked me deeply. Every member of the delegation was welcomed with garlands of flowers except the Japanese. It was 1955; ten years had passed since the war, and I felt the people of the Philippines still harboured a deep hatred and resentment toward the Japanese.

All the members of the MRA delegation were invited by President Magsaysay to the presidential palace the next day. I had to present the Japanese delegation and left the Manila Hotel for the palace by taxi. 'If you are going to meet with the president of the Philippines,' the taxi driver said to me, 'you had better see one place on the way.' He stopped the taxi outside a ruined church and said, 'Innocent people were burned to death here.' There were charred black stones inside on which victims had scratched their wills with their fingernails. I was shocked, and my first thought was, 'I didn't do it.' Then came another voice: 'You attended the Naval Academy, so as a member of the Japanese armed forces you share the responsibility.'

I stood there and committed myself to God. 'I will give my life to fight for Japan so that the same mistake will never be made again.' Half a century later, I still have the burning belief that I must fight for my country in this way.

President Magsaysay was very warm and grasped the importance of MRA, and for years his conviction was taken up by his successors. The MRA musical *The Vanishing Island* was performed to a packed audience. After the play, there were to be speeches by Niro Hoshijima, MP (who became speaker of the House of Representatives) and Kanju Kato, a Socialist MP who, because of his fiery nature, was called 'Fireball Kato'. When they began to speak, the audience exploded and shouted back in Japanese with hatred, but when Yukika Sohma interpreted their heartfelt apologies for the past, with the same passion as the speakers, the entire theatre became deathly still and then burst into thunderous applause.

After the show, all the Japanese were standing in a corner of the theatre. A great many Filipinos surrounded us and told us how they had been made to suffer by the Japanese during the war but had found forgiveness for Japan that evening. People from both the Philippines and Japan were moved to tears. One person in a wheelchair came up and said, 'I was healthy and normal but at the end of the war a Japanese soldier cut both my legs off. I had decided I would not speak about it as long as I lived, but when I heard leading Japanese sincerely apologising this evening I decided that though I cannot forget what happened to me I can forgive.'

Not right, not left, but straight

In 1958, Prime Minister Nobusuke Kishi called Buchman on the phone. Kishi was facing tremendous opposition in Japan influenced by agitation from the leftist camp. The prime minister explained the seriousness of the situation. Frank listened very carefully and said, 'Please go not right, not left, but straight.'

On one occasion when Kishi was paying an official visit to several European nations, he brought with him to Caux Mrs Kishi and Takeo Fukuda (who later became prime minister) and his wife, together with Mr and Mrs Saburo Chiba. Later on, I was invited to work with these three statesmen and found out that Prime Minister Kishi had the idea of establishing diplomatic relations with Korea. Prime Minister Fukuda worked ardently to create heart-to-heart relationships with the ASEAN nations—the so-called Fukuda Doctrine. For his part, Saburo Chiba initiated the creation of the Asian Parliamentarians Union.

After he stepped down as prime minister, Kishi met President Park Chung-Hee of the Republic of Korea, and although President Park could speak eloquent Japanese, in those days circumstances did not allow him to do so. So I was invited to interpret Japanese into English, while a Korean interpreted from English to Korean. The main purpose of this meeting was to start to talk over how we could begin to normalise diplomatic relations between the two nations. Right at the beginning, Kishi expressed his heartfelt regret over the difficult years when Korea suffered because of Japan. As I was interpreting, I remembered that when Kishi had come to Caux he was very interested in the fact that Germany and France were beginning to build a new relationship through apology and forgiveness. After this discussion between him and President Park, normalisation talks were handed over to the Ministry of Foreign Affairs and the Japan-ROK relationship became normalised.

As prime minister, Kishi officially apologised to the ASEAN nations for what Japan had done during the Pacific war, and again at the joint meeting of the Australian Upper and Lower Houses he similarly expressed his regret for Japan's actions. The Veterans' Association of Australia was organising a demonstration against Japan, but after hearing Kishi's apology they cancelled the demonstration, and soon afterwards the way was opened to normal diplomatic relations.

King and elevator boy

Frank Buchman was invited by many nations around the world, and his musical groups were received enthusiastically wherever they performed. World War 2 ended in 1945 but the world was divided into the eastern and western camps, and people were worried that we might face the same kind of disaster we had been through before. When we went around the various nations, leading politicians, industrialists and labour leaders were included in the delegation. And since I was president of a university student body, I was welcomed as a student leader. When we were invited to present our musical plays, the international group would visit places such as city halls, labour unions, and gatherings of university students.

It was like water flowing into a dry desert, since everybody was longing for ideas on how to keep peace in the world. And since every year the MRA world conference was held on Mackinac Island in the US and/or at Caux in Switzerland, national leaders also visited these places. When, as in the case of Japan, management and labour from leading industries participated together and found answers to their conflicts, whole nations began to wonder, 'What is the secret?'

In this way, top government people began to be interested, and kings and queens, presidents and their first ladies, prime ministers and their wives did too, and news of this was always announced enthusiastically to the cast of the musical and the international delegates. Then when we talked to people we would mention 'this country's king' or 'that country's president'. In other words, we became swollen-headed.

Frank came back to Europe and visited Milan, in Italy. I was with him when we got into a hotel lift and the elevator boy said, 'Hi, Frank – welcome back to Milan.' Frank called him by his first name and asked, 'When do you get off work today?' 'This afternoon, Frank,' he answered. Frank invited him to his room for tea. I was invited, too. When I entered, the boy was sitting there already. He was the only guest, and we explained MRA to him with the same conviction and passion as we would to kings and queens. I also spoke from the heart in telling him of my commitment to repent when I pledged myself to God in the Philippines.

Asian Parliamentarians Union

Saburo Chiba once visited Frank in Tucson, Arizona. After that, Chiba and I began to plan how to organise an Asian Union. One problem was the Japanese foreign aid programme that was typical of the bureaucratic attitude in government. Japan gave away huge amounts of money and material assistance, but always with self-serving strings attached.

Chiba, who had many friends in Asia before the war, was deeply concerned with this situation. Japan was trying to provide aid but was resented by the receiving nations because of this attitude. After talking this over with Prime Minister Kishi and Takeo Fukuda, Chiba and I were chosen to make the rounds with the object of organising such a Union. In the discussions that followed, the ODA programme among other matters was discussed with parliamentarians from the Asian nations and a list of priorities was drawn up. Almost no one in Japan realises how dangerous it was for our country when Mao Zedong and Chou En-lai made an all-out effort to oust Prime Minister Kishi and create a successful revolution in Japan. Kanju 'Fireball' Kato and his wife, Senator Shidzue Kato, together with Yukika Sohma, stood by the prime minister when the Japanese Parliament was surrounded by demonstrators who were attempting to overthrow the government.

It is very hard to convince people now how Frank Buchman protected the democracy that God had given us by taking his message to leaders and others during those days. This was why Prime Minister Kishi and his team strove so hard to build free and peaceful Asian nations.

Speaking at the ASEAN Conference in Malaysia, Takeo Fukuda, then prime minister, emphasized the importance of 'heart to heart relationships'. Later, he became chairman of the Asian Parliamentarians Union and his heart-to-heart relationships became a household term among the APU nations. I accompanied Fukuda when he toured the ASEAN nations, and saw for myself how he gave his own heart to education and population problems. In Kishi I saw a man of strategy, in Chiba one of initiative, and in Fukuda a man who won hearts. They were the right men at the right time and all played important roles.

* * * * *

Caux Round Table

The whole world was bashing Japan. Every nation was attacking the country because it was enlarging its share of products in their markets. The Japanese were puzzled. We were taught: 'Work hard to produce better and cheaper products. Work hard to sell and increase your market share so you can sell better and cheaper products.' So the Japanese worked hard and single-mindedly. And the harder they worked the angrier the world became.

Frits Philips, chairman of the Dutch company Philips, felt strongly that something should be done. His company had a special relationship with Matsushita and he knew many Japanese industrial leaders. He invited European, American and Japanese business and industrial leaders to Caux for a round table discussion. This came to be called the 'Caux Round Table' (CRT). Ryuzaburo Kaku, chairman of Canon, responded that 'Japanese should live and work together for the common good.' He talked with top leaders of Japanese industrial companies. The Federation of Economic Organizations of Japan, and the Japan Committee for Economic Development responded and numerous companies took the need for social responsibility and ethics seriously.

Many nations joined the Caux Round Table, and it soon became clear that Western nations have a tendency to reason and theorise while Japan tends to emphasise the importance of the process and the result. People at the CRT meetings found it difficult to understand what the Japanese were thinking as they tended to just sit there and say very little.

Not long after the CRT was formed and the meetings were still going on, I talked with the late Peter Hintzen, a son-in-law of Frits Philips. 'How about giving one whole afternoon for the Japanese group to report?' I suggested. The CRT responded favourably and Mr Kaku spoke about how one must begin by building unity among the managers of a company, then between management and labour, and expand that to other Japanese companies in the same field, and eventually to the whole world.

Frank Buchman taught that, 'Unless you know what the other person is most interested in, you cannot make friends.' It is an invaluable lesson. Basic moral and ethical principles are vitally important in every level of our lives.

6

Seeds of Change for Africa

by Peter Hannon, Suzan Burrell, Amina Dikedi-Ajakaiye & Ray Purdy

Peter Hannon is an Irishman. At Oxford he met men from all over Africa who were to become leaders of their countries. He then spent thirty years in that continent. Author of *Southern Africa – what kind of Change*? This chapter was much helped with the assistance of Suzan Burrell, whose father, George Daneel, was one of those who pioneered Initiatives of Change in Southern Africa after meeting Buchman.

IN the great move towards the independence of the majority of African states which marked the 1950s and '60s, the impact of Buchman's work was considerable. Nigeria, Ghana, Congo, Kenya, Sudan, Morocco... the list could continue, each with a story to tell.

Some sample vignettes: the visit of Dr Nnamdi Azikiwe, President of the National Council of Nigeria and the Cameroons, to Caux in 1949. As the leading voice of Nigerian nationalism at that time, he went to London with fresh proposals for steps towards self-government within fifteen years, but was cold-shouldered by the Colonial Office and told to go home and co-operate.

The press attacked him. One newspaper had his full page photo, headlined 'Black Mischief'. Frustrated and bitter, his organisation decided to send delegates to any body which would provide them with a platform, so he was on his way to address the 'Congress of Peoples against Imperialism' in Prague, and then go on to Moscow.

Whilst in London he was invited to spend an evening in a private home. There he learnt about Moral Re-Armament. 'It was the first time I had ever been treated as an equal in somebody's home in this country,' he commented. He accepted an invitation to visit Caux on his way to Prague. At the conference, where I had the privilege of acting as his aide, he became aware of the abundant evidence that human nature can change. At the end of three days he was able to say, with deep conviction, 'It's not a question of whether Nigeria is right, or Britain is right, *but what is right for Nigeria*. Our prayer for Nigeria is, 'Through God's guidance the people of Nigeria shall be redeemed from the servitude of hate, fear and suspicion. The torch of absolute honesty, purity, love and unselfishness shall flame anew.''

He returned direct to Nigeria, being met at the airport by some of his political opponents. His chain of five newspapers spread his new challenge. The *West African Pilot*, under a headline 'The Spirit of Caux' wrote, 'The questions on every lip are therefore these: Is the African capable of realising his destiny? We believe he can. But in that belief we submit that both leadership and followership require the spirit of Caux... That is the only gateway to African freedom.'

Step by step, moves went forward towards independence with 'Zik', as he was universally known, eventually becoming the country's first President.

Ghana was also directly affected. Gerald Henderson, who came to know one of the country's key figures, writes:

'The Tolon Na was a distinguished Muslim leader from the north of Ghana. Before independence in 1957, in what was then the Gold Coast, he was president of the Northern Territories Council and a member of the Legislative Assembly.

'Dr Kwame Nkrumah was President, while Tolon Na sat on the Opposition Front Bench, along with a number representing the Ashanti Region in the central part of the country. The Ashantis were threatening to secede in reaction to Nkrumah's government. They were seeking to get the North to join them.

'At that time an international team of Moral Re-Armament was touring Africa, performing plays at the invitation of African leaders, many of whom had been to Caux, such as Dr Azikiwe. The team flew on from Nigeria to the Gold Coast. The Speaker of the Legislative Assembly, Sir Emmanuel Quist, agreed to have showings of the plays under his patronage in the hall where the Legislature met. Many of the legislators, including Tolon Na, came to see the performances. He was so impressed that he agreed to lead a delegation from West Africa a few weeks later to the international conference at Caux.

'Four of the international team, including myself, were encouraged to stay on in Accra. I met the Tolon Na on his return from Caux and was fascinated to hear from him what a difference it had made in his life. He told how Frank Buchman and his colleagues had welcomed the delegation on arrival. Then, quite early on in the conference meetings, he was asked if he would introduce the West African delegation from the platform, which he did.

Apparently one of the speakers had commented on the cost of dishonesty to the nation. He told me that, as he was coming down from the platform, Buchman, who was sitting nearby, asked him quietly, 'Tolon Na, when did you steal last?'

'He related to me that 'It was as if the whole world was asking me that question. I blushed! But I went on as if nothing had happened. I then went to my room and lay on my bed. My whole life began to go in front of my eyes. I remembered how, as a child, I had taken money from my mother's purse. When I was at school I had taken paper and pencils from my teacher. When I became a teacher, I took books from the school library and I remembered that some of those books were still in my house. When I came to Caux, I felt I had a big part to play in this work, but I never realised that I would need to change.'

'As a result of this experience at Caux he had also noted down the names of people to whom he owed apologies. On his return to Accra he attended a meeting of the Legislative Assembly. Tolon Na walked across the House and shook Nkrumah by the hand and spoke to him. The local press reported on this as an act which prevented the break up of the country, and possibly even the risk of civil war.

'The Tolon Na, though he did not agree with all that Nkrumah stood for, felt that it was in the interests of his people and the country that it should stay together as one.

'He was very keen that his colleagues from the North in the Legislature should understand what Buchman stood for. One afternoon, in the heat of the day, there was a knock on the door of the home where our small MRA international team lived. We were having a siesta! Who should be at the door but Tolon Na, followed by the majority of the Front Bench members of the Opposition in the Legislature. Without delay, he said to me, 'Tell them the story about Frank Buchman and Bill Pickle.' Which we did, to the best of our ability. Bill Pickle had been a local hostler and janitor at Penn State University, who peddled liquor to the students. Buchman had been offered a job at the College not long after his profound personal experience of change. Excessive drinking was a huge problem on the campus.

'Buchman had developed the practice of giving an hour at the start of each day to seek God's leading for his life. In that time of quiet he got the names of particular people, students and others, whom he should help, first personally, and then to bring change to the whole College. Some students began to change and cut with their addiction to drink, much to the anger of Bill Pickle.

'But Bill was one of those Buchman felt led to care for. It was not easy. He found that Bill shared a love for horses! Buchman's care, and his ability to win his confidence, along with his vision for him, resulted in Bill agreeing to join him and students at a conference where many told stories of profound change in their lives. Bill decided to change and asked Buchman to help him write letters of apology to people he had wronged. This had a profound effect on the College when he returned. Tolon Na wanted his colleagues to understand the relationship between a change in individuals and the work of bringing change to a nation and the world. As he once commented, 'I decided to live Frank's way of life.'

'Tolon Na went on to be Ambassador and High Commissioner for Ghana after its independence in 1957 in several countries, ending up in Nigeria at the time when the military took over from Nkrumah in Ghana. But as he was so trusted as a person, the new regime asked him to stay on in his post.'

'The people of Africa have a message to give to the world.'

In 1955, a further group of African politicians, educationalists and student leaders attended the Caux conference. They absorbed much at the conference, but then felt that it was time for them to go home. Frank Buchman, however, was very aware of the pressures they would face in bringing new leadership to the continent. Were they adequately prepared? He invited them to meet him.

Manasseh Moerane, vice-president of the African Teachers Association of South Africa, tells what happened: 'Dr Buchman told us of a thought that had come to him during that night. 'The people of Africa have a message to give to the world. It will come to them, out of their hearts and experience, in the form of a play.'

'We accepted the challenge. We got together and listened, too, for God's direction. The plot of a play began to evolve and in three days it was written. On the seventh day it was on the stage. We called it *Freedom*, and, unknowingly, we were catapulted into history. Within a few months *Freedom* was seen by thirty thousand Europeans in London, Paris, Bonn, Berne, Geneva, Helsinki, Copenhagen, Stockholm, Oslo and Milan. In London's West End the audience gave it a ten minute ovation. The demand for *Freedom* became so great that we decided to make a film. Over two thousand people contributed sums. It meant sacrifice for all the actors and technicians, none of whom received any pay. Some gave up their jobs. I had to risk losing mine, and forfeiting the right to a pension.'

It was costly, but it forged leaders who spoke to their continent. When Dr Kwame Nkrumah, as President of Ghana, paid his first official visit to Nigeria, Dr Azikiwe showed *Freedom* as part of the programme at the State banquet. In Kenya, former Mau Mau fighters arranged with President Jomo Kenyatta that *Freedom*, dubbed into Swahili, be shown to a million people throughout the country in preparation for the first national election.

Freedom epitomised that element Buchman brought to his challenge to change: to expand the vision which people have for themselves and for what they can do. As the Psalmist puts it: 'Lift the veil from my eyes that I may see the marvels which spring from You.'

'People around you seem to change'

To illustrate Buchman's fundamental conviction that every forward step depended on conviction and commitment in an individual, one can move to the south of the continent, to Cape Town.

In his book, *Frank Buchman's Secret*, Peter Howard describes what began there. 'In Italy, Queen Sophie of Greece heard that Buchman planned to visit South Africa in 1928. She gave him letters to the Governor-General, the Earl of Athlone, great-uncle of the present Queen.

'In Cape Town, Buchman presented his letters. He talked with the Governor-General for an hour. Then Athlone took him out to the motor-car that was waiting. But as the door of the car was opened, Athlone said, 'We haven't talked about the thing that interests me most. What I really want to know is how you get hold of a man like George Daneel and change him. You've not told me. Come inside again.' So the two men turned and went back indoors, to talk further for several hours.

'George Daneel was a Springbok, the name given to men who play rugby football for South Africa. They are national heroes. Daneel comes from the heart of Afrikanerdom. His background and straightforwardness were such that cabinet ministers of the day heeded him. He was studying for ministry in the Dutch Reformed Church. He came to take morning tea with Frank Buchman. He said to him 'People around you seem to change.'

'Buchman replied, 'Of course. Don't they change when they are around you?'

'Daneel had to say that they did not. Buchman said, 'Why is that?'

'Daneel decided that he would stay to lunch and talk more. Then he stayed to tea. Then to dinner. Then he stayed for life. He found an answer that day to selfish habits that had robbed him of the power to change people.'

He began to work together with men like Bremer Hofmeyr, another brilliant young Afrikaner who, as a Rhodes Scholar, met Buchman at Oxford and, as a result, told his friends that he planned to give the rest of his life to bring an ideology to Africa and the world.

Fast forward twenty five years. Daneel, now a minister in the Church, with a devoted congregation, had married and had a family. But the challenge of what one might call Buchman's 'divine restlessness' remained with him. Buchman was never satisfied with the status quo, however good. He was always searching for God's further steps for himself, and for all those he met. It made him at times an uncomfortable, if stimulating, companion.

Daneel had maintained his links with Buchman's

worldwide work throughout the war, as an army chaplain in North Africa and Italy, and in other parts of Africa. He was now asking himself if God had wider responsibilities for him. He joined Hofmeyr and others at an inter-racial residential conference held in Northern Rhodesia. Such events were not possible at that time in South Africa. One of those present was Dr William Nkomo, founder and first President of the African National Congress Youth League who believed that 'the hope for the African lay only in a bloodbath where every white man would be slain or driven into the sea.' Whites called Nkomo a Communist; he called them Fascists.

Then he heard Daneel speak, saying publicly that it was the feelings of racial superiority in white men like himself that were creating the conditions for producing bloody revolution. He said that he had been wrong and that he was giving his life to work for a South Africa where all had a full and equal part. Nkomo said, 'I have always been a revolutionary, and have spent much of my life in the struggle for the liberation of my people. Here I see white men change, and black men change, and I myself have decided to change. I realise that I cannot love my people unless I am prepared to fight for them in a new dimension, free of bitterness and hate.' Some months later Daneel and Nkomo spoke together to a packed audience in Cape Town City Hall. The *Cape Times* headlined, 'Black, White, on MRA Platform'. It was a new voice for South Africa.

Daneel pursued his vision. He resigned: from the security of his position in the ministry, and, with a wife and children to support, he stepped out in faith. Others, black and white, joined him. Nkomo played a leading part in the writing and filming of *Freedom*. Together with

Daneel, they gave their challenge to other parts of Africa. And wider afield: they took a group of white and black South Africans to Northern Ireland. And everywhere their message was the same: what was needed was more than racial harmony; it was for every man and woman to commit themselves for life to finding God's will for their country and its leadership.

It was not easy for Daneel. Many of his own people resisted the challenge. But as a new realisation of the stature of Nkomo grew in him, he felt it was important that white leaders of his country should meet him and grasp what he saw for the future of South Africa. But the way did not open easily, so he desisted. Then Nkomo died.

This hit Daneel hard. He said, 'I had not done what God had told me because I was still bound by fear of what my own people would think. I decided that, from then on, I was going to be completely at God's disposal no matter what my friends or my people would think.'

One morning, in 1974, Daneel felt God prompt him clearly: 'An international conference for the Moral Re-Armament of Southern Africa, for all races, for all parts of Africa, to be held in Pretoria'. It seemed impossible, but he had learnt to be obedient and not just to rely on his own comprehension. Doors opened in a remarkable way. The Government, unexpectedly, agreed that it could happen. Delegates crossed borders normally tightly closed, coming from Nigeria, Kenya, Mozambique and further afield. Leading blacks and Afrikaners were among 400 of all races who stayed for a week together in a hotel in the heart of the capital, Pretoria. Many new insights were gained and decisions reached, for the emphasis was not on theory or the passing of resolutions, but on the experience that attitudes could change and new aims be found.

Daneel was musing about this later. One black nationalist leader had asked to talk with him, not a usual role for a Dutch Reformed Church minister. Daneel said, 'Why he should have asked for me I honestly don't know. But I do know that, for me, there is now only one thing that matters. That is what God wants, that He actually is in charge, for my future, my time, my country, as priority before any other loyalty. And that goes for everybody.' And his wife, Joey, added, 'I knew what it would mean. No fixed income, no security of home or comfort, and the responsibility of three small children. At first, fear took me over. But then God spoke in no uncertain terms; 'You cannot accept Christ only as your Saviour; He must be your Master, too.' Then a miracle: I became a free human being.'

This freedom of total commitment gave Daneel authority when he spoke to the General Synod of the Dutch Reformed Church. The editor of a British publication which reported his talk wrote in introduction: 'This is not a political statement. It is moral and spiritual truth. Acceptance by us in Britain of its challenges would alter social, economic and political attitudes in *this* country. We, too, could then surprise the world.'

Daneel said, in part, to the Synod, 'The future of our country is in the balance. Changes are inevitable. The question is what kind of change is it to be? Voluntary, as a result of repentance, or violent change, by force. Fear should never be the main motive to put right what is wrong. We must do it because God asks it. Many of us feel we are free from race prejudice. But what about our fellow citizens who ill-treat blacks? They are our flesh and blood. As Christians we are called to identify ourselves with them as if equally guilty ourselves and in need of God's forgiveness. Of course Africans need to change, as we do. But we cannot allow our Afrikaner pride to prevent us searching our *own* hearts and asking God to bring about that transformation in human relationships which our country needs.'

Daneel wrote with these convictions to Prime Minister Vorster and later had a meeting with him. 'But,' he said afterwards, 'he didn't give me much chance to explain my stand, and I felt nothing had been achieved. But that was not the end of the matter. Shortly before his death he visited a great friend of his and during their conversation he mentioned my letter, adding, 'Daneel was right, after all."

And increasingly other voices in Afrikanerdom spoke out in similar, courageous terms. They prepared the conscience of many among their people, so that when Nelson Mandela was released, Prime Minister De Klerk was able to take steps which took the world completely by surprise in handing over power, and carrying the majority of his own people with him.

Daneel died in 2004, at the age of 100. He lived to see the birth of the new South Africa, with all the challenges that it now faces.

Buchman was once asked, 'What do you regard as the greatest sin?' He replied, 'The sin of limited expectations'. To the end, Daneel exemplified what Buchman fought for; a willingness constantly to be stretched in obedience and in vision.

* * * * *

Amina Dikedi-Ajakaiye, a Nigerian, living in the UK, helps develop future leadership for Africa through the Clean Africa Campaign, having worked in 26 nations on that continent. She believes in telling stories about Africans making a difference, and is a founding member of Creators of Peace, a women's initiative.

I MET the idea of IofC as a student at a teacher training college in Nigeria. My lecturer, John Ifoghale Amata, was one of the first Africans to meet Dr Frank Buchman in the 1950s. These were years when many countries across Africa were agitating for independence from colonial powers. I was fascinated by the story of how Frank challenged the 'angry' Africans to write a play based on their experiences, that would help usher in a smooth transition of power from colonial rule to self-governance. A play *Freedom* was written and acted in Caux and later made into a film. I remember travelling across Nigeria showing the film in different Youth Service camps. Many responded to the change of heart of the principal character, Mutanda, performed by John. And whenever he was introduced to the audience, it was electrifying! Many often stayed back to ask him questions. His personal story of change gave credibility to his part in the play. The film is still in popular demand and is relevant to situations across Africa.

I have often said how I wished I had met Frank Buchman. What did he see in the Africans he met? What did he mean by 'Africa is the answer continent'? I could not make sense of it and found it hard to believe – not with all the conflicts that have happened in many of our nations since independence. Through the influence of John Amata and his brother Isaac, I came to realise that for Africa to truly become the 'Answer Continent' we have got to turn the searchlight inwards. Change begins with me. It meant putting right my relationship with my father and caring for him unconditionally. This freed me to be part of a growing number of men and women right across Africa who have dedicated themselves to bringing about effective and lasting change.

From the stories told of Buchman and people who worked with him, I learned the need to work with others, to build a team and expect the best from everyone irrespective of their background or past. John introduced a group of about 30 students in their twenties to the concept of 'As I am, so is my nation!' We became a team and travelled to different parts of Nigeria with a new production, *The Next Phase*. At each occasion we mingled with the audience at the end of the play and people were fascinated by this group of young people passionate about bringing change in the nation: not what many youths really do in their 20s! From this group have emerged leaders in different spheres of life occupying responsible positions nationally and internationally. By allowing each of us to discover our part in God's grand plan, John helped us find our calling in life.

From big campaigns in Nigeria, I went further afield – to Kenya, Uganda, Tanzania, Ethiopia, Sudan, South Africa, Zimbabwe, Sierra Leone, Ghana and Cameroon. I have also worked with Africans in diaspora from countries like the Democratic Republic of Congo, Rwanda, Burundi, Angola, Liberia, Lesotho, Cote d'Ivoire, Somalia, Eritrea, Burkina Faso, Niger, Togo, Benin, Senegal and Chad. The work of Initiatives of Change has offered many Africans who come in contact with the organisation the opportunity to find an alternative to revenge and taking up arms. In Ghana, for example, the local team was instrumental in initiating peace talks in a town called Bortianor – an area that was historically torn apart by two groups fighting over a chieftaincy position. After delicate negotiation, the main protagonists acknowledged their past mistakes, forgiveness was found and restitution made.

One can rightly say that part of the legacy of Dr Buchman is in the rebuilding of nations coming out of conflict. Countries in Africa that are emerging from conflict are working at strengthening the moral and spiritual dimensions of democracy, so challenging selfish interests and corruption. A country like Sierra Leone is rebuilding both the social and political infrastructure after more than ten years of conflict. John Bangura, a Sierra Leonean refugee now living in Denmark, started an NGO, 'Hope Sierra Leone', to conduct joint training with the police, the military and civil society groups. The course – Moral Foundations for Democracy – is a trust-building exercise aimed at bridging the gaps created by the protracted war.

On a recent visit to Sudan, I met women who are divided along ethnic, religious and cultural lines due to the prevailing political environment. They made a commitment to let go of the culture of blame, and recognise and repent of their own part in sowing and passing on the seeds of discord to the next generation. During one of the workshops we showed the film, *The Imam and the Pastor*, which depicts how a Christian and a Muslim who had sworn to eliminate each other's faction, found forgiveness and are today working together for peace and reconciliation around the world. This encouraged the Sudanese women from all walks of life to reflect on how they could use the ancient truths of their two religions to promote peace in their country. One, a Christian, had vowed never to set foot in the Muslim part of the country. But after the workshop in the south, she decided through the leading of the spirit to travel with the visiting team to the north, after 18 years!

One of the aims of IofC is healing the wounds of history that ferment the cycle of revenge, especially where cultures and civilisations meet.

The stories are unending. From not understanding the thought expressed in the 1950s that 'Africa is the answer continent', I now believe that it is achievable – when the passionate faith of Africans can be translated into social responsibility. Secondly, when greed will no longer drive the leadership in Africa, and be replaced by integrity and accountability. I believe that answers will come when we can celebrate our diversity instead of it being a source of conflict. Africa will be the answer continent when more stories of people making a difference are told to the world.

* * * * *

The story of Arthur Norval

Ray Foote Purdy, an American who met Frank Buchman in 1919 and became one of his closest associates, spent a year in South Africa, 1932-33, at the invitation of people who had been influenced by the visit of Buchman's young 'Oxford Group' in 1929. The following extract from Purdy's memoirs illustrates how links between 'the intimate and global' resulted from the intensive type of personal evangelism that Buchman encouraged.

THE University of Pretoria had been created by the Act of Union in 1910 to be a national university as the symbol of unity between the Dutch and English people. Here, using both languages, were supposed to live in peace and amity those who eventually would become leaders of the nation.

The university was part of the vision the first prime minister, Louis Botha, and of his aide, General Smuts, at the turn to of the century, to create the new South Africa following the Boer War and to accept the consequences of their defeat at the hands of Britain. During the thirty years since the Boer War there had been a growing feeling on the part of the nationalist group among the Afrikaans-speaking people that this would never continue and that as soon as it was possible in this two-stream theory of co-existence between Dutch and English, there might come a time when the Dutch would achieve the superiority and take whatever steps were necessary to expel the British from the Union and create a new state along the lines of the Irish Free State, separated from the British Commonwealth.

This leadership had finally in 1931 come to power at the election of the nationalist leader General Hertzog as prime minister. General Smuts' South African Party went into opposition. At this point the Nationalists thought that the best symbol of permanent superiority would be to expel the British from the University of Pretoria as the first step to their expulsion from any kind of power in the Union. And so there was a strategy at work led by Arthur Norval, at that time professor of economics on the staff. He burned with bitterness and even the casual reader of the newspapers saw the tremendous power which he exerted at that time.

Don't take sides, take responsibility

We were naturally asked what our attitude was as far as the work of Frank Buchman was concerned to these two sides and our only guidance was, 'Don't take sides. Take responsibility.' Little by little we began to learn the issues.

At the evening services at the St Andrews Presbyterian Church, many of the Dutch came to talk with us. One of those was William Hofmeyr, the head of the leading boys' school in Pretoria and one of the famous educators of his day. He had the conviction that it would be right to get together for an evening in his home some of those who were in educational and political prominence. Some fifty of his friends came, and among those was Arthur Norval and his wife. His wife had become much interested in the work we were doing and was convinced that her husband would find an answer to the problems which were gnawing in his heart if he were to come. With great patience and persistence she succeeded in bringing him to the back of the meeting in the Hofmeyr home. He was an unwilling listener to what was said by George Daneel and myself at the meeting, and, though gripped in spite of himself, then left without being introduced.

Some two weeks later, however, he came to an evening meeting in a different part of the city and afterwards came to me and asked for a talk. Knowing who he was, I thought that one of two things would happen. Either he would threaten me with the need of immediate departure from the nation, or else he would tell me things that he had never told anybody before about himself. Hoping that the second alternative was the one moving his spirit, I suggested a drive in the country. So we got into my car and drove to the mountains surrounding Pretoria and talked for two hours. He told me how he had gone to Leiden in Holland to the university and lost his faith in God, of how the one thing which moved him was the death of his father in the Boer War, so that he burned with hatred against the British and would do anything to avenge his father's death. He used to get out his father's bloodstained coat to feed the fire of his bitterness. He said, 'I have the feeling that I am being prayed for and that I would like to expose myself to a knowledge of God if He existed. If He did exist, I would have to fight as hard in South Africa for unity as I am now fighting for division. What would you do if you were in my position?'

A sound proposition

I said, 'I would be a quack if I tried to tell you what to do, but I do believe from my own experience that God can make it very clear to you.' I felt that this was the decisive moment in the interview, with the survival of peace in the nation probably at stake. After a few moments of silence I said to him, 'If you want to come to our home quietly for an hour every morning for a month, to take unhurried time to listen and write down the thoughts that are deepest in your heart during that time, whatever you feel is the right step to take for that day, I will help you take it.' He said, 'That's a sound proposition. I'd like to accept.' And so every day for the next month he came to our home and we had a time of unhurried listening together, writing down the thoughts that came to us about ourselves, about the nation and about the future.

Clearly day by day he began to see what it meant to change his own life in accordance with the absolute moral standards and what God's plan might be for him and for South Africa. His heart and mind began naturally to go toward solving the problem of bitterness, separation and hate in his own life, first with an honest apology to his wife, a full discussion on a totally new basis, then with the two men – one of whom was president of the university of Pretoria – who were at the centre of this strategy of national division. He decided to be honest with himself and his colleagues about his motives and objectives and then to go before the council of the university staff and tell them that he would like, whatever he did in the future, to do it on a sound Christian basis.

The newspapers immediately attacked him and called him an arch-hypocrite, saying that they knew of his activity for division and now he was trying to cover it with a cloak of piety. It was a bitter blow, and his first experience of what it meant to stand under the glare of merciless publicity imputing motives to him which were certainly not there. He came to me the next day and said, 'I would like to know everything that you know, by book or experience, about the Cross of Christ; because I am going away for a week alone to think over what I am meant to do with my future, and I would like to take with me the best material you have on the subject.'

He returned at the end of the week with the clear conviction of what he was meant to do. He drew together in our home leaders of both the Afrikaans and English groups and suggested that they should form a joint committee to invite the leaders in the city and nation to explore and apply the new spirit he had discovered to the critical problem facing the nation. Those who were united in this conviction printed an invitation in English and Afrikaans, sending it to all of the national leadership, the Members of Parliament, the Cabinet, leaders of the Church and Dutch- and English-speaking communities. 1,100 people went to the meeting in the City Hall. Norval himself courageously spoke for 25 minutes, giving the experiences he had had to date with an answer to bitterness and hatred and fear. He spoke in English, which he had vowed he never would use in public. I remember sitting in the meeting with the chief of staff of the army,

General Brink, who said, 'What this does is to transform the entire picture of the situation in South Africa. And if these principles were to be applied it would change both Afrikaans and English alike.'

Forces were set in motion that made many of the national leaders reconsider their whole position. Tielman Roos of the Supreme Court had the conviction that with this spirit it might be possible for him to control 25 of the nationalist votes and with General Smuts as Deputy Prime Minister form a coalition Cabinet to lead the nation. Smuts did not accept this proposition but in return had the courage to go to General Hertzog and suggest the same thing to him, offering to serve as his Deputy Prime Minister in a coalition government. He said, however, that there was no use in making this a political marriage of convenience. 'It must be a politically united move in spirit and in strategy, and it will mean that you and I will have to go to every leading centre in South Africa and make that clear.' This they did.

The result was that from the brink of civil war there came to birth within six months a coalition government, including 114 out of 132 in Parliament. And this government lasted for six years until the outbreak of the Second World War.

On the day we left South Africa, after a wonderful year there, we were having tea in the lounge of the parliament building in Capetown with Denys Reitz, the right-hand man of General Smuts and Minister of Lands in the Cabinet. As we sat there, many other Members of Parliament came to tea. In the centre was a table of four. They were General Hertzog and General Smuts with Havenga and Duncan. The latter two were the brilliant and able assistants to Hertzog and Smuts at the last conference they were to have before Smuts went – with the economic destiny under the new government of South Africa in his hands – to the Commonwealth Economic Conference in London in 1933. The four men were talking and laughing together as firm friends. Reitz said to us, 'There's nothing in the world that can explain what we see at that table but a Damascus Road experience.'

7

Frank Buchman's legacy in French-speaking Africa

by Frédéric Chavanne

translated by Mary Jones

Frédéric Chavanne, a full time worker with Initiatives of Change in France, spent his childhood in Morocco. Today he works on relations with the Muslim populations in France and North Africa and is involved in a reconciliation programme in the Great Lakes region of Africa.

IN the mid 1950s a group of young Africans went to the Caux international conference centre in Switzerland. Frank Buchman felt he must set them a task which was bigger than themselves. Through them Africa could speak to the world. He proposed they write a play about the essential lessons learnt during their visit to Caux. In a few days *Freedom* was born, first as a play, then as a full-length film. More than half a century later this film is still used by men and women who bring the same message. It is their hope that war, corruption and bad governance are not beyond remedy and that the solution lies in a change of motivation and behaviour, beginning with their own.

We shall confine ourselves here to the French-speaking

countries of Africa, although one could cite more examples from Kenya, Nigeria, Somalia, Sierra Leone, Zimbabwe, South Africa, etc, *in addition to those described in the previous chapter.*

The initiatives of these French-speaking African men and women took them to play a part in the post-colonial era in Morocco, Tunisia, Cameroon and former Belgian Congo. After a long period of inactivity, things started up again in the 1990s. In Tunisia and Cameroon, a work was done with young people to implant a new spirit of responsibility and integrity. In the Ivory Coast an association was formed to launch a campaign for hate-free, clean elections. In Burundi and the Democratic Republic of Congo there is a small group at the forefront of the peace struggle. They reach out to ordinary citizens as well as the leadership, who are often overcome by the scale of the problems. They proposed guidelines and key attitudes to restore hope of recovery and a way out of crisis. There is of course still a long and difficult road ahead but there is hope.

What was it in the thinking and approach of Frank Buchman that set these people on the move? What are the keys that made them act? To what extent are these factors crucial in confronting Africa's problems today?

* * * * *

DURING DECOLONISATION

Each of the following stories is about someone who was deeply touched or found peace of heart over some difficult experience, was spurred into positive action or gripped by a vision of what could be done to help resolve the problems they faced:

Charles Assalé: uniting political forces in Cameroon

In 1957, Charles Assalé from the Cameroon was due to represent his country at the United Nations Trusteeship Council in New York. At the invitation of a young compatriot, Delphine Zanga, he took part in an international Initiatives of Change gathering at the United States centre in Mackinac Island. He left with a very different view of France and considerably less aggressive. The speech he made at the United Nations was surprisingly moderate and brought a change of attitude in the French representative, Jacques Kosciusko-Morizet. It was the start of a relationship of mutual respect which was to facilitate the process of decolonisation. On his return, Charles Assalé became reconciled with his main political opponent, Ahmadou Ahidjo, thus helping to assure the country's political unity. He himself was appointed Prime Minister, remaining in that post for five years. He said that Moral Re-Armament was the Unknown Soldier in Cameroon's war of independence.

Mohamed Masmoudi: facilitator in Tunisia's independence negotiations

In 1953, Mohamed Masmoudi, representative of the Tunisian nationalist Neo-Destour party, was touched by the humility of the French he met at the Caux centre. Replying to a letter from his mother saying she was asking Allah to bless him and to curse the French, he replied that it was no longer necessary to curse the latter.

Following this, a meal was arranged in a private house in Boulogne-Billancourt, France, for Masmoudi to meet Jean Basdevant, official spokesman of the French government in charge of the Tunisian desk. The atmosphere was icy around the table until the moment when Masmoudi spoke of his change of heart towards France. Something clicked between the two men in the course of a private conversation they had after the meal. Each time negotiations between France and Tunisia reached deadlock, the two men would meet away from the official discussions, and on the basis of the new trust between them, seek ways to re-open the dialogue. 'Without meeting this way,' Masmoudi was to say later, 'we would be engaged in a war without mercy against France.'

Morocco: behind the scenes of the Glaoui's volte-face

Summer 1955. The fiery young nationalist Ahmed Guessous was brought to Caux by French people who had found a new attitude to Moroccans. Like all leaders of countries fighting for independence, he had good reasons to hate the occupiers. However, it was the hatred he held against one of his compatriots which exercised his mind. 'I am as far from God as from the person I hate most' was the remark which hit him. 'Go towards your worst enemy and he will become a keen protector,' he also read in the Qur'an. He returned to his country determined to do something to resolve the serious crisis between his country and France. 'Guessous wanted to reconcile everybody with everybody,' commented Philippe Lobstein, one of the Frenchmen who took him to Caux.

Through this Guessous not only became free of his hatred of the French but also of the Glaoui, a great Moroccan figure who went along with the occupiers and whom most Moroccans considered a traitor. The new openness in his heart and mind made him ready, unlike his political friends, to respond positively to an appeal from the Glaoui's son, Abdessadek, who was making tentative overtures to resolve the Moroccan crisis and still save his family's situation. The deposition of Sultan Ben Youssef – the future Mohammed V – by the French, who had exiled him to Madagascar, had been supported by the Glaoui.

Guessous helped make the contact with the Istiqlal, the main active political force in the independence struggle. He was present at the meeting between the Glaoui and representatives of that party which culminated in the statement by the Glaoui, as unexpected as it was sensational: 'I ask for the Sultan to be returned from exile to his throne, since he alone is capable of bringing calm to the people.' This statement abruptly ended the Moroccan crisis.

Si Bekkai

Less has been told about another great Moroccan figure, Si Bekkaï, highly respected in Morocco. When he went to Caux in 1953, the independence struggle was at its height. At the time Ben Youssef was deposed, he had been the only pasha (a local position conferred by the sultan) to resign in protest.

After the Aix-les-Bains talks in search of a compromise to resolve the Moroccan crisis, Si Bekkaï wrote to Frank Buchman: 'In these negotiations, I assure you I have never lost sight of the four standards of Moral Re-Armament.' It is interesting to read this letter alongside remarks made by Pierre July, one of the French political team who was also at Aix-les-Bains, who expressed amazement at the honest and conciliatory positions taken by Bekkaï. Bekkaï was appointed Prime Minister in the first government of independent Morocco.

At a private audience in January 1956, King Mohammed V expressed his appreciation to the Moral

Re-Armament delegation: 'I wish to thank you for all you have done for Morocco, Moroccans and for me through testing years. You have noble principles of virtue, love for one's neighbour and unselfishness. They are right and they are the principles of Islam. My wish is that they become widespread in Morocco and in every corner of the world.'

Congo: easing the tensions

At the beginning of the 1960s, a Moral Re-Armament team spent several months in the Congo. The film *Freedom* was shown to the young leaders who had just formed their first government, as well as widely throughout the country. 'Thank you for what you are doing for Africa,' said Patrice Lumumba, prime minister of the first government of independent Congo, after he had seen the film, 'You give Africa its rightful stature in the eyes of the world.' The songs of three singer-composers from MRA, the Colwell brothers (from the United States), were broadcast on radio in French, Lingala and Tshiluba. They contributed to forging a united country at the height of the Cold War when the struggle for control threatened to cause its total break-up.

During this troubled period marked by outbreaks of aggression and inter-ethnic massacres, the ideas in the film were to make their mark on several men who adopted positions or took initiatives designed to help bring calm and avoid killings. Two men in particular, Albert Kalonji and François Lwakabwanga, combined efforts to reduce tensions between their ethnic groups (Lulua and Baluba) which threatened to eliminate each other.

Two of the actors in the film *Freedom* had the idea to

go and visit Jean Bolikango who had just been defeated in the presidential elections. According to his own testimony, this visit dissuaded him from following a course which would have led to bloodshed and gave him fresh courage to calm his own supporters down.

Being at the right place at the right time is one of Buchman's key ideas. We cannot do everything, but we can try to see the thing we must do to make the difference. This implies a belief that we are not just acting in our own human strength but that we can be led and used beyond our imagination.

* * * * *

IN THE FACE OF AFRICA'S CHALLENGES TODAY

Bringing peace to the Great Lakes region

Since the year 2000, three men have been committed to a long term effort to bring an end to war in the Great Lakes region of Africa. They are Michel Kipoke and Thomas Ntambu originally from the Democratic Republic of Congo and Bonaventure Nkeshimana from Burundi. They grasped the significance of Frank Buchman's message. Their aim: to prepare minds and bring people together. Their method: to help people heal the wounds of the past, be freed from their fears and open about their own vulnerability. Patiently and methodically they created bonds of trust with political figures from opposing sides, chiefly in Burundi and the Democratic Republic of Congo, but also in Rwanda.

Between 2000 and 2004 they organised round tables with leaders of all three countries. In March and June 2003, two round tables brought together protagonists in the Burundi conflict. One of the rebel groups, the CNDD-FDD, has since rejoined the political process. Two of its leading members have said that Caux was a decisive factor in achieving this result. The 2005 elections put this party in power. The other rebels, the Palipehutu-FNL, the last rebel group still operating, signed a cease-fire agreement in September 2006. A work of living alongside the leaders of all parties continues in an effort to consolidate the still fragile peace, especially by re-establishing bonds of trust between people on opposing sides.

Cameroon: training tomorrow's leadership

With the creation of a local association in 1991, Initiatives of Change has taken off again in Cameroon. This is thanks to two men known for their personal integrity: Victor Anomah Ngu, oncologist, specialist in the fight against AIDS and former Minister of Health, and Pierre Oko Mengue, senior civil servant, now retired. Together they have mobilised a small team to work on strengthening the moral fibre of the country. They invite their compatriots to consider to what extent they contribute to Africa's sickness, to step out of the victim or assistance mentality and to rediscover the hope that each person can play an essential part. Pierre Oko Mengue does not hesitate to tell his latest story of change, the repayment of debts long forgotten, honesty with his wife over marriage infidelities or the hurt pride of a father taking a new look at his authoritarian approach. 'Initiatives of Change is the practical workshop of my faith,' he maintains. 'The dynamics of a changed life begin with a decision, however small.'

Initiatives of Change films have been shown on national television. In 1994 a pan-African gathering took place, drawing representatives of other Initiatives of Change teams at work on the continent. And importantly, the local team organises frequent forums to train citizens and particularly youth in taking responsibility. On one occasion the subject was 'family life'- a prime laboratory for learning about dialogue and democracy! Another of their preoccupations is to unite the English-speaking and French-speaking populations of Cameroon.

Tunisia: unity across the Mediterranean

Hatem Akkari, professor at Sfax University in Tunisia, has just opened the Centre for Dialogue and Culture in the setting of a family library he has been creating for years. His aim: to give a sense of responsibility and initiative to the youth, open their minds to different horizons and form bonds beyond the shores of the Mediterranean.

He leads a group of youth to whom he tries to give meaning in life over and above the question of career. He develops a close relationship with these youngsters, many of whom are or have been his pupils, and ends up as their confidant and counsellor. Together they learn to deal with their conflicts, debate world problems and learn from visiting foreign speakers. They also welcome in their group students from other countries who are all too often ignored by the Tunisians.

But perhaps the most important lesson they learn is to be interested in others for their own sakes. Some of these pupils go on to become teachers and bring a wholehearted commitment to their work. There is a certain enthusiasm within the group, a desire to give their best and do something useful for society. This is in contrast to many of their peers (in Tunisia) who are often disillusioned, with no vision for their future and dreaming only of leaving the country in search of a dubious Eldorado under different skies.

* * * * *

THE SIGNIFICANCE OF PERSONAL CHANGE

Transformed lives across Africa

In the context of these briefly recounted events and initiatives, many lives have been transformed: Nadine, the former rebel, who rediscovered how to laugh; Don Bosco, who gave up his radical opinions; the political opponents who share with each other their deepest convictions and carry their respective loads together. Time and again, we have observed that crucial moment when suddenly someone becomes aware that his attitude is part of society's problems!

There is Nelly, for instance, who lived in Europe but had wanted to see her Banyamulengue brothers (Congolese Tutsis) eliminated. 'If I had been in the country,' she admitted when she apologised to one of them, 'you would not be alive today!' Then there is the officer from Chad, overcome to realise he could be free from the perpetual desire for revenge. Or yet again, the Cameroon student who gave up the lucrative business of forging diplomas, identity cards and false birth certificates.

'It is we citizens who are the main obstacle to democracy,' claims Pierre Oko Mengue. 'Every ethnic group thinks it can demand what it wants from anyone in that group who has a responsible position. Let us free our ministers from being ethnic hostages!'

'National unity is not decided by decree,' confides one Rwandan. 'If some subjects become taboo, the pressure mounts and we end up with an explosion. We have been the dumb society, denying the ethnic problem instead of facing up to it.'

'A wall of mistrust, scorn and hatred has grown up between us,' said Lucienne Munono from the Democratic Republic of Congo. 'Without realising it we slide into aggressiveness. The very violence I decry in my country is also in me. It is destroying us. When I put someone in a category with which I feel unable to work, I exert a kind of violence.'

Those who are committed to bring this change of attitude to decision-makers have developed a quality and way of life which cannot just be turned on. Sometimes it has taken years of contact with Initiatives of Change teams for them to be ready for this task.

It is through the simple acts and attitudes of individuals working on their own or in a team that they succeed in building trust and provoking a change in outlook which eventually has repercussions on the political and social life of their country. 'When men change, situations change,' Buchman used to say.

Attentive listening

'One of the first things I learned with Initiatives of Change was about listening,' admitted Michel Kipoke, one of the pioneers of the reconciliation programme in the Great Lakes region of Africa, who tragically died in June 2007 on returning from a mission to Burundi. 'Before, all I thought about was preparing my argument in order to win against the other side.' This ability to listen became his chief tool and drew round him opposing elements in the conflicts affecting the whole Great Lakes region. In October 2006, he travelled to the east of the Congo where General Nkunda, a redoubtable figure who had read a memorandum on the Congolese situation written by Michel, was determined to meet him. 'When I read this document,' the general told him, 'I realised there were still people capable of listening to us.'

However, Michel Kipoke did not come with ready-made answers. He was convinced that every person carries within him the answers for which he is looking. 'The people I talk to appear very sure of themselves and their positions at first. Quite often they end up themselves raising the subjects which worry them and sometimes even come to confess problems weighing on their conscience. I act as a kind of mirror.'

Michel liked to recall something Frank Buchman said to some young people he was training and sending out on mission. 'What interests me is not what you said to the people you were talking to but what they had to say to you.'

Listening to the inner voice

The practice of taking time in quiet, as Buchman taught, remains the essential basis of the work done in his name. Thomas Ntambu, who is involved in the mission for consolidating peace in Burundi, makes it a daily discipline. 'Every morning at 5 o'clock I have a quiet time,' he told us. 'I read my Bible and I think about what has happened the day before in case my conscience reminds me of some thoughtless thing I said or something which might have caused hurt. I also look for key ideas to help me in the interviews planned that day.' Imagine the kind of society we would have if everyone resorted to a daily self-examination!

This sensitive availability to people and constant questioning of oneself, one's gestures and reactions, leads to a stripping away of self, ever greater dedication and not least to clarity about people and their motives.

Honesty about motives

'The evil we were fighting in our political opponents was eating away at our own people,' Thomas Ntambu went on. A former soldier and rebel fighter, he had been chief of military operations for the Marxist group whose aim was the overthrow of the Mobutu dictatorship. He dreamed of power, villas, luxury cars and women. He was also hungry for justice. He wanted to replace one political or ideological system with another. In Initiatives of Change he found a new hope that men can change and the conviction that without this change all revolutions would end in disappointment.

This clarity about himself helps him not to set himself up as judge or censor. 'When I discovered what the Burundi rebels had suffered, I felt very small,' said Thomas. This ability to make someone feel welcome and not to judge, is this not part of Buchman's message? Anyway, we recalled the vision Buchman had for every person with the infinite belief that each one could play a vital part. During the inter-Congolese talks in Addis Ababa, where I accompanied Thomas, I could see that he had that same vision which draws the best out of people.

The person who has the courage to talk about mistakes and inner struggles and yet remain faithful to what his conscience dictates, holds a power which is infectious. He appeals to consciences. In the course of the round tables with protagonists of the Burundi conflict, one former minister spoke of his personal responsibility in the tragedy which has afflicted his country for the last thirty years. 'I did not take part in the 1996 coup d'etat,' he told us, 'but by my attitude I gave support to the people who judged that the new president could not remain in power.' He had the courage to apologise publicly to the president who had been driven out by the coup d'etat.

In Cameroon, Victor Anomah Ngu, talking to a group of students, referred with great humility to the mistakes made by politicians like himself. A minister who admits his mistakes! Stupefaction on the part of the students and an immediate wave of sympathy. The discussion was no longer about denouncing the mistakes of the other side but about considering what everyone could do where they were. Cynicism gave way to hope.

* * * * *

LONG TERM ACTION FOR THE CONTINENT

The strategy worked out through the programme Reconciliation in the Great Lakes region could be a model for action across the African continent. The key concept is 'living alongside'.

Identifying and reaching the key people

Through his experience in American universities and in China, Buchman had learnt the importance of discerning who were the key men on whom the solution to a problem might turn. In the same way, as the team at work in the Great Lakes region meet people from very different backgrounds, they too look out for those who could make the difference.

The team then works at creating bonds of trust with these people. There is one condition – to have no hidden agenda. 'No man who puts his own interests first can think for the nation,' recalls Michel Kipoke in an expression he made his own from reading the biography of the South African, William Nkomo, a man strongly influenced by Buchman's ideas.

Offering a framework and atmosphere which encourages reconciliation

The next step is to bring these people together in a framework and atmosphere which encourages honest sharing. That is what happened with Mohamed Masmoudi and Jean Basdevant, with Charles Assalé and Jacques Kosiusko-Morizet, with Albert Kalonji and François Lwakabwanga and, more recently, with key figures from the Great Lakes region.

At the last round table in April 2007 with thirty-three key figures from Burundi, the first two themes proposed for discussion were: 'Talking about one's hurts' and 'Being freed from one's fears'. It was not a question of reaching political agreements but rather of building the relationships which make peace agreements possible and above all applicable.

Longer term, as was seen in Southern Rhodesia during the seventies with the 'Cabinet of Conscience', the aim was to form a group of representatives from every political and social sector desirous of finding just solutions for all. Such a group can act as a catalyst in proposing approaches and points of reference acceptable to all.

Anyone can be the missing link in a chain of contacts which may change the course of history. That is the tremendous hope handed down by Frank Buchman. It offers a credible alternative to those who only believe in the balance of power or for whom violence seems the only way to settle the injustices of which they feel themselves to be victims.

8

Political Dynamite in Australia

by John Bond & Mike Brown

For the past decade John Bond has taken leadership in healing the harm done to Aboriginal Australians by cruel and misguided past policies. He was the Secretary of Australia's National Sorry Day Committee and the Journey of Healing from 1998 to 2006. In 2007 he was awarded the Medal of the Order of Australia for this work.

Mike Brown, a member of the International Council of Initiatives of Change, is a writer/trainer from Australia, currently living in India. His book, *No Longer Down Under – Australians creating change*, features chapters on Kim Beazley and the movement for justice for the Australian Aboriginal people. For twenty years Mike has been active in the Australian reconciliation movement and in 2000 he received the Non-Indigenous Person of the Year award in his State.

EVERYONE wants their politicians to be honest, but many doubt that this is possible. Kim E Beazley, who served for 32 years in the Australian Parliament, made honesty his policy. His Cabinet colleague Bill Hayden, later Governor-General of Australia, wrote: 'I don't believe that absolute honesty is possible, but Kim came closer to it than anyone I knew.'

Beazley grew up in poverty in Western Australia, but thrived at his local school. 'We didn't have shoes,' he remembers, 'but we could quote Wordsworth.' He became active in the Labor Party, and entered Parliament in 1945 at the age of 28. Prime Minister Ben Chifley said he would 'go a long way'. Beazley agreed, and soon his arrogant lecturing in the House gained him the epithet 'The Student Prince'.

However, when Beazley retired, he had been elected to his party's second highest office and, as Minister for Education, initiated far-reaching reforms to education. The *Melbourne Herald* wrote that he had been 'beyond any dispute, one of the best Members of Parliament Australia has ever had'.

The turning point came in 1953, when he reached a crucial moment in his personal life and public career. 'I have made a decision,' he said, 'to concern myself daily with the challenge of how to live out God's will: to turn the searchlight of absolute honesty on to my motives; to try to see the world with the clarity of absolute purity; to take as radar through the fog of international affairs absolute love.'

Hardly usual language for a politician. And in Australia, the ramifications were soon being felt. 'No one with even a slight working knowledge of politics could fail to delight in the confusion that could result from even one of our politicians resolving to be absolutely honest,' wrote one political columnist, commenting on the 'political dynamite that might be set off by Mr Beazley's practical sincerity and absolute honesty'.

Destroy him

Others were not so delighted. 'Facing the prospect of political destruction at this moment is young Kim Beazley,' reported Alan Reid, doyen of Australia's political journalists at that time. 'Powerful, office-hungry individuals fear that his idealism and his current determination to pursue the truth, whatever the price, could cost the Labor Party the next election. The story they are assiduously and effectively peddling is, "Beazley has lost his balance." So the word has gone out, "Destroy him."'

But they did not destroy him. Beazley was ultimately elected by his party to its second highest office, and was Minister for Education in two of the three terms which Labor has had in government since then. More important, the 'system' – that nebulous blend of structures, laws and attitudes – shifted under the sustained impact of Beazley's effort and conviction, particularly with regard to education and to Australia's humiliated and often persecuted minority, the Aborigines.

Power is dangerous

'He has always had intellectual force and clarity,' wrote the political correspondent of *The Australian*. 'He is undoubtedly Labor's – and probably Parliament's – best orator.' But Beazley himself feels that intellect in politics can be suspect. His experience is that 'power is dangerous when intellect kills the conscience in the exercise of authority, and safe when conscience governs the -intellect'.

Through a process of struggle in his own spirit and mind, one basic conviction has emerged: 'The most practical point in politics is that there is an intellect, God's intellect, beyond the perception and self-interest of man.' This was not theory, but experience. It had started with that decision to 'concern myself with the challenge of how to live out God's will'.

Beazley had been chosen as one of ten MPs to represent the Australian Parliament at Queen Elizabeth's coronation in 1953. Intrigued by the ideas of Moral Re-Armament, he stopped at the conference centre in Caux, Switzerland for a week on his way home. Two weeks... three weeks went by, and he was still there. 'What I saw at Caux was far more significant for the peace and sanity of the world than anything being done at that time in Australian politics,' he says.

It was a process rooted in personal change. As Beazley says, 'Moral Re-Armament is the ultimate in realism, for it suggests a simple experiment that anybody can try – the experiment of searching for God's leading, of testing any thoughts that come against absolute honesty, purity, unselfishness and love, and carrying those which meet these standards into practical action.'

Beazley himself was brought face-to face with the 'ultimate realism' of that experiment during those days in Switzerland. A friend had suggested that he should seek God's guidance, having 'nothing to prove, nothing to justify and nothing to gain for yourself. Then your mind will be free.'

'What a shockingly subversive thing to say to someone in politics,' Beazley says. 'I had been proving how right I was at every election, justifying everything we had ever done, and gaining political power for myself was the minimum I must do.'

But Beazley could not escape the challenge. He began to recognize over the following days that 'the life of a morally re-armed man is no cheap subscribing to principles, but costly restitution, the apology which is costly to our pride, and definite decisions'. The process was started by sitting down and writing a letter to his wife.

Betty Beazley was a successful sprinter, holding an Australian women's record for ten years in her event. 'Some things in that letter I knew already,' she says. 'Some I had guessed, but some I did not know. I felt a wonderful sense of relief and trust after reading it.'

While disentangling the web of deceit in his family life, Beazley found he was tackling the same web in his political life. 'I thought of my father. He had the problem of drink, and I had not given him my heart. I realised I had treated some people in my party with that same problem in the same way. I had not helped them with my superiority and contempt.'

Then came a tough thought for a politician: 'You have formed the habit of not being absolutely accurate in political statements.' As he put it to the conference in Switzerland, 'I have always congratulated myself that my campaign speeches were objective. I objectively analyzed the government's mistakes, but never their virtues. I have come to realize that this is one of the most mischievous forms of lying in politics.'

During those days God had seemed to be challenging basic motives: political ambition, self-will and pride. He had seen that his university education had made him aloof from the working class, though his father had been a trade union member and Beazley himself had been raised in poverty. As a Labor MP representing the port of Fremantle, he would often visit the waterside workers for political purposes. Yet he never wanted to know them socially or to have them in his home.

But it was not merely an exercise in self-examination. Gradually Beazley had begun to see what God might require of him in the future. One thought had stuck in his mind: 'If you live absolute purity you will be used towards the rehabilitation of the Australian Aboriginal race. Purity is the alternative to living for self-gratification, which kills intelligent care for others.'

In terms of definite action, he had the thought, 'If Aborigines are not acknowledged as owning land, they will negotiate from a position of weakness. If the dignity of land ownership is acknowledged, they will negotiate from a position of strength.'

At that point, in 1953, Aborigines had no civil rights and no voting rights in Australia; they lived in appalling conditions in complete subjection. They did not own one acre of land – and few white Australians cared.

Within months of returning from Caux, Beazley got Aboriginal land ownership on to the Labor Party platform. In government, 20 years later, Labor initiated legislation for land rights. Although their battle is far from over, Aborigines now have freehold title to approximately 188,000 square miles in two states in Australia, and are negotiating for more.

Restoring dignity

The Beazleys began to invite Aborigines to their home in Perth. 'Over numerous meals, they enlightened us a great deal about Aboriginal thinking.' For almost two decades on the opposition benches of Parliament, Beazley continually sought the guidance of the Holy Spirit on how to restore the dignity and rights of the Aboriginal people. In 1961 he toured the far north of Australia as part of a Select Committee on Aboriginal Voting Rights, whose work laid the foundation for full voting rights for Aborigines in 1968.

Labor was elected to government in December 1972, and Kim Beazley became Minister for Education. On the first morning in office, he wrote down in his time of meditation: 'To deny a people an education in their own language is to treat them as a conquered people, and we have always treated the Aborigines as a conquered people.' Then came ideas for action: 'Arrange for Aborigines to choose the language of Aboriginal schools, with English a second language.'

He discussed the thought with his wife. Then at 3pm that day he told the new Prime Minister, Gough Whitlam, of his thought. On the 5pm national news, Whitlam announced as government policy a bilingual programme of education for Aborigines. Until that day, in some States teachers could be penalized under law for teaching in an Aboriginal language, or any language other than English. When Beazley left the Ministry, education was being given in 22 Aboriginal languages.

For Beazley it was but one further step in a conviction formed twenty years before, by no means the only step. Appalled by reports of widespread malnutrition and disease among the Aborigines, with other Federal and State ministers he set in motion a government programme to tackle the disasters of leprosy, yaw hookworm, trachoma, alcoholism and malnutrition. Aboriginal adult education had become another focus.

Soon after the end of his time in office, the Australian National University awarded him an honorary Doctorate of Laws, citing particularly his contribution in the areas of Aboriginal affairs and education. 'It has become popular over the last years,' reads the citation, 'to recognize the contribution of the Aboriginal people to this nation... and the injustices that have been done to them. But over the last half-century this was far from popular. In that time few people have done as much, and none have done more than Kim Beazley, to bring about that change in attitude.'

Healing an ulcer

In education, the citation highlighted the impact of his Ministry, during which tertiary education was made free, Federal grants to schools increased sixfold, a wide-ranging scholarship scheme according to need was established for handicapped and isolated children, and existing study grants for Aboriginal children were extended. 'However,' the citation continues, 'Mr Beazley's greatest contribution was not the expenditure of money, but the healing of an ulcer that has festered in our society for close to 200 years. Sectarian bitterness, which focused on schools and their funding was dealt a death blow by needs-based funding which Mr Beazley introduced.'

These reforms, including the giving of State aid to church-run schools, was indeed a sensitive political and social issue, and their introduction came only after a long and sometimes bitter public and political debate.

Though that legislation has become the mainstay of education funding policy since, Beazley feels that the credit was not his. His policy had been shaped by the inspiration gained during his 'quiet times', a spiritual discipline he practised every morning, whether in the heat of government or during long years in opposition.

This practice also gave him a sense of inner direction about the concerns of his wife and three children, whom he saw only briefly at weekends. Stress is an occupational hazard for any politician, and often families suffer. Beazley's family was on the other side of the continent from

Canberra, and the arduous 2,000-mile journey back to his electorate and home added to the strain.

'Those early years were so turbulent,' remembers Betty Beazley. 'I had care of the three children most of the time and when things went wrong, Kim would be met with a spiel of anger from me immediately on his return home.' She was given the thought to tell him the good things on his return, then, when he had rested, tell him the things that had gone wrong and work out with him what to do about them.

When her husband became Minister for Education, she felt that having given 25 years to bringing up the children, the next 25 years she should be by his side. It meant renting a second home in Canberra, where they could entertain and care for his colleagues and his Aboriginal friends.

Every child's needs must be met

Each morning, she and her husband would exchange the ideas given them in 'that first quiet hour of the day' when they sought God's guidance. Betty remembers Kim telling her of one thought which became the basic motivation of his education policy: '*Every* child's needs must be met.'

In the hurly-burly of politicking, it is the conventional wisdom that those who stick to scruples will be taken for a ride. Beazley disagrees, and survived 32 years in Parliament to prove it. 'If you are devoted to God's guidance,' he says, 'you are not out to destroy people; your political environment is not strewn with corpses. The fact that you are not lethal but gracious in your relationships makes a big difference.'

That difference had been noted in Beazley's case. Before his experience in Caux, one correspondent wrote of his 'lecturing Parliament in a hectoring, sneering tone which earned him almost universal dislike'. Upon his retirement he could hardly have been more respected on both sides of the House. The Speaker of the Parliament, Sir Billy Snedden, a member of the opposing party, paid tribute to him as 'a fine parliamentarian and a great Australian'.

But it was not a matter of being popular. Beazley saw there was a choice involved. 'If you do not accept the importance of conscience, you accept only the importance of power,' he says. 'This question of motive is the key to social advance. I have spent 28 years in opposition, and I have come to believe that the true function of an opposition is to out-think the government at the point of its successes. Only then can alternative competitive policies be framed and social advance take place.'

A senior public servant in the Prime Minister's department said of him, 'What a poor reward it would have been for the nation if Kim had pursued the cause of personal power during those years in opposition, because it was as much in opposition as in government that he brought progress and healing. Great issues, such as the welfare of the Aboriginal people and the preparation of Papua New Guinea for independence, were brought into focus from the opposition side of Parliament.'

In the years since, there have been important steps towards justice for Aboriginal Australians. Even though the Government in which he served was defeated by a conservative Government, the new Government implemented the programme developed by Beazley and his colleagues. As a result, today Aboriginal people own 15% of the land area of Australia. The art of Aboriginal Australia has flourished, and now brings in millions of dollars annually to Aboriginal communities. Aboriginal people are slowly taking their place in the professions, as doctors, lawyers, politicians.

Throughout the 1990s, a nation-wide programme of study circles created the opportunity for tens of thousands of non-Aboriginal Australians to talk deeply with Aboriginal people. This brought a whole new level of understanding and empathy. Perhaps this was seen most clearly when, in 1997, a national inquiry reported on the effect of the policies under which tens of thousands of Aboriginal children were removed from their families, and placed in institutions and with families in an attempt to assimilate them into Western culture. These policies, which were implemented until the 1970s, had tragic consequences, and the report, *Bringing Them Home,* exposed the tragedy.

Sorry Day and a Journey of Healing

The Government tried to ignore the report, and refused to apologise for the harm done. Many Australians were offended by this refusal, and took it upon themselves to apologise. A million people took part in a Sorry Day held a year after the *Bringing Them Home* report was issued. In response, Aboriginal people launched a Journey of Healing, offering all Australians the chance to help the healing process. This has spawned hundreds of community events every year since then, bringing together Aboriginal and non-Aboriginal communities in initiatives aimed at healing the effects of these cruel and misguided policies.

However, Australia still lags far behind comparable countries such as Canada in redressing the wrongs of the past. Racism towards Aboriginal people is still rife, and

Aboriginal people find it far harder than others to find employment, and to receive services which other Australians take for granted. Aboriginal people still die 20 years younger than the rest of the community. Other countries have shown that tragic health conditions among their indigenous community can be overcome, and the reluctance of successive Australian Governments to invest adequate resources in improving Aboriginal health is an indictment on all Australians. Also, there has been a stop-start approach to developing a representative national Aboriginal organisation, which means that the Aboriginal community has a wholly inadequate voice in national affairs.

So there is much work yet to be done. But a new spirit is abroad. Many Australians of all races have realised that they don't have to wait for Governments; that they can work for healing and justice for Aboriginal people. Therein lies the hope that the Aboriginal community will become healthy, educated and prosperous, and so be enabled to make its full, unique contribution to Australia's national life. And Beazley made a significant contribution to the growth of this spirit.

Kim Beazley's son, also called Kim, followed his father into Federal politics and held senior Cabinet posts in Labour governments under Prime Ministers Hawke and Keating, and for some years was the Leader of the Opposition. He reflected his father's passionate concern for Aboriginal Australia.

This article was written before Kim Beazley died, in late 2007. Three former Prime Ministers attended his funeral. Obituaries appeared in all Australian newspapers, and many overseas. They referred to him as a pioneer of Aboriginal land rights, and his legacy of educational reforms. But above all they focused on his faith and his integrity. The London Times described him as 'one of Australia's most respected politicians' The *Sydney Morning Herald* headlined its obituary 'Integrity and principle beyond political success'. 'His faith came before politics,' wrote the West Australian.

It was a faith intimately involved in the affairs of the nation. As the *Melbourne Age*'s obituary concluded, quoting Beazley: 'There is sanity from the Holy Spirit beyond human ideas of justice. The thoughts of God, given primacy in the life of man, bring to the innermost motives the virtue of mercy, and with it a cure for hatred that can turn the tide of history. This is the essence of intelligent statesmanship.'

9

India's Journey towards New Governance

An Indian Perspective by V C Viswanathan

V C Viswanathan came from Kerala in South India. He was president of the Students Union at Madras University when Frank Buchman visited in 1953. Inspired by what Buchman and his friends had to say, Viswanathan began applying Buchman's ideas in his first job with Caltex Oil Company. Later he decided to give his full time to the work of Moral Re-Armament for some years before becoming in turn marketing manager for two different tyre companies in Madras and Delhi.

FRANK Buchman's love for India was kindled very early in his life. He noted in his diary in January 1902, 'Today a visitor told us, "Had I my life to spend over again it would be spent in India. There are magnificent opportunities there for the young man." I would so much like to go to India.' He was 24 years old.

'You will be guided beyond your wildest dreams. God has a unique part for you and your work in India... You are needed in India. You can create an organism here which would decide the future of the world.'

These were some of the thoughts Frank Buchman had in Mumbai at the start of an historic six-month visit to India in 1952–53. 'What are we to think of such thoughts, written down in the night some decades ago?' wonders Garth Lean in his well-researched biography *Frank Buchman: a Life*. Reflecting on this, I believe Buchman's coming with an international team was a divine intervention, which helped turn the tide in the ideological struggle.

Buchman's longing, when he was 24, was fulfilled 13 years later. His mother tried to dissuade him from leaving America then, as the First World War had started and it was not safe to travel by ship because of German torpedoes. Buchman insisted, and reached India safely via Colombo in 1915. He stayed six months, travelling extensively throughout the country from Travancore in the south to Rawalpindi in the north and from Bombay to Calcutta, criss-crossing the sub-continent several times. He met and became a friend of many including Rabindranath Tagore and Mahatma Gandhi. He had long walks with Gandhi on the sea beach in Madras where he stayed three days. Gandhi had just come back from South Africa and was not then a central figure in India's political life. Buchman wrote that 'walking with Gandhi was like walking with Aristotle'.

Nine visits

Buchman made nine visits to India. On his second visit in 1924-25 he met Gandhi again and many national leaders including Mohammed Ali Jinnah, Jawaharlal Nehru, C Rajagopalachari and the Ali brothers at the Congress party convention at Belgaum. Later he visited Gandhiji at the Sabarmati Ashram and met him again in Bishop

Foss Westcott's home in Calcutta. Buchman wrote prophetically to a friend, 'He (Gandhi) is no longer a political leader, but the sphere of his influence will be sainthood and a compelling one at that.' Buchman was a true friend and maintained a close association with three generations of the Gandhi family. Years later in June 1956, speaking at the MRA world assembly at Caux in Switzerland, Devadas Gandhi, one of Gandhi's sons, said, 'I do not think there is any single message for the world today that has so much significance as MRA. You are embarked on a most essential if difficult mission, and if you fail the world fails. The basis of MRA is fundamental and calls for the highest courage and patience. You face opposition and criticism. But I believe, with you, in persistence, and the good seeds you have sown will certainly come to bear fruit.'

Gandhiji's grandson Rajmohan Gandhi, speaking on the occasion of Buchman's 80th birthday said, 'Think of Frank Buchman and you must think of countless ordinary people of Asia, Africa, America and Europe of every colour, culture, creed and background who count him as their true friend. His secret has always been his intense care for people and for nations and his ability to see what, under God, they can become. To be with him is an experience – you know that you are the only person that matters for him. So it is with nations. While others protest, criticise or are cynical, he has always had the faith born of experience in his own life, that the most difficult man or the most divided nation can change and demonstrate an answer. This vision is actually being realised in many lands.'

Buchman made a positive impact on the lives of many Indians and non-Indians. David Young in his book *Ini-*

tiatives of change in India – Observing six decades of Moral Re-Armament,* gives many interesting anecdotes. One is the story of the change in Lionel Jardine, a senior member of the Indian Civil service in 1933. Four generations of his family had served in India since 1806. His wife Marjorie and her family, too, had a long connection with India.

The transformation in Jardine's life and his decision to live by the absolute standards of honesty, love, purity and unselfishness and to seek God's guidance by listening to the inner voice had a ripple effect on the lives of many including Dr C Chandra Ghosh, leader of Forward Bloc, a breakaway wing of the Congress Party, who believed in the use of violence if necessary for winning India's independence. Jardine has given accounts of his encounters with many people of varied backgrounds in his autobiography, They called me an Impeccable Imperialist.

From autocrat to servant

Gandhiji once told a British friend, Roger Hicks, about Jardine, 'You remember you were telling me stories last time about the Revenue Commissioner in Frontier Province? Well, I had the Chief Minister Dr Khan Sahib investigate them and they are all true.' They talked about others who had met Buchman in Oxford in 1934 and whose lives had been completely transformed. They had found a new purpose and motive in life. In the words of Dr C C Ghosh, 'From being an absolute autocrat he (Jardine) became an absolute servant of the people.' Gandhiji said that this was the most important thing happening today and observed, 'Politics has become a great game of chess. We know the value of the pieces and we know the

* Grosvenor Books 2003

possible moves. But if men's motives and values change, like those of the Revenue Commissioner and others, then the whole board is upset and we begin again.' He went on to say, 'Go tell the Viceroy from me that if we have this spirit, remembering all his wartime difficulties, we could find agreement in half an hour.' Hicks carried out Gandhi's wish, but sadly the Viceroy's views of the Mahatma were too set at that point for him to accept his offer.

Over the years many Indians from varying backgrounds had met Buchman and colleagues like Peter Howard and Roger Hicks, and had attended MRA conferences at Caux in Switzerland. Impressed by the change brought about in people and situations through the application of MRA ideas, a powerful national committee of Indians wrote to Buchman inviting him to bring a team to India:

> *'We unite in asking you, most earnestly, to come yourself this winter to India and to bring with you an international team that we may profit by your experience. Together we must succeed in turning the world from crisis to cure and in demonstrating an overarching ideology for Management and Labour.'*

Left and Right for East and West

In response to this invitation, Buchman came with four plays and an international team of 200 people from 35 nations. They stayed in India for six months journeying across India, visiting Bombay, Ahmedabad, Delhi, Lucknow, Hyderabad, Madras, Bangalore, Calcutta and Srinagar.

On his first day in New Delhi, Buchman and his team visited Raj Ghat and laid a wreath in honour of Mahatma

Gandhi. Later Buchman had the rare honour of addressing a large number of members of both houses of Parliament in the Lok Sabha presided over by the Deputy Speaker. In his address he expressed his vision for India, which appealed to the hearts and minds of many parliamentarians who heard him.

An All-Asian Assembly was held in January 1953 in New Delhi. Speaking on that occasion Dr Buchman gave his New Year message to the people of India:

> *'Men are hungry for bread, for peace, and the hope of a new world order. Before a God-led unity every last problem would be solved. Hands will be filled with work, stomachs with food and empty hearts with an ideology that really satisfies. That is what Moral Re-Armament is out for. It gives faith to the faithless but also helps men of faith to live so compellingly that cities and nations change. Nations where everyone cares enough and everyone shares enough, so that everyone has enough will pattern a new social and economic order for this and all future generations.*
>
> *'A nation at peace within itself will bring peace to the world. A nation that makes What is Right regnant in personal, industrial, political and national life will pioneer the next historic step of progress and destiny for all mankind.'*

President Rajendra Prasad received Buchman and his full team at the Rashtrapati Bhavan. Dr S Radhakrishnan (later President) also invited him and his friends for tea. On January 3rd Prime Minister Jawaharlal Nehru came to tea and talked for half an hour with Buchman at Jaipur house, which had been made available by the Prime Minister. Pandit Nehru was visibly moved when the international chorus sang India's national anthem and other songs, especially the 'Song of India'.

One of the MRA plays was performed before 20,000 workers at the annual session of the Indian National Congress at Hyderabad. In Madras initially some students picketed the theatre with placards and leaflets using slogans taken from Tashkent and Moscow broadcasts. But soon the general enthusiasm of the public for the MRA plays lured the protesters inside and the agitation faded away. In fact, the public interest was so overwhelming that the cast had to give open-air performances to which thousands came. The Vauhini studio in Madras built a special stage, the largest in India, and on some days the cast performed thrice to accommodate the huge crowds that waited patiently.

In Calcutta the disparity between the rich and the poor and the clash of class war were even more apparent to the visitors. But soon the MRA team won the hearts of many belonging to all classes including several trade union leaders. Sibnath Banerji, president of the 800,000 strong Socialist movement – the *Hind Mazdoor Sabha* – was drawn to MRA when he saw the plays and met people like Geoffrey Daukes (UK), Gordon Wise (Australia) and Cecil Morrison, 'the Happy Baker' from Canada. As a young man he had made his way overland to attend Lenin's funeral in Moscow in 1924 but communism did not capture him. He was a true champion of the workers and the poor. He became an active supporter of the work of Moral Re-Armament in India and the world. Another remarkable trade union leader who became a life-long fighter for MRA was Satya Narayan Banerjee.

From Calcutta the team went west to Srinagar. Sheikh Abdullah, then Prime Minister of Kashmir, came with his wife and sons to see the MRA plays. He told Buchman, 'You have here the answer for India and Pakistan. It takes patience, I saw the answer in the plays and it is God.' His wife added, 'When I saw the play, I knew the spirit of God was there. It is something you don't run into much in the world today and we are grateful.'

A new phase

David Young's book, *Initiatives of change in India*, tells of the outcome of Buchman's visit and the continuing action in India and its outreach through changes in the lives of many. Some of the landmark events were:

1) The Moral Re-Armament World Assembly at Caux in 1953 was attended by a large delegation of Indians consisting of students, trade unionists, parliamentarians, industrialists, educators and leading citizens who were enlisted as a result of Buchman's visit to India. Their experience at Caux is best expressed in the words of one young man: 'My experience at Caux was beyond all expectations. I saw the dawn of a new civilization – a world free of hate, prejudice, greed and exploitation. Men and women of every faith, race, class and colour from over fifty nations, from every continent had assembled there. Meeting real people who had experienced change in their own lives and as a result helped to bring about vast social, economic and political transformations convinced me that MRA was the way to build a new world order of equity and justice.' He like many others decided to be part of this global revolution.

2) The work of Moral Re-Armament in India entered a new phase when Rajmohan Gandhi returned to India in

1957 and decided to give his all to it despite great opposition from his family and well-meaning friends. After graduating from St Stephen's College, New Delhi, he was sent by his father to Britain for training in journalism on *The Scotsman*. His father sought Buchman's help to find a good MRA home where he could stay in Edinburgh.

The quality of life of that family and their care made a deep impression on the young man. He decided to live by the ideas they lived. In his words, he says, 'For me change meant contrasting my life with the absolute standards of honesty, purity, unselfishness and love. It meant returning money to the Delhi Transport Undertaking for travelling on their buses without tickets. It meant apologising to a friend for jealousy because he was successful and popular. It meant writing to my old school principal to seek forgiveness for cheating in an examination. It meant being completely honest with my parents about how I spent my time and the money they gave me. It meant a decrease in my interest in myself and an increase in my concern for others. Every morning it means for me having a time of Quiet during which my conscience or the inner voice or God's voice can clarify my motives and help me see where I needed to change and show me how I can change others.'

He was faced with a difficult decision when his father suddenly passed away. Being the eldest son there was considerable pressure on him to take up a job and take care of his mother. His maternal grandfather, C Rajagopalachari, a close associate of Gandhiji and India's first Indian governor-general and elder statesman, impressed upon him his filial responsibility. With his own ability and family background there were many positions the young Gandhi could aspire for.

G D Birla, a leading industrialist and family friend who owned the *Hindustan Times*, invited Rajmohan Gandhi to join as assistant editor of the newspaper of which his father had been the Chief Editor till he died. It was a position that carried considerable prestige and power apart from being a comfortable and secure job. Rajmohan Gandhi turned down the offer. He said, 'When Mahatma Gandhi came back from South Africa his family urged him to continue his legal practice. Instead he put aside his private plans in order to free the country. Now there is a bigger job than freeing one's country. The job is to save the world from dictatorship, corruption and war. I am going to put MRA in the first place.'

3) A visit to Caux in 1954 by a Kerala delegation consisted of leaders of different communities including Mannath Padmanabhan, leader of the Hindu Nair community, and P.T.Chacko, a Catholic and leader of the Congress party in the Kerala Legislature. It led to a new understanding and unity among the leaders of different communities ending factional fights within the Congress party. Kerala had made history in 1957 when for the first time in the world a Communist government was elected to power through a free democratic process. Mannath Padmanabhan spoke at Caux: 'Communism has grown in the world because we have not heeded the teachings of Lord Krishna, Buddha and Jesus Christ. We have had religions, moral principles, and lofty ideals. Prophets and sages have talked about them for thousands of years, but we have not lived them. As we stand united to get rid of selfishness, living purity and dedicated to God, our efforts will be crowned with success. Frank Buchman is a guru. He has rediscovered the fundamental and noble principles that

will lead mankind to a better life and prosperity. The key is to change men. It is the only way in this atomic age.'

4) At a press conference held in New Delhi in August 1963 Rajmohan Gandhi, together with leaders from Kerala, spoke of a bold plan to rouse India's millions to fight for Moral Re-Armament with the same passion with which they sought political liberation. The statement declared: 'As deadly as the danger from China is India's internal disease. It lies in jealousy, impurity, hate and fear. They have produced divisions, bribery, drift and frustration. Unchecked they will lead inevitably to anarchy and dictatorship.

'A force of Indians is determined to strike at the root of our national disease. These men and women are pledged under God to change the character of our nation. The aim is to make Moral Re-Armament the dominant force in all spheres of our national life – politics, administration, business, education and defence.

'Our aim is a new social order where man no longer cheats, insults, worships, corrupts or exploits his fellow man. Where a nation is united because families are united. Where men and women live as sons and daughters of God. To create this new order across the world must be the united aim of our nation. The fight for a clean, strong, united India will need more dedication and sacrifice than the struggle for freedom required.'

A March-on-Wheels

5) They announced that a vigorous nationwide campaign, a March-on-Wheels, to alert and enlist India's millions in the battle for Moral Re-Armament, would start on October 2 from Kanyakumari for Delhi. 'Our aim is to make

India a nation of one heart, one mind and one goal. Conscious of our shortcomings, but trusting in the power of God, we are pledged to fight for this revolution, whatever the cost may be... We urge every patriotic man and woman to join with us in the battle.'

The marchers consisted of a core of committed Indians and included a number of foreigners. Over a period of seven weeks, the team of 75 people travelled in buses from Kanyakumari (at the southern tip of India) to New Delhi, stopping at towns and villages through the states of Kerala, Mysore, Madras, Hyderabad, Orissa, Bengal, Bihar and Uttar Pradesh. They spoke at meetings to every kind of person – students and workers, industrialists and trade unionists, peasants and tradesmen, citizens and leaders, men and women. To everyone the message was the same. The creation of a strong, clean and united India required people to be different. Rajmohan Gandhi's challenge to all was simple:

- Accept absolute moral standards in your own life and allow yourself to be used to give a lead for the country.
- The ordinary man who listens to the inner voice can do extraordinary things.
- An India clean, just, strong, united and honest at home, proclaiming boldly and fearlessly a revolution beyond communism and anti-communism for the entire world, is the India we shall fight under God to create.

The climax of the March was the Moral Re-Armament Assembly of Nations that opened at Vigyan Bhavan, New Delhi, on November 24.

The creation of 'Asia Plateau'

6) The idea for building a conference and training centre for Moral Re-Armament came out of the experience of conducting training camps for young people who had responded enthusiastically to the challenge of building a clean, strong, united India. Impressed by the remarkable change in the youth and inspired by their vision for India, citizens of Panchgani including municipal councillors, teachers and senior citizens urged Rajmohan Gandhi, Russi Lala and others that a permanent training centre for training the youth should be built in Panchgani, and offered to help find a suitable site.

The building of the centre was an act of faith from the word go. First steps for purchasing the land were taken in 1965. Construction started in January 1967 and the first phase was completed in January 1968; the second phase in January 1969 and the third phase including the large auditorium, meeting rooms, dining and catering facilities were completed in early 1972.

For four decades now men and women, young and old from all walks of life, of all classes, races and religions have come to Asia Plateau from all over India and other countries of Asia, Africa, Europe, North and South America and Australia and have experienced here, a change in attitude, motivation and behaviour. Many found a new vision and a new purpose for their lives, making a difference in their personal lives, families, work places, communities and their nations.

A leading Indian newspaper called Asia Plateau 'a beacon of hope'. An Indonesian youth leader said, 'Asia Plateau may lie in India, but it belongs to Asia.' The *Sunday Standard* wrote, 'The Moral Re-Armament Training Centre is destined to change the hearts and minds of the people. From here will come out trained men and women, their ambitious task to remodel a nation. It will help mould the youth of India for the task of leading India, Asia and the world; give industrial labour the necessary training to fight not only for a fair day's wage but also for a fair day's work; help traders and industrialists to put people before profit; train teachers to revolutionise the educational pattern; give the peasants sufficient training... and instil in every man and woman the need to care for the family, the neighbours, the community and the world.'

Buchman always believed that the ordinary man inspired by God could do the extraordinary thing. Perhaps those who are a bit out of the ordinary can make an even more far-reaching mark.

It was worth having a try

Initiatives of Change multiplies through the inspired initiatives of all kinds of people. One day in late 1973 a letter arrived at Asia Plateau, Panchgani, from the chairman of a big textile company in Mumbai. He asked if, now that the Centre was completed and operational, he could send his 5,000 employees in batches for training in Moral Re-Armament. You can imagine the kind of discussion that took place over this letter! Could the Centre take on this assignment? Were the facilities there for handling this? Above all, who would provide the training and the faculty for these industrial people?

Some wanted to reply that while they would love to respond positively to his request, they did not feel ready and equipped to undertake this. Another suggestion was that perhaps God might be wanting to open a door and if advantage of this was not taken, other openings might be missed.

Eventually one of the Trustees at the Centre said he felt it was worth having a try. If the experiment worked out, he said, well and good. If it failed, all that would suffer would be our pride.

And so, as a start, it was agreed to plan for three seminars, one a month for three months for groups of about 75 employees in each batch. It was suggested to the chairman that each batch should consist of a cross section of staff from senior managers to shop floor workers. They would live and eat together at the Centre irrespective of their positions in the company and all would be treated equally. For an Indian course at that time this was unusual.

A further request was made that a few representatives of other firms should also be invited, to have the chance to evaluate similar actions for their respective companies. All this was agreed and the first three seminars were fixed. In order to help carry these seminars some people from industry, who had experience of personal change and its application at the work place, were asked to come and assist.

After the trial seminars it was agreed to continue, and to hold about ten such courses a year. From those who attended the first seminars came an unexpected request. Because of deep changes which took place in some of the participants some of their wives wanted to know how this happened and could they attend and learn more. They wanted to know what had changed their husbands in regard to simple things like over-drinking, overspending money and not helping in family issues. And so it was agreed that wives could accompany their husbands, if they wished, and the company would underwrite the extra cost because they recognised the value of truly supportive wives and families.

A knock-on effect was that more and more companies began sending their employees, as well as in many cases having follow-up programmes in their factories, and a new industrial culture developing in the country. This was particularly noticeable as big and well-known companies began to send their staff. And this goes on to this day.

Man management as key to maintaining morale

Another quite different development took place at Asia Plateau through the visit one day some 15 years ago of an Army Brigadier from nearby Pune. He had been on holiday at an adjacent hill station and called in to find out what went on when passing a very attractive campus with elegant buildings and fine gardens. At the time he was commanding the Army Institute of National Integration (INI).

It should be mentioned here that the Army has always had a high regard for man management as key to maintaining morale in the Service. And of course the reputation of the Indian Army is high from campaigns of the Second World War in North Africa, Italy and Burma until the present day. The first Indian Chief of Staff, General K.M.Cariappa, had supported the visit of Buchman to India in 1952/53 and continued to do so until his death.

The setting up of the INI in Pune was in pursuit of maintaining this high standard in the Army and ensuring the unity on which efficiency greatly depended. The Indian Army, the fourth largest in the world, is made up of personnel from many different ethnic, language and religious backgrounds, as is India as a country. Units have their own faith leaders as appropriate to the make-up of the unit. In the Western world these are the equivalent of Army chaplains. In India they belong, of course, to the Hindu, Muslim, Sikh and Christian faiths depending on the unit concerned.

The INI was established so that these faith leaders could understand the other faiths as well as their own and thus provide a framework of unity for the Army. So the INI holds month-long courses of some fifty people in each course. This was the establishment which this Brigadier was running at the time of his visit to the Centre at Asia Plateau. Before leaving he asked whether it would be possible for him to send those participating in an INI course to the Centre for a day to study what training was being given. This was agreed and the first batch duly arrived. The result was so satisfactory that the Brigadier asked if this kind of visit could be included in the programme for every course. Not only was this readily agreed, but after a number of such visits, they were extended to two days so that the participants could get the maximum benefit. And thus it has continued to this day.

Ethical governance for the country

Another initiative resulted from the visit to Asia Plateau some three years ago of a man called Prabhat Kumar. He had been Cabinet Secretary in Delhi and on retirement had been Governor of one of India's States. Now retired from that last assignment he came as an onlooker at a programme at the Centre and was impressed not only by the spirit of the participants but also the changes which took place in the people attending. He began considering the application of this kind of training to members of the Indian Administrative Service (IAS), which provides the framework for running the country at all levels.

In teamwork with another retired Cabinet Secretary he proposed bringing together some 30 or 40 IAS officers for four days to find out whether these men and women felt that it was something of value in their work and for running the country. To establish 'ethical governance for the country' was Kumar's aim, and it could only happen through the readiness of these IAS officers to practice the ethic themselves.

The first group who came together were fully in favour of this being a regular element in the training and life of their cadre. So a second such course was fixed and has just been completed. Some comments illustrate what it meant to them.

With forty years of experience in the Civil Service, Prabhat Kumar spoke with deep conviction and passion. He said that the four days spent together have enabled everyone to think together as a community. Looking back over the corridors of time, he said, good practices were in vogue at the dawn of Independence. There was sufficient space for the civil servants to operate. Good practices were legitimatised without illegitimate interference by the politicians. This phase of mutual respect continued till about the end of the '60s. Phase two came into being after that. Vagueness and formality crept into the service. The politician took the decision and civil servants merely implemented his diktat. Kumar felt that internal consistency has to be re-established and the areas clearly marked out for a politically neutral civil service.

Transparency International has ranked India 83rd out 133 in their table of honest government. The most potent remedy for change is the 'Sunshine of Information', Kumar felt. Ethics is a personal option. One has to be prepared for flak and also to flourish with the new choice.

He urged participants to give priority to project thinking and stressed the importance of micro-management of projects especially in backward areas, as this would solve the problem of poverty in Indian villages, prevalent even after fifty years of independence.

As the five days of togetherness were brought to a close, views ranged from 'excellent' to 'awesome'. Some participants were of the view that it is not only the positive stories which should get highlighted but also the stories of struggle. Shailaja Chandra, senior IAS officer and ex-chairman of the Public Grievance Commission articulated a powerful keynote address on the role of IAS officers in everyday life. One very relevant point made by her which set everyone thinking was, 'Ends matter as much as means', saying that the core of conduct must have strong embedded values. She also emphasised that high ideals of honesty, duty and truth must always be upheld in public life. While achieving these ends a personal benchmark could be set. She concluded by saying that ethical leaders must select public good over personal gain.

The vision of the initiators of this programme is that it will provide a groundswell of change in the governance of the country with one by-product being that India will move up in the ranking in the Transparency International table as well as giving the population renewed confidence in the administration.

10

Ordinary Brazilians doing Extraordinary things

by Luis Puig

A former trade unionist in Guatemala, Luis Puig represented his country at the ILO in Geneva. He met Frank Buchman in 1952, and has worked full time for Initiatives of Change since 1956. He was with Varig Airlines for 22 years. Married to Evelyn, from Austria, they have two grown-up sons.

'Frank Buchman said to us that Brazil is not only meant to export the best coffee to the world but also the best idea!'

THE familiarity with which tough, poor, hard-working port workers from Rio de Janeiro, Santos and Recife referred to Dr Buchman sounded pretentious when I first heard it. But as I got to know them and their friends, I realised that Buchman's ideas had become part of their lives. Some of them had met and talked to him at international MRA conferences in Mackinac or Caux.

Carlos Anselmo, leader of the coffee packers of the busy port of Santos near São Paulo, astounded his socialist comrades when he admitted having used union funds for himself. He apologised and submitted his resignation.

He said: 'As a socialist I want to help build a new society but I cannot do it if I am dishonest.' At first there were angry cries demanding punishment and expulsion, but the mood calmed when a fiery older communist fighter intervened. 'Be quiet! Who among you would have the courage to do what comrade Anselmo just did?' The resignation was accepted nevertheless. After that some wanted to know what had brought about the change in Carlos, and a new spirit began to develop in the port. Carlos and his wife were later invited to different parts of the world to talk about their new-found ideas. A São Paulo woman, wife of a top industrialist, travelled with them at her own expense to serve as translator.

Reign of terror

Rio port workers were tough. When a group of Buchman's colleagues arrived in the city, the headline in the papers was 'Reign of terror in the port'. Shortly afterwards, a group of thirty workers was invited for an evening in a flat which had been rented for the work of Moral Re-Armament. Among the group were members of rival factions at war with each other.

In the course of the evening a young man from Europe asked, 'God created the world, isn't that true?' The men nodded. 'If so, he must have a plan for the world.' They nodded again. 'How do you find it, then?' 'We don't know,' they said. 'Well,' he continued, 'we've discovered that if we take time in quiet, God very often puts a thought in our heart.' Then it was suggested the men be quiet. After a while Damasio, the toughest of the trouble-makers, said, 'God told me, 'Damasio, sell your two revolvers; one knife is enough."' Others in the room felt that was a strange thought to come from God. Nevertheless, next day Damasio sold them and 18 months later most of the guns had disappeared from the port. That night there had probably been more revolvers in the room than men!

Together with people from other walks of life, the Santos port workers invited a group of their colleagues from Rio to come and hear about what they had found. The Rio men were divided and would not at first sit or talk together, one lot representing the official legitimate union, the other representing an unofficial breakaway union. The latter included extreme radicals and trouble-makers. Yet later, the two groups returned home united, having ironed out their differences. Months later the two unions merged. The largest paper in Rio carried the headline: 'For the first time ever, democratic elections in the port of Rio.'

'Frank' instead of the more formal 'Dr Buchman' was the name used in other sectors of society, for instance by Luiz Dumont Villares and his wife Leonor Diederichsen Villares. Luiz was president of Aços Villares, then the biggest private steel mill in Latin America. The couple financed a planeload of port workers, trade unionists and industrialists to fly to a world assembly for Moral Re-Armament. Buchman helped them to become a purposeful fellowship of friends. 'Brazil is not only meant to export the best coffee to the world but also the best idea,' he said.

Senora Villares later donated a beautiful house that for many years served as a centre for MRA in São Paulo, Brazil's largest city.

'Men of Brazil'

Honesty with their wives, with their bosses and with each other, together with vision for their country, were the experiences brought together in what became the film

Men of Brazil. In it, each man acted his own part in the true story. Highly motivated, these men and their wives, some illiterate, did something that surprised and interested other sectors of society. The film was made possible by the voluntary work of professionals and generous contributions from different parts of the world. Dubbed into 23 languages it has been shown on nearly every continent, especially in the ports. At present the Hindi version is part of a regular programme of industrial seminars for workers and personnel managers taking place in Panchgani in the west of India, at the centre for Initiatives of Change in that vast, populous country.

The legacy of Frank Buchman in Latin America crops up in unexpected places. His visits to Mexico, Chile and Peru, decades before, had given him a taste of life in the continent. I was in Mexico City some years ago. One afternoon we were visited by a taxi driver who had heard we were there. He had driven Dr Buchman around years before. He was an old, quiet man. He said, 'My life has never been the same since I met him.'

Buchman's influence passed through the port workers to leaders of the favelas, the shanty-towns which have proliferated (over 600) in the city of Rio de Janeiro. Brigadier Antonio Muniz and his wife, recently returned from an MRA conference where they re-found their Catholic faith, invited some of the port workers of Rio to their home to meet with favela leaders he knew. The port workers talked about what changes in their lives meant for them and for conditions in the port. They were quiet together and one favelado leader said, 'We must tell the State Governor that the favelados are not one million problems but two million hands which can be put to work.' With this conviction, and with stories to tell, they arranged to meet the State Governor. After listening to them, he said, 'For the first time I'm confronted by a group of men who are united with a clear purpose. We can work together.' The State provided money and tools, and the favelados the hard work. The favelados also asked to be in charge of the work, which was accepted. Two and a half years later nearly half a million people from the slums had been re-housed in decent homes.

At the same time an industrialist and a port worker decided to go together from one favela to another, most of them spread through the hills or *morros* of the city, to project the film *Men of Brazil*.

A bright outcome if...

When Peter Howard, the British sportsman and journalist who had taken over the leadership of MRA after Frank Buchman died, visited Brazil in 1965, he brought the challenge of Buchman to a new level. He spelled out clearly what a dark future was reserved for the country if moral standards were not lived out by the men in power. But he also outlined the bright outcome for Brazil, in terms of social equality and improvement, if men and women put their lives under God's authority. Using experiences from his own life he talked directly to those who were most feared at the time, the military and other supporters of the dictatorship that ruled the country. He was listened to and utterly respected in all circles.

Howard took seriously Luiz Pereira, a very simple man, leader of Morro São João favela. Pereira took seriously what he learned about Frank Buchman. Pereira grasped that anyone anywhere can listen to the inner voice, change, and then help others to change and work together to transform social conditions.

One day while at work, Luiz had the thought that the Minister of State in charge of social conditions should hear about his project for re-housing the people of his own favela. Pereira picked up the phone and was put straight through to the minister, an army general (the military were in power at the time). He listened to what Pereira had to say. The general mobilised materials and a work force. The result can be seen today, thirty years later, in a group of modest apartment buildings owned and managed by the former favela people.

Over the years Pereira has passed on what he learned with conviction and passion to other leaders and inhabitants of the favela communities of the city. Every month or so, he takes groups to the 'Sitio São Luiz', 50 miles north of Rio, a place considered by many to be the centre for Initiatives of Change in Latin America. Taxi drivers have often joined them, as well as industrialists, trade unionists, military figures and all kinds of people who had captured Buchman's spirit.

Rio taxi drivers were notorious for taking tourists 'for a ride', as well as overcharging the locals. Their vehicles were often dirty and badly kept. They frequently quarrelled over the best parking spots to attract passengers. Some were exploited by greedy proprietors.

One man, Americo Martorelli took Buchman's ideas seriously. He quit drinking, and he and his wife had a frank, honest conversation. He said, 'I don't want just to be a better man, I want to take these ideas to my colleagues.' He and others had earlier tried to organise a taxi drivers' co-operative, but without success. They had wanted to do away with the unfair sums charged by the taxi owners and, eventually, to own their own cars. Now they were able to work things out.

Two taxi co-operatives were established when other drivers caught the same spirit and attitude that Martorelli had found. One of them even included the absolute moral standards of MRA in its bylaws. Each co-operative could have a maximum of 250 people, according to regulations. The news of success spread. Today there are countless taxi co-operatives with different groups copying each other, all based on the same principles as the first two, even if they never heard of Buchman or MRA. Each co-operative has an ethics committee that judges any misconduct by a member. In a city of eight million people, something definitely changed for the better.

The second generation of port workers now play their part. One of those who was in his teens when *Men of Brazil* had been filmed is now vice-president of the Board of Initiatives of Change in Brazil. Another, the son of the first elected president of the United Port Workers' Union, is now the only black instructor at the top military officers' training establishment of the country, the Escolar Superior de Guerra. He lives by the principles he learned from his father. Another who grew up in the port says, 'If it wasn't for the ideas (of Buchman) passed on to me by friends in IofC, I should be a man without a future and without principles.' He has become a prosperous lawyer. He says, 'People often expect me to handle their affairs in a devious way. I tell them about the right way, which I learned in MRA. They leave my office happier and I am able to take honest money and a free conscience back home.'

The port workers took their experience to Argentina, invited by the Minister of Labour; to Italy, invited by the Bishop of Bari; and to India, Canada, the USA and other parts of the world. The legacy of that extraordinary man Frank Buchman lives on!

11

Buchman's Inspired Ideology for America

by Jarvis Harriman, Bob Webb & Dick Ruffin

Jarvis Harriman heard about Moral Re-Armament from his father, whose faith as a clergyman was renewed after meeting Frank Buchman. After serving overseas in World War 2 Jarvis worked with MRA in the US and Canada, Switzerland and across Europe and the Asian continent. He and his wife now live in Tucson, Arizona.

MY FATHER was an Episcopal clergyman; he was appointed to a key parish in the heart of Philadelphia, where the wealthy used the church for weddings and funerals, and supported it financially, and the white- and blue-collar working people in that neighbourhood came to worship. Dad was deeply discouraged, professionally and spiritually, with the state of 'organised religion'. He felt it was running on empty.

Then one day he met Dr Frank N D. Buchman and his 'Oxford Group'. They challenged him to begin a revolution himself. He quit chain-smoking, cold turkey. He began to be real with his wife and his kids. He became a dynamic Christian. This interested me, at age 10, enough to join him some mornings in his study to 'listen to God'. I wrote down a few thoughts – starting with confessing to the neighbourhood drugstore owner and his wife that I had stolen bits of candy from them, and paying them what I thought I owed. There were other similar things – I was in fact a thief, from my neighbours, from my school friends. I apologised and made what restitution I could.

Time went on. I tried living this quality of life in college; when war came, and a college-deferring program, I enlisted. Two weeks after graduating I was in uniform. Officer training was offered; I 'listened' to my inner voice, and decided to let the army do what it wanted with me. A commission, with the war obviously coming to a climax, seemed to me more of an ego-trip than a help to the army. I was sent to be trained as a medical laboratory technician and assigned to a pioneering unit in the treatment of battle fatigue cases, and spent a year on Saipan in the Western Pacific, until the war was over.

On Saipan three things struck me: 1) air-raids of a thousand planes at a time were coordinated on our island, a tremendous effort of industrial production and military precision; 2) there were 500 ships in our harbour in preparation for the anticipated invasion of the Japanese homeland; and 3) we were building on neighbouring Tinian Island a 10,000-bed hospital in anticipation of the casualties we would suffer in that invasion. My conclusion was: I want to spend the next years of my life working to see that this terrific capacity to produce, to coordinate, to go all-out to achieve a major objective – be used to build a better world. I decided to spend my time with Moral Re-Armament, which had become the programme of the Oxford Group.

This was an intellectual decision, although rooted in

my inner being. I went to work with MRA out of a great mix of genuine convictions, for which I certainly thank God. I cannot however say that it represented a spiritual awakening, a road-to-Damascus revelation. It was a natural consequence of all that had gone before. In subsequent years, to see people like Irène and Victor Laure at work, to get to know individuals like Max Lassman (the French Jewish member of our Caux stage crew), and people like John Riffe and his family move forward in their new life – these things moved me to keep doing what we were doing to put this message before people where they could see and feel it. Events like working in Washington with the musical *The Good Road* to support the passage of the Marshall Plan through the US Congress; like staging it in bombed-out cities of West Germany and then in London; like taking *Jotham Valley* through America and then Ceylon, India and Pakistan; and working hand-in-hand with an amazing group of men and women from all over Africa to put their play *Freedom* on the stage; and then *The Crowning Experience* with that unique personality Muriel Smith and her white team-mate Anne Buckles, first on stage and then into a film – these have been worth anything I could do with my life, and without earning a penny out of it!

And now, we are in a different era. I'm 84 years old; life has moved on. The world is very different. What is the legacy of Frank Buchman in his own country, America?

Alcoholics Anonymous

AA stands as a pioneer effort at self-help, on how to tackle one's addiction to alcohol, and by inference, other addictions. It got its start from the work the Revd Samuel

Shoemaker did with alcoholics as an outreach of his training with Frank Buchman. Their efforts are acknowledged especially by Dick Burns, a lawyer living in Honolulu, who has written extensively on the subject as 'Dick B'.

It is to be hoped that this practical way to break the hold of alcoholic addiction will continue, as it has for some seventy years, to be a tremendous blessing to thousands of men and women across the world as well as in the United States.

From isolation to a world view

Buchman's work in America in the 1930s was enriched by the presence of dozens of men and women from across the globe. They tackled America's problems of labour and management disputes that threw roadblocks in the way of production of materials vital to the war efforts growing in Europe, so that ships, tanks, planes and guns could flow to Europe which badly needed them to fight the Nazi war machine. They helped to develop instruments to inspire the country to live in a threatening wartime situation – the musical review *You Can Defend America*, with its handbook of the same name, and the industrial drama *The Forgotten Factor*. These theatrical productions and the printed materials with them were used enthusiastically by the growing movement called Civil Defence Councils, which the federal government called into being in almost every community across the country. The presence of these overseas workers and the efforts that they put forth were a living bridge that helped America move from isolation to full involvement in the war.

Not to be forgotten in this legacy is the wartime book by Daphne du Maurier, *Come Wind, Come Weather*, in which she gives stories of similar effects of related shows and handbooks, *You Can Fight for Canada, Battle Together for Britain*, and *You Can Fight For Australia*.

I've really raised two points here: 1) the presence of Buchman's international workers during World War 2 in the United States helped to move the US out of its isolationist mood and toward its present stance as a global power involved in global issues. And 2) Buchman's work used musical revues and drama – the theatre – to give a message that was enthusiastically accepted by cities and towns that needed a programme for strengthening a war effort and building teamwork in industry to make that effort effective.

The Evangelicals

Buchman's own personal message was deeply Christian – the experience he had in Keswick, in England's Lake District in 1908, was a powerful personal experience of the cross of Christ.

But his message, as Moral Re-Armament developed over the years, was much simpler and proved to have universal appeal. In the 1950s his appeal to Christians, Muslims, Buddhists, Hindus, Jews, atheists, Marxist-Communists was universal. The elements he stressed were:

1) If you want to see the world different, the place to start is with yourself. Look at your life honestly in the light of absolute moral standards of honesty, purity, unselfishness and love; take time to see where you have fallen short of these standards, specifically; apologise for and if possible make restitution for the things you have done that have hurt other people.

2) Buchman felt, along with many men of faith in world history, that, as Abraham Lincoln once said, when

the Almighty wants to let him know something, He finds a way to do it. To listen to the divine spirit can become as normal as breathing.

There is in human experience a conscience, an inner voice, a divine leading – it goes by many names – but when a person takes time to listen in an attitude of openness, willingness, or prayer if that is your 'thing', then thoughts come, whether dramatically or simply, which we can recognise as not of oneself. To share these thoughts with trusted friends, to check them against those absolute standards, can lead to new and fresh things happening. Some will call this divine guidance, some our conscience, but it can lead to remarkable results. It can also lead to disaster, as we see with pathologically delusional people, so it is a phenomenon that needs careful and honest handling!

Throughout his life, and in the world conferences in Caux in Switzerland and in other settings, Buchman found that his simple message of the four standards, honest apology, restitution, the inner voice in peoples' hearts – and projecting this quality of living on a world stage – 'As I am, so is my nation' – appealed to people of all faiths and none. They felt a common bond of humanity and purpose with him; they could stand with him, and work with him. He would be of great help to the evangelical Christians who alienate so many in a modern secular world and our internationally-derived nation. This could be the most significant aspect of Buchman's legacy in America today.

Labour and Industry

This is hard to deal with, although John Riffe, who was to become the executive Vice-President of the AFL/CIO, in one sense was the best example of a man going through a drastic change in his life, and of applying that to major problem areas involving labour and industry. MRA unintentionally worked against Riffe by trumpeting his work as the work of MRA. This alienated much of the labour movement.

But the fact remains: for many involved in industry, the simple concept of 'Not who is right but what is right' became a fresh entry into industrial disputes, and, coupled with the idea of the four standards and listening for the inner voice, became a fresh way of solving seemingly irreconcilable situations.

This is a key part of Dr Buchman's legacy in America. It can come into play again and again as time goes by, and needs to be cherished and nourished.

An economics of the spirit

One of the crying needs in the world today is for a fresh expression of one of Buchman's key thoughts: There is enough in the world for everyone's need, but not for everyone's greed; if everybody cared enough, and shared enough, wouldn't everybody have enough?

This line of thinking could be America's great gift to the world. (It may fall to India, whose thinking people may well move out ahead of us in pioneering revolutionary economics like this.)

George W Bush enunciated a policy of 'compassionate conservatism' in his run for the presidency in 2000. What a shame that he did not have the fortitude or imagination to flesh that thought out, as Buchman tried to do!

But it remains for some nation or people to do so. Think of what a concrete demonstration of compassionate conservatism could mean to the Chinese, who are caught between a concept of a planned society and the freedom of a market economy. What if they could see that a free market economy did not mean unbridled greed, and could mean instead a concern that every hand had meaningful work to do, every stomach had food enough, and every heart had an idea that really satisfied!

Reconciliation

Buchman and his teams worked to heal the wounds of World War 2 in Europe, in offering a hand to bring Germany back into the family of nations, and by lifting labour-management relations to a new level in Europe and in the US. And despite the deliberately- stated intention of the Communist International to take over the means of production in Britain, France, Germany and Italy, they found MRA's creative ideas trumping them in cities and factories and labour halls all over Europe. These things today go by the widely recognised phrase 'conflict resolution', and institutions of higher education are offering degree courses in it across the world. Buchman spotlighted the price of such reconciliation, that someone had to start by accepting what it meant in his/her own life. It was not free; it had a real cost for the one willing to begin.

Irène and Victor Laure were a prime case study in this. They were lifelong socialists, and labour leaders, and fighters in the French Resistance against the Nazis. What it cost Irène, in particular, to stand in front of groups of labour people, management, politicians, and just plain individuals, to admit to the hatred of the German people that had consumed her, and of the managing class – and what it meant to ask forgiveness for those tremendous feelings as her part in building a new tomorrow – no one will ever know. Those who lived alongside her could see it, though. It was real, it was tangible. It was not done on the cheap.

And so it will always be, if it is to be genuine. It requires a surrender of self, of pride, of my own will, of all temptation to blame, and a total willingness to take responsibility for my own part in divisions. It cannot be faked.

We must see that the world does not go blithely along with 'reconciliation' on the cheap. It is our legacy to pay this price ourselves, and to hold others to it who would go this way.

* * * * *

Robert Webb, born and reared in Mississippi, is a former Washington Bureau chief, news editor, senior editorial writer and columnist for the *Cincinnati Enquirer*. Earlier, he was associate editor of the *State Times* in Jackson, Miss. and on other newspapers in the South.

FOR years I ignored the brute evil of the ruggedly segregated society around me. As a child of the Deep South, born and reared in Mississippi, it hadn't bothered me that schools, rest rooms, water fountains and neighbourhoods were segregated, that blacks were supposed to 'know their place' and stay in it. It hadn't bothered me that most jobs of consequence were denied them. The 'Southern way of life' was my lifeblood, but I sorely needed a transfusion.

Small wonder that as a journalist there in the mid-1950s I succumbed to the siren voice of those militantly opposed to the US Supreme Court's May 17, 1954 decision outlawing segregated schools. As associate editor of the State Times in Jackson, Miss., writing editorials and columns, I was the eager conduit of the region's traditional views on race.

All the while I considered myself Christian. But the transformation I so badly needed came after I accepted an invitation to attend a Moral Re-Armament conference in 1957 at Mackinac Island, Michigan. There I heard stories of lives revolutionised when men and women listened to their inner voice and measured their past and present by the absolute moral standards of honesty, purity, unselfishness and love. I was deeply moved. These people had something I wanted.

One afternoon I saw the film *Freedom* – written by Africans – that was to drive a stake into my racist heart. As the film ended, I knew I had to apologise to the first black man I saw for the way we in the South had treated his race. As it happened, the first such man was an African of middle age. He had a face that spoke great wisdom. I apologised and will never forget his response: 'After the apology, what?' I have been trying to answer that question ever since.

Before leaving Mackinac Island, I sat down with those four moral standards. A host of wrongs I'd committed sprang to mind. Among them: cheating in high school, cheating on my expense account as a reporter for a New Orleans newspaper, and misuse of the darkroom of my hometown weekly where I'd worked one summer. Moreover, I'd maliciously attacked in print the aged editor of the competing afternoon newspaper in Jackson. I'd even committed offences I thought violated federal law. I made restitution as best I could.

When I confessed my cheating to my high school principal, she invited me to speak to a student assembly. After a glowing introduction by the school superintendent I stood up and said, 'I'm here because I cheated in high school,' then discussed the answer I'd found. I reimbursed the New Orleans newspaper which, in turn, donated the funds to MRA.

One of my toughest chores was the confession I had to make to the US Attorney in Jackson. Thankfully, he didn't prosecute. And wonderfully, each act of restitution brought an inner liberation of indescribable joy. With this experience, I knew God would always guide me if I listened and obeyed. One of the first thoughts I had after leaving Mackinac Island was to write a fellow Southerner – Dr Martin Luther King, Jr. He replied quickly with a beautiful note.

Clearly my life changed radically. I tried to give readers the vision of an America forging a model for all the world of how people of every race and background could work together. I spoke and wrote to heal rather than hurt, to unite rather than divide. I reached out to African-Americans as never before. The unexpected closure in 1962 of the State Times led me in 1963 to Cincinnati and a crucial new front in the battle for a new world.

Answering deep despair

My vision broadened quickly with that personal transformation. At Mackinac Island I'd glimpsed a new world extending far beyond the South with all its turmoil. But that wider vision also made clearer my vision for the South. With Mississippi friends similarly committed, we began to seek that inner wisdom for what to do. How could we make a difference? For one thing, we brought to Jackson the film – *Freedom* – which had so transformed my heart and mind. As well, we enlisted the help of others, including Bremer Hofmeyr, a former Rhodes Scholar, and his wife, Agnes, from South Africa, long a part of Buchman's work. We arranged a private showing of *Freedom* for the then governor, James P Coleman. Bremer introduced the film with the compelling story of how Agnes' father, a farmer in Kenya, had been buried alive by the Mau Mau then rebelling against the colonial government and how she had overcome her deep despair, vowing to work all the harder to answer bitterness and hatred wherever it exists.

Coleman was impressed by Hofmeyr as having had 'something to say' the moment he opened his mouth. He joined Bremer, Agnes and their friends for lunch after the film and asked that it be shown to members of the state legislature. So it was.

But strong winds of resistance to the 1954 high court edict were blowing in 1957. Little Rock, the Arkansas state capital, became the storm centre when on September 25 President Dwight Eisenhower ordered the Army to escort nine black students through an angry crowd into Central High School. Earlier, a federal judge had ordered their admission but on September 20 Governor Orval Faubus used National Guard troops not to ensure their entry but to keep them out. Little Rock Mayor Woodrow Mann sent a telegram to President Eisenhower four days later asking for federal troops to maintain order.

Compared to some parts of the South, Arkansas had been a relative oasis on race. As early as September 1949, for example, the University of Arkansas School of Law was racially integrated. In January 1951, the Little Rock Library board opened its doors to blacks. So it was not too surprising that the Little Rock School Board said, five days after the Supreme Court's de-segregation decision, that it would comply.

But Faubus placed himself squarely against the National Association for the Advancement of Coloured People (NAACP) and its Arkansas division president, Mrs L C (Daisy) Bates, to join those strongly opposed to integration. He called a special session of the legislature in August 1958 to pass a law enabling him to lease public schools to private corporations to escape the federal mandate. The next month, Arkansas citizens voted 7,561 for and 129,470 against de-segregation. Public high schools in Little Rock were shut down, leaving 3,698 students to fend for themselves.

Little Rock quickly gained global attention as a bastion of defiance. But some few from the city found their way to the MRA centre on Mackinac Island. They returned determined to bring a fresh spirit to the city and state. But if Little Rock became a symbol of defiance it was also the spark for a rising tide of hope in America, as catalyst for a play The Crowning Experience, and subsequent film with the same title.

'The crowning experience of my life'

British author Michael Henderson sets the stage in his 1996 book, *The Forgiveness Factor*. He recalls black leaders beginning to attend the Mackinac conferences in the 1950s:

'Then in 1955 an international conference was held in Washington, DC,' he writes, 'more than a thousand people from 41 countries attended. A new dimension of racial unity was one of the themes. Among the blacks present from the United States was Mary McLeod Bethune, the 17th child of a family of former slaves, founder of Bethune Cookman College and a former advisor on minority affairs to President Franklin Roosevelt.

'She said on that occasion: "There are 16 million people like me in America who have been dreaming, praying, working, toiling, sacrificing, forgiving for an hour like this. Only a basic change of heart in men and women of all races can handle the present integration program in the US. Law and law enforcement alone can never do it. The task of morally rearming the nation is the greatest job to which any of us can apply our energies and talents. To be part of this great uniting force of our age is the crowning experience of my life."'

Out front in a wheelchair sat Mrs William P Wood of Richmond, Virginia. Her parents had been slave owners. 'She asked if she might speak,' Henderson writes. 'Rising from her chair, Mrs Wood apologised for the racial prejudice she had felt. "I am glad to take this opportunity to shake hands publicly with someone of your race, because I helped to build racial bitterness. I have decided to commit the rest of my life to building bridges between the two races."' That historic encounter was captured in *The Crowning Experience*, based on the life of Mrs Bethune, which then led to the film being shown in theatres in America and elsewhere.

'The impetus for the creation of the musical was an explosion of violence in Little Rock . . . in the autumn of 1957 over the integration of black and white schoolchildren,' Henderson recalls. Thus ironically, what happened in Little Rock led to a historic breakthrough in Atlanta when *The Crowning Experience* opened with two performances there in June 1958 in a civic auditorium with de-segregated seating for the first time.

One who attended was the Jewish owner of the Tower Theatre, in Atlanta, who was so moved he invited MRA to bring the play to his theatre for performances with no colour bar. The play, starring Muriel Smith, the American mezzo soprano, as Mrs Bethune and British actress Phyllis Konstam as Mrs Wood, ran five months. Ralph McGill, then editor and publisher of *The Atlanta Constitution*, was reported to have said that to assess fully all it meant to the city would have required several pages in his newspaper.

Clearly Atlanta was on a new road. 'Atlanta will never be the same again,' said Colonel A T Walden, a pioneer black lawyer quoted by the *Atlanta Daily World*. 'The atmosphere throughout the city, the shops and buses changed and was the talk of the town.' Atlanta, setting for the Civil War movie classic, Gone with the Wind, escaped the violence that devastated other cities in the civil rights era.

Muriel Smith's personal story and how she came to play Mrs Bethune was extraordinary in itself. An African-American from Harlem, she was a stellar performer at or near the peak of her career when she attended in 1957 her first MRA conference on Mackinac Island, the one where her life was to take a new direction. She'd created the role of Carmen Jones on Broadway in the 1940s, starred in *South Pacific* and *The King and I* and rejected Sam Goldwyn's repeated efforts to land her for *Porgy and Bess*, feeling it demeaned her race.

But for all her mounting fame and overtures from Hollywood and London, Muriel abandoned her career to help bring a new spirit to the world through the plays and films of MRA. So as her voice rose in song and conviction in *The Crowning Experience*, she brought that new spirit to the country: 'The world walked into my heart today, black man, white man, red and yellow, the statesman yes and the ordinary fellow, they all walked into my heart...' With its marvellously upbeat rhythm, 'The World Walked Into My Heart,' especially as sung by Muriel, doubtless opened many hearts.

'The end of a hundred years' civil war'

Meanwhile, the film *Freedom* made its way to Little Rock with a group from various African countries. One who saw it was Mrs Bates, the NAACP president and nemesis of Governor Faubus. Afterward, she and a group of Arkansans from both races went to MRA's Mackinac centre. It was there she decided to visit Faubus. In his book, Henderson says, 'Unknown to her, he had also seen *Freedom*.' Their meeting resulted in a handshake between them that Henderson said moved a CBS radio commentator, reviewing 1959, to label it 'possibly the most significant news event of the year, which marks the end of a hundred years' civil war in the United States of America.' While racial tensions remained and violence had not ended, there were glimmers of a new dawn.

With Dr King's non-violent Gandhian crusade for racial equality well underway, a new young president, John F Kennedy, took office in 1961 with an inaugural address in which he said, 'Ask not what your country can do for you but what you can do for your country.' King got to know him and with others of like mind impressed on him the urgency for new civil rights law. They convinced Kennedy, but an assassin's bullets in 1963 took him away before he could get Congress to act – a challenge left to his successor, Lyndon B Johnson.

Clearly the face of America has changed since the 1954 school decision, with African-Americans not only voting but also helping run their cities, states and the nation as officeholders. They occupy key positions in business and industry, education, mass media and other sectors of life. As well, they mix and mingle with people of all colours and from many backgrounds as America becomes increasingly diverse racially, ethnically and religiously. But divisions remain.

As the African-American historian, John Hope Franklin, 91, told a crowd at the 2006 National Book Festival in Washington, DC, 'We are trying to become a nation of equals but we haven't got there.' If often subtly expressed, racial discrimination remains. Many, if not most, African-Americans experience it to some degree. So do Americans of other colours and creeds.

That's why the American civil rights era, in reality, is not over. And that's why another Buchman legacy – Richmond, Virginia-based 'Hope in the Cities' (HIC) – was launched in 1990 by the city's political, business and community leaders. Its mission was to bring racial healing to the city that was capital of the Confederacy during the Civil War. But it became a national network in 1993 when those leaders organized the *Healing the Heart of America* conference, chaired by Richmond mayor Walter T. Kenney, which drew a thousand participants from fifty US urban centres and twenty foreign countries. Racial issues at the centre of many of the toughest urban problems – in housing, education, policing, community relations and public policy bearing on families – were examined. The Richmond Times-Dispatch gave the event heavy, prominent coverage.

Integration was for many largely a myth

The genesis of Hope in the Cities was the conviction of Rob and Susan Corcoran, long a part of the work Buchman initiated, to move their family from Britain to Richmond 26 years ago. They chose a home in a largely African-American neighbourhood where they soon made warm friends who joined them in their mission. Among them were Collie and Audrey Burton, community activists who became an integral part of HIC. So was Mayor Kenney. The Corcorans and their friends recognised the racial divisions remaining in their city long after the Supreme Court's landmark school de-segregation decision and passage of two major federal civil rights laws.

They were divisions typical of most cities in the North as well as South. The most obvious indications of those divisions were the suburban rings, fed by white and some middle-class black flight, around core urban centres. Integration was for many poor black families largely a myth. While de-segregation was the law, de-facto segregation, largely from racially segregated housing, remained. This flight of more affluent families to the suburbs left many core city governments and school systems perennially short of funds. Richmond was not exempt from these demographic forces.

But with the arrival of Hope in the Cities, Richmond began to feel more hopeful! HIC leaders soon saw the needs there were not confined to the city proper but extended into three suburban counties. White flight had taken much of the city's taxable wealth to the suburbs. Where needs were greatest – in the inner city with its concentration of poverty and crime – resources were far from adequate, as failing schools and ailing social services attested. So with HIC taking the initiative, an annual Metropolitan Richmond Day was established to bring city and suburb together to explore the area's needs in hopes of forging solutions on an area-wide basis. The event brought 500 participants from the city and its three-county suburban area together on 12 November 2004 in the fiftieth anniversary year of Brown vs. Board of Education regarding integration in schools.

In an article in the *Richmond Times-Dispatch* at that time, Don Cowles, then HIC co-chair, wrote, 'Thousands of citizens have mobilized through hundreds of initiatives and have invested tens of millions of dollars each year to mitigate the damage caused by our segregated society. These heroic measures are making a difference, but they are inadequate. A new way is required.' He said the current system creates loser and winner schools at a time when 'we must find a way to make all of our children winners.' Cowles was with Alcoa/Reynolds Metals Co. as chief legal officer, chief human resources officer and president of one of its business units in 2002 when he took early retirement and began his involvement with IofC.

Corcoran, as national director, and Cowles as executive director, became in 2006 co-leaders of Initiatives of Change, HIC's parent. 'In asking us to lead the organisation, Initiatives of Change has affirmed its mission to work for hope, healing and transformation in America's increasingly diverse national community,' Corcoran says. 'We are developing a focused and cohesive strategy which makes better use of our human and financial resources...Building trust and new vision across the divides of race, religion and class is a vital part of our work. We will continue to promote dialogues and collaborative citizen action. Offering leadership formation and skills building to individuals and groups who are attempting to address key issues in their community is a priority.'

If indeed the Supreme Court's 1954 school decision inaugurated the modern civil rights era in America, that era, as historian John Hope Franklin makes clear, is by no means over. Buchman's work clearly played and will continue to play a key role in the extent to which that era leads finally to genuine equality for all Americans.

* * * * *

Dick Ruffin is a graduate of Yale and Oxford Universities, and a former Rhodes Scholar from Virginia. At Oxford, he encountered the ideas of MRA and applied them in his work on the staff of the US Secretary of Defence. He later served as executive director of Initiatives of Change in the United States for 23 years and is now executive vice president of IofC International.

I grew up in Norfolk, Virginia, part of a large extended family steeped in southern lore. My father, a lawyer, was particularly proud of his great-grandfather, Edmund Ruffin, a noted agriculturalist whose ideas helped restore lands exhausted by the over-cultivation of cotton. He had five plantations around Richmond, Virginia, and campaigned ardently for the preservation of the institution of slavery on which the plantation economy depended. His fame led the Governor of South Carolina, the first state to secede from the Union, to invite him to fire the first shot of the Civil War at the federal fort in Charleston Harbour.

Unconsciously, I absorbed much of that pride, and also some of the prejudice that accompanied it. However, being at the same time embarrassed by the lionising of my slave-holding forebear and the constant idealisation of the ante-bellum south, I convinced myself that I was somehow above the raw prejudice that I saw around me. I became blind to my own deep-seated prejudices. This blindness was unexpectedly reinforced by the extraordinary decision of the State of Virginia to adopt a policy of 'massive resistance' to the US Supreme Court's order to integrate its public schools. This defiance led to the temporary closure of Norfolk's public schools, and provided my mother the opportunity she wanted to enrol me in a northern school. So I took my last two years of high school at Choate, a distinguished northern prep school in Connecticut. It was but a small step from there to Yale University, breaking the long family tradition of going to the University of Virginia.

My time at Yale was during the Kennedy years of the early 1960s. It was easy then to suppress or ignore unacknowledged attitudes of superiority and to adopt the liberal ideals popular on campus. These influences, plus guilt about my southern heritage, led me to become active in the civil rights struggle. It was not long before I had the privilege of spending an evening with Martin Luther King, Jr. I also took up other liberal causes at Yale, consciously turning away from my southern heritage. What I didn't realise at the time was that while my politics had changed, deep-seated prejudices remained.

These only began to come to light during my postgraduate years at Oxford University in England, where I went on a much-coveted Rhodes scholarship. An encounter there with another American Rhodes Scholar led me to question my motives and attitudes more deeply. 'How can you make a better world,' my friend asked, 'if you insist on remaining the same yourself?' At the time I was deeply involved in public challenges to the Vietnam policies of President Johnson. Our complaint was about

Johnson's so-called 'credibility gap'. My friend, one of several new friends influenced by the ideas of Frank Buchman, calmly asked whether there were such credibility gaps in my own life.

With a little reflection, the gaps gradually came to mind. I held high principles, but lived quite differently. I campaigned against the exploitation of blacks, but was quite prepared to exploit women for my pleasure. I thought of myself as an honest guy, but withheld many truths about myself from my parents and from many of my friends. I said one thing to one group of friends, but something quite different to others. Slowly, I began to understand why one college roommate had called me 'bluffing Ruffin'. So I began to face these gaps and to do what I could to close them. In the process, I saw that my liberalism masked hidden prejudices and was unconsciously a defence against facing uncomfortable truths about myself. The process was like peeling the layers of an onion. The more I was honest with myself, the more I saw of the hypocrisy and deception in my life. And the more I faced these truths, the freer I became to be true to myself.

Why so patronising?

A few years later, after completing my military service, I joined forces with a multi-racial team led by Richard Brown, a black American professor who had also been deeply influenced by Buchman's ideas. We were visiting nine prominent individuals who were making significant contributions to ending racial discrimination across America. Brown's aim was to support their efforts and to inspire them with our own stories of change. In our group was a South African black, the son of a courageous organiser of African miners and currently a post-grad student at Columbia University. One day when we were preparing for a visit, Peter turned to me and asked, 'Dick, why are you so patronising?' I was dumfounded and angry at what seemed to me a wholly unjustified accusation. But I had learned to reflect on such personal challenges rather than to hit back. A simple thought came into my mind. 'You treat black people as if they are less knowledgeable and less responsible for this country and the world than you feel yourself.' I shared this insight with the others and another layer of the onion was peeled.

Later still, I began to see yet deeper levels of prejudice. The context was a major conference in Richmond, Virginia, led by Richmond's mayor Walter T. Kenney, an African-American. The conference, organised by Initiatives of Change, called the nation to honest conversations on matters of race, reconciliation and responsibility. Its aim was to start a process that could heal the deep wounds caused by three and a half centuries of racial discrimination. This caused me to reflect more deeply on my own heritage and on the unconscious attitudes that had come to me as part of the legacy of Edmund Ruffin.

I recognised, for example, that in thinking about the Civil War – what was called the 'War between the States' in my family – I was far more conscious of the humiliation suffered by white Southerners at the hands of the North than of the far deeper pain and loss suffered by the enslaved Americans. They simply did not figure in the narrative. Their reality was ignored, their true feelings denied. Preoccupation with the perceived arrogance of the North had blinded me, and millions like me throughout the South, to the emotional toll of slavery and of the long history of continued discrimination in its aftermath.

At a deeper level, I also recognised that a more persistent legacy from Edmund Ruffin was a minimalist concept of the potential of African-Americans. I had little vision for what black Americans would contribute to American life and culture and political life. While undeniable black accomplishments had forced some revision in my thinking, I saw that I, and many others like me, needed nothing less than a revolution in our expectations for what African-Americans could give to our common country.

It has taken me many years to peel the layers of unseen prejudice, and the journey continues. In the same way, it may take years of painful, honest conversations between black and white Americans to identify and remove the barriers that even now prevent African-Americans from making their maximum contributions to American society. There is no more important task before the American people, for our capacity to help heal a broken world depends finally on our ability to heal the deep wounds embedded in our own nation's history. As we make real progress in this task, I believe that we will unleash powerful forces for reconciliation that will have impacts far beyond America.

12

Clean Elections – Target for Taiwan

by Ren-Jou Liu and Brian Lightowler

Ren-Jou Liu was born in Taiwan, and has worked with Initiatives of Change since 1984. He has been running self development programmes for more than a decade, with the aim of inspiring and enabling individuals to overcome personal challenges in life. He has witnessed encouraging transformation and healing in many lives over the years.

Brian Lightowler was born in UK, a Cambridge University graduate, mountaineer, journalist and Initiatives of Change full-time worker for 54 years in Europe, North America, Asia and Australia. Author of *Corruption: Who Cares?*

GENERAL Ho Ying-Chin, commander of the Chinese forces at the end of the Second World War, received the Japanese sword of surrender on 9 September 1945 from General Okamura Yasutsugu, Japanese military commander in China, acting on behalf of the Japanese government. Ho later gave this sword to Frank Buchman in recognition of his work for the Chinese people and the world. Speaking in the Upper House of the Japanese Parliament in 1951, the general emphasised this further when he said, 'Moral Re-Armament is the only basis for lasting peace for China and Japan. It is priority.'

Ho attributed the collapse of the Nationalist Government in China in 1949 to corruption and immorality, saying that if the leaders of China had 'loved their country more than they loved their mistresses' the outcome could have been different. In Taiwan, he with other leaders invited the MRA Statesmen's Mission with the powerful musical play *The Vanishing Island* to Taiwan in 1955. In this Statesmen's Mission were leading political figures from Africa, Asia, Europe and North America. Their message was real and simple. For example, Mohamed Masmoudi, later a Tunisian cabinet minister, standing alongside the French Secretary of State for Air, Diomede Catroux, said, 'Without Moral Re-Armament, we would be involved today in Tunisia in a war to the death against France... Tunisia would be a second Indo-China.' General Ho in welcoming the visit said, as reported by Dr Daniel Lew, then a member of the Chinese delegation to the United Nations, 'This visit is unprecedented in the history of China. Never has such a group as this come to China, or to any other Asian nation, before. Even to our brethren on the Chinese mainland, your visit has brought comfort and hope.'

In 1956 Frank Buchman visited a number of Asian countries including Taiwan where he met General Ho and others convinced of the need for a new spirit as expressed through Moral Re-Armament. Following these visits an international conference took place in Baguio in the Philippines which brought together leaders from the Philippines, Japan, South Korea, and Taiwan. General Ho said to the press, 'What and I and others have striven for in ten years of post-war diplomacy and failed to achieve has been accomplished here in ten days; speaking for democracy this is the work we are meant to do for many years ahead. The reconciliation between Koreans and Japanese is the most important event of this conference.'

The democracy referred to by General Ho did not begin to arrive in Taiwan until much later in the 1980s, with the opening up of the political system to political parties other than the ruling Nationalist Party. However, through the general's efforts (he died in 1987 aged 97) and the efforts of Dr Daniel Lew and many others, by the late 1980s a group of people committed to MRA had developed. One of this group was Ren-Jou Liu, a high school mathematics teacher, whose life had been changed to faith in God through a number of talks with Dr Lew. As Taiwan moved towards a democratic system, Liu became convinced that the corrupt practice of vote-buying had to be tackled frontally and publicly before the elections took place for the first time for the National Legislature scheduled for 1992.

Confronting the mood for vote-buying

Speaking later in Caux in 1995, he described how MRA launched a Clean Election Campaign a few months prior to the 1992 national elections. He said:

'Towards the end of 1992, when the first complete electoral reform for legislatures was scheduled, one could predict that the main political power would move to Parliament. In May, one day as I was having lunch with two members of the business community, they were both very worried that the mood for vote-buying would favour only ambitious politicians and enable financial groups to enter Parliament in great numbers, thereby worsening future politics. Business opportunities in Taiwan would become even more unfair. Fair competition and management and the development of the economy would certainly regress, the general environment would worsen and very soon Taiwan would lose hope.

'The next day during a time of reflection, I had a strong inner thought to initiate a clean election campaign. After discussing this with friends and colleagues in Moral Re-Armament in Taiwan, we decided that over the next five years, MRA would go all out to promote a clean election campaign.

'As an individual, I publicly announced that I would never enter politics or take part in any political elections at any time, in order to prevent people from thinking or believing that I had any personal ambitions. I also stated that I would never become a politician.

'The Campaign had a four-point strategy:

1. Strive for joint action with non-government groups and religious groups;
2. Win the trust and support of the ordinary people;
3. Work for a positive response from the media and the public;
4. Make sure that the government keeps its promises in carrying out reforms.'

Taiwan's *Global Views Monthly* interviewed two of the Campaign's leaders, Liu and Jack Huang, a legal adviser to several major enterprises. The magazine reported: 'It was Liu who conceived the idea of launching the 'anti-corruption movement'. Some friends criticised him as a Don Quixote but he persevered. His conviction that 'human nature could be changed' inspired others in MRA to join him.' The article added that Huang's tactical skills had won the full co-operation of 68 other civic groups who also became partners in the campaign. In response to criticism, Liu responded, 'We are not engaged in a political struggle.'

Indeed, all those running the Campaign, he said, were personally committed to maintain political neutrality; seek no personal advantage or gain; generate no hatred towards the corrupt but inspire love of country as the motive for action; and run the public demonstrations peacefully and with joy.

As the weeks went by the impact of the Clean Election Campaign grew and became 'a raging fire', according to *Global Views Monthly*. The Minister of Education, Mao Kao-Wen, wrote to 4.2 million parents of schoolchildren in support of the Campaign. He said that the behaviour of parents influenced the development of their children's character and none of us would wish our children to cheat in school exams. Parents must set the example and refuse vote-buying. *The China Post*, Taiwan's largest newspaper, supplied free advertising space for the Campaign and printed stickers, leaflets and slogans. By the time of the vote, some 670,000 voters had committed themselves in signed statements neither to accept a bribe for their vote nor to vote for any candidate who offered a bribe - practices which had been commonplace for two generations. Of the 350 candidates for the Legislature, 162 signed pledges against vote-buying. President Lee Deng-Hui and Prime Minister Hao Po-Ts'un received members of the Campaign and personally handed over their signed pledges against vote-buying and bribery.

Victory of people power

The results of the Legislature elections were hailed by the media as the miracle of the Clean Election Campaign or the victory of people power. Five billionaires who had stood as candidates offering all sorts of incentives were defeated – and in those same electorates the highest number of votes went to candidates who had supported the Clean Election Campaign. The ruling party, the Kuomintang (KMT), lost heavily and the opposition Democratic Progressive Party (DPP) doubled their number of seats. The General Secretary of the Kuomintang resigned.

The Campaign was certainly one factor in the swing of public opinion against vote-buying. It also helps explain the broad public support for the then Justice Minister Ma Ying-jeou's crackdown on corrupt practices in the city and county elections of March 1994. Twenty-three were arrested, including a speaker, a deputy speaker and nine councillors from city or county authorities on charges of buying votes or accepting bribes. They were found guilty and *The China Post* reported that Ma's move had been 'like an earthquake measuring more than six on the Richter scale, rocking not only the main opposition Democratic Progressive Party but also the Kuomintang'. Ma said in an interview with Brian Lightowler that the Clean Election Campaign had a positive effect on his crackdown campaign. In fact the two campaigns had interacted on each other.

Following the arrests, the regional chairman of the KMT resigned. A senior official of the KMT pointed out that if Minister Ma continued his relentless attack on corruption the grassroots structure of the KMT could collapse. A group of KMT legislators warned Ma that if that happened he would be held responsible. Ma responded by telling the Legislature that anyone believed guilty of vote-buying would be prosecuted, regardless of his background and political affiliation. The fight against corruption was not for personal show but an ongoing national policy. Nevertheless political pressure from within the ruling KMT on the President led to Ma's eventual departure from the Ministry of Justice. He told Lightowler, 'After three years of crackdown as the minister I was able to prosecute more than 5,000 government officials and 7,500 people involved in vote-buying. The conviction rate when I left the Ministry (and most cases were still pending) was 40 per cent.

'833 city and county councilmen were investigated and 341 prosecuted. In one county of 60 councilmen, 54 were prosecuted. Eleven councilmen in Pindong County were disqualified after being elected. If we pursue things persistently in a very determined way we can really get things done.'

But it was not only Ma's determination and that of the prosecutors and investigators that produced results; it was also the quality of personal integrity. Ma said that from an early age he had guarded against any form of cheating or corruption. So when he became Minister of Justice, his conviction for personal integrity broadened, so that it was 'not only for myself and those around me but also for the people of the country'.

The Prosecutor-General said on Ma's departure as Justice Minister that if he had been able to stay on for a further three years, Taiwan would be a very different place. In December 2002 Ma won a second term as Mayor of Taipei and is likely to be the KMT's candidate for President at the next elections.

From 1992 to 1997, the Clean Election Campaign was in action at every election – national, city or local. Hundreds of teachers and university students volunteered for training for the Campaigns, conducting public meetings, demonstrations and seminars. After 1997 the success of the Clean Election Campaign led to the setting up of an officially sponsored campaign against vote-buying and other forms of political corruption.

The Campaign's present Vice-Chairman, Buddhist Master Shihjingyao, is also a member of Taiwan's Central Electoral Committee. Evaluating the campaign, he acknowledged that Ma had suffered a political backlash and had been forced to step down. But, he went on to say, 'We have been telling the voters that this country belongs to us all. It is up to us to help create a political environment based on clean elections and sound politics so that we can have politicians of good character working for the good of our country. This kind of responsibility belongs to each and every citizen.'

The Financial Times (London) reported that the December 2001 elections were the cleanest in Taiwan's history. The China Post conducted a poll two days after the election and found that 70.1 per cent of those questioned considered that vote-buying had been greatly reduced and were satisfied that the election was fair.

The effectiveness of the Taiwan Clean Election Campaign led to similar campaigns in Brazil (1994), Kenya (1997, 2002 & 2007), the Solomon Islands (2006), and Sierra Leone (2002) following the civil war and a further campaign in 2007.

13

Frank Buchman and the Muslim World

by Imam Dr Abduljalil Sajid

Imam Sajid is a leading British Muslim of Pakistani origin and presently chairman of the Muslim Council for Religious and Racial Harmony, UK. He is also chairman of the UK Chapter of the World Conference of Religion and Peace and of the task force for the European 2008 Year of Inter-Cultural Dialogue.

IN 1964, when studying at Punjab University in Lahore, I was set a project on the subject of Honesty in World Religions. I found material on every faith but I had difficulty in finding the answer to the question, 'Do Christians have any moral standards?'

In the British Council Library I was shown a book called *Remaking the World*, the collected speeches of Dr Frank N D Buchman, an American Lutheran Church minister. Buchman was descended from Swiss immigrants who settled in Allentown, Pennsylvania (and in fact, one of his ancestors, Theodore Bibliander, was the first translator of the Holy Qur'an into a European language).

I was surprised to discover that Buchman not only believed in morals, but felt that a true Christian should aim to live by *absolute* moral standards. He summarised these as honesty, purity, unselfishness and love - a formulation he learned from the scholar Henry Wright. Was not this, I thought, exactly what the Prophet of Islam, peace be upon him, described in the teaching of the Holy Qur'an and Ahadith (sayings of the Holy Prophet of Islam)? Buchman's speeches revealed a picture of a man who was fearless, frank and yet humble. It left a big impression on me, though I did not take it any further at the time.

My family comes from Rajanpur in the Punjab, near to the borders of all four provinces of Pakistan. I was born on 1 November 1947, the year Pakistan was partitioned from India at the time of Independence. We were a simple family and I was one of 14 siblings. I was fortunate in getting schooling and was the first of my family to go to university and get a degree.

My first teaching post was at the University of Dhaka, then the capital of East Pakistan. When it became Bangladesh in 1971, people like myself from West Pakistan were in danger of a backlash from those forming the new administration of the country. However colleagues in Dhaka University helped me to leave and return to Lahore where I was able to find employment in the university.

There, one of my tasks was to invigilate for the university examinations. At the time cheating was rife among the students, and I decided to take a stand, in the face of violence and threats. As a result the students mounted a demonstration against me outside the Vice-Chancellor's office. Fearing riots and loss of life, the Vice-Chancellor asked me to lie low and later arranged for me to take a further course of study in the UK at the London School of Economics and Political Science (LSE).

After completing my studies I was offered a job, so my wife and children joined me. We started in East London and five years later we moved to Brighton where I started the first mosque in the town, and later an interfaith group as well as a Council for Ethnic Minority Groups. I was appointed a local magistrate and got to know people at all levels of society.

Encounter with Initiatives of Change

In 1985 as a result of an interview I gave on local radio I received a letter from a Richard Pearce, who was working not far from my mosque. He had been impressed by the interview and wanted to meet me. Sometimes we would pass in the street at the end of the day as we were both returning home. However, I was so busy I did not feel I could spare the time to talk to him. He was a New Zealander working temporarily in Britain, so he got a local friend, David Young, to phone me to fix an appointment. Not wanting to offend, I asked to be excused on account of the pressure of work. However when he persisted, I said, 'Look, if you can come at 6 am, I could spare half an hour.' I was confident that no Englishman would agree to an appointment at that hour. But they called my bluff!

The great surprise for me was that both these men were familiar with Frank Buchman's work of Moral Re-Armament. They invited me to meet other friends and attend some meetings of the local MRA group. Later I participated in a conference at MRA's international conference centre at Caux in Switzerland.

I warmed immediately to what I found in Caux. It had echoes of the world community of common humanity – the 'Ummah' – which every Muslim believes in and aspires to create. I found people living together, caring for and thinking for each other. All wanted to serve and achieve a common aim, to repair what was wrong in the world. Everyone took part in the running of the centre and the practical arrangements. People listened to what others expressed rather than only trying to get across their own view. Above all there was a determination to tackle the difficult problems in the world and the evil lying behind them. They worked by identifying the needs in the world and then to create contexts in which people involved in them might change their attitudes.

Who was Frank Buchman?

All this prompted me to find out more about Frank Buchman. What could I, as a Muslim, learn from him and the way he worked? Was it relevant to my own commitment and convictions? I began to get a fuller picture of what Dr Buchman had created through this international team of people. In 1938, as the European nations were rearming militarily, he launched a campaign to deal with the causes of war in the human heart, under the heading of Moral Re-Armament. I learned the way in which they worked, namely through identifying the needs in the world and then creating contexts in which key personalities in different situation might find a new perspective.

I discovered Buchman was a man of faith, who deeply believed that God would guide those who listened and were ready to obey. But his faith was not exclusive. He would have endorsed what Mother Teresa said: 'What we are all trying to do by our work is to come closer to God.

We become a better Hindu, a better Muslim, a better Catholic, a better whatever we are, and by being better we become closer and closer to Him.'

I left Caux after that first visit feeling that here was an action I was called to participate in, something which encapsulated the dream every Muslim would want to be part of.

European Experience

In 1992 I accompanied Gerald Henderson, an MRA full-time worker from Liverpool, on the first of two visits to Germany. Though I had previously been to Germany a few times on interfaith projects, I had a special interest in doing this because I had heard that before the Second World War Buchman had visited Germany many times. He had tried very hard to reach some of those who had set their sights on creating a powerful but godless country, which eventually took the world into war. After the war, he took important steps to help rebuild the country and its links with the rest of the world. In 1948 he took a musical revue with an international cast with the title, *Es muss alles anders werden* (Everything must be different). To a defeated and downcast nation it brought hope and a new aim, particularly in the industrial areas where the communists were trying to exploit the sense of hopelessness by offering a Marxist solution. Some of the hardened, committed communists began to see in Moral Re-Armament a new way forward.

Buchman's Vision for Muslim World

During these many encounters with people and meetings, whether in Britain or in other countries I learned something of the friendships Buchman made with Muslims from many countries. One such person was the late Mohammed Fadhel Jamali of Iraq. Jamali had a distinguished career in educational and political fields and he paid heavily for his readiness to stand up for his convictions in the face of political pressure. In 1945, as Iraqi Foreign Minister, he was present in San Francisco at the founding conference for the United Nations. He played an important role in the drafting of the Charter of the UN, standing up for the rights of those nations (like his own) who were under some form of mandate. However, he remarked that his meeting with Frank Buchman was as important to him as his part in the drafting of the Charter. Buchman had invited him to see a play, *The Forgotten Factor*, which portrayed the solution to an industrial dispute. Jamali was captivated by the theme of the play, 'It's not who is right, but what is right'. He wrote afterwards, 'I'll never forget it! It made a lasting impression on my mind and spirit. It showed how violence is not the way, but that the road to just and lasting peace lies in forgiveness and in the admission of mistakes, both in families and in politics.' He kept touch with Dr Buchman and was inspired by his vision for the Muslim world to be a 'girder of unity for all civilization'.

Never afraid of controversy, Jamali spoke out in April 1955 at the International Conference of Asian nations at Bandung, Indonesia. It was at the height of communism's bid for world power and the discussion was on the question of disarmament. He made this statement: 'Physical disarmament is not enough: the truth is that what the world needs is ideological disarmament. Achieving that, we must work on the basis of moral rearmament and physical disarmament whereby men of all races and nations with clean hearts, with no rancour or hatred, approach each other with humility, admit our own mistakes and work for mutual harmony and peace. It is then, and only then, that the world will turn into one integral camp with no Eastern or Western camps.'

Healing the Colonial Past

Others who counted Dr Buchman as their friend included Abdul Khalek Hassouna, Secretary General of the Arab League, as well as his predecessor Abdul Rahman Aziz. Si Bekkai, a prime minister of Morocco at the time when the Pasha of Marrakech triggered a miraculous change in relations with France which led to independence for Morocco, was another. Mohamed Masmoudi, a cabinet minister in newly-independent Tunisia, said that his meeting and friendship with Buchman and the resulting link he was given with France had been instrumental in the bloodless achievement of independence by his country.

The founder of Pakistan, Quaidiazzam Mohammed Ali Jinnah, responded to Buchman's aims. In London in 1946, Jinnah saw *The Forgotten Factor,* the play which had moved Jamali so much. The portrayal in the play of the tough employer as a man who 'would not budge' amused him and he laughed out loud – the first time his companions had even seen him smile since arriving in London. Over dinner with Buchman afterwards, Jinnah, referring to the play, told Buchman, 'Apology – that is the golden key.' Later after independence had been achieved, though with a great loss of life and property, Jinnah admitted that he had not expected the violence which erupted, and he apologised to those who had suffered so much.

Senior Sudanese have become involved including the late Mohammad Salih Shangitti, former Speaker of the

Sudan Parliament and a very influential person in newly-independent Sudan. Another, who was first introduced to Moral Re-Armament in his student days in Oxford, is Sayyid Ahmed El-Mahdi, the senior surviving grandson of Mohammad Ahmed El- Mahdi.

The present Chairman of IofC in Malaysia is Tan Sri Hajjah Saleha Mahammad Ali, who met Buchman when she was a student at London University soon after the end of the Second World War. Since her return to her own country she has prominently advocated close teamwork between Muslims and others in IofC. Another more recent visitor to Caux was Sabri Koci, then Mufti of Albania. He was accompanied by the Minister for Religion and spoke there of his experiences of God taking care of him during the 22 years he had spent in prison when the Communists were ruling his country. He said that he sensed the spirit of Islam pervading Caux. Buchman's hope had always been that Muslim countries should become 'a belt of sanity to bind East and West and bring moral rebirth'. That, I thought, is a very big challenge, not only to me as a Muslim, but to us all.

Personal experiences of forgiveness

In Caux I learned the importance that Buchman and his fellow workers attached to the principle and practice of forgiveness, which Muslims also consider vital. The Holy Qur'an enjoins Muslims to 'pardon and forbear' in all our doings. In recent years, I have some experience of facing criticism and setbacks. In 1996, events at the Dyke Road Mosque and Islamic Centre in Brighton tested my own practice of forgiveness to the limit. I was Director and Imam of the mosque at the time. I had tried to help some people to gain British citizenship and given them training in Islam. However, they came under the spell of a radical preacher and began veering towards violence. They disapproved of my policy of trying to work with people of all backgrounds. Finally they challenged my leadership and took over the mosque by force in 1998. What, I wondered, should I do? I discussed the options with the Trustees of the mosque and, having made all possible legal moves, the only way forward seemed forgiveness. It was not easy, as the temptation to try and hit out was strong. However I have managed to resist that temptation.

* * * * *

Muslim/Christian Teamwork in Middle East

At an IofC conference in 1997, I forged a deep friendship with an American, Bryan Hamlin, a veteran IofC full-time worker who had developed remarkable touches with people in both Palestine and Israel. Subsequently I made two visits there with him for the purpose of inviting Muslims and Jews to conferences in Caux. I learnt from Bryan the secret of living with an open heart and using our honesty to change people. It enabled us to reach people whom few foreigners could meet and to bring to bear the factor of openness and reconciliation in an otherwise often closed society. As I did this I thought of many instances from the life of the Prophet which we can all benefit from. One example of this was the value of a time of silent reflection, of prayer and of seeking God's guidance, which is underlined in the Holy Qur'an. What an important element Bryan and I found this to be in our travels together! Often when we were uncertain of our next move, we would feel the 'nudge' of the Almighty showing us the next step.

Recently in Brighton we have made use of a remarkable film, which portrays a fine example of peacemaking in Nigeria. *The Imam and the Pastor* is the true story of Imam Muhammad Ashafa and Pastor James Wuye whom I first met in 2005 in Caux. It was when they were leaders respectively of Muslim and Christian militias in Northern Nigeria in the early '90s that the Imam felt he was not following the principles the Holy Qur'an preached. He struggled within himself but eventually approached the Pastor, who rebuffed him. However he did not give up, but tried a second time, and gradually they began to establish a relationship. Since then they have co-founded an Interfaith Mediation Centre, leading task-forces for reconciliation to places of religious and ethnic conflict in Nigeria and beyond. In working for peace and reconciliation together they have become closer than brothers and have impacted thousands of people in their country with the prospect of change.

Visit to Australasia

In 2006, my wife and I spent three months visiting Singapore, Indonesia, Australia, New Zealand and Fiji at the invitation of IofC teams in these countries. We addressed public meetings, gave interviews and met religious and political leaders, university teachers and interfaith activists. We also went to Pakistan as part of a British Council project of visits to Muslim countries with particular reference to the role of women in Islam. Talking to, and being interviewed by a wide variety of people, was a new role for my wife, Jamila. What came out was her deep belief in home-making and family-building. It is a role that she loves and gives her whole heart to. As she often said, 'The world is full of greed and hate. We must give our time and energy in guidance from God to serve humanity above ourselves. As the Holy Prophet of Islam said, the best among you are those who serve others selflessly so that we can create a world around ourselves which is greed-free and hate-free.'

What struck me from our visit to Australasia was the value of teamwork through bringing together people of different backgrounds and experiences and giving a chance for them to share their examples of change in order to help others find similar changes in their own life. The accumulated effect of this is to start change reactions which can lead to the change in nations, as we found in the case of retired politician Kim Beazley, whom we met in his home town of Perth. I decided to try to follow this example by setting ten others to work, rather than trying to do the work of ten people myself.

Dr Charis Waddy was another person whose example made a deep impact on me. I met her late in her life after she had spent a lifetime working with Moral Re-Armament – something she continued to do until her death. Brought up in Jerusalem, where her father was head of the Anglican school, she was the first woman to study Arabic and Hebrew in Oxford University. It led to her making friends with many people from the Middle East. She told Frank Buchman, 'The West has much to learn from Islam and many will find enrichment in the effort to understand it.' She wrote many books, using her pen to reach people through her writing. I liked her booklet, *The Skills of Discernment*, which showed her profound understanding of human nature and the ways in which people can be changed, much of which she had learned from working with Frank Buchman.

Task for the future

For so many Muslims, the attacks on the World Trade Centre and the Pentagon on 11 September 2001 were deeply shameful. The killing of so many innocent people was itself a terrible shock. But the fact that it was described as being done in the name of Islam was even more shocking. With many others I tried to make amends for this act. But above all I gave much thought to the reason lying behind such an outrage.

We are encouraged in the Holy Qur'an to carry out self-criticism, to reflect and search for fresh and creative ideas. I thought back to Frank Buchman's actions after the Second World War and the ways in which he reached out to the German people, particularly offering alternatives to those, like the communists, who sought to exploit anger and defeatism. Was not the next task for people like myself, to find ways of providing hope and a positive way forward to young Muslims who were driven by hatred and bitterness to carry out acts of violence and even suicide to draw attention to their passionately-held views? And to help those who have the power to affect world events take decisions that are beneficial in the long-term for all parties? These are tasks that need the best minds and actions of us all, and that Muslim and non-Muslim can to take on together.

In conclusion

When I read Frank Buchman's emphasis on the four absolute standards of honesty, purity, unselfishness and love, and listening in prayer to seek God's direction, I thought that these might have come from the following principles every Muslim learns from the Qur'an:

Be honest: *Engage yourself in efforts for the way of God courageously and honestly. (Qur'an 22:78, 16:92)*

Be pure: *And those who guard their chastity except with their spouses....they shall inherit paradise to live there forever. (23:1-11)*

Be unselfish: *Do not follow your selfish desire and do not come near to fornication as it is a serious, sinful and shameful act. (17:32)*

Be loving: *Learn in the name of God... God loves those who love others. (2:195, 9:108, 96:1)*

Change: *God will not change the condition of a people until they change themselves. (13:11)*

Obedience: *Listen and obey. (64:16)*

14

Action emerges from Silence – a Russian view

by Grigory Pomerants

Grigory Pomerants was born in 1918 into a Jewish family in Vilnius, Lithuania, but his family moved in 1925 to Moscow where he graduated in Russian language and literature. Through his thesis on Dostoyevsky being judged anti-Marxist he was not admitted to post-graduate studies, but is now a well-known Russian author. He fought in the Red Army against Hitler, was twice wounded and twice decorated. Despite five years imprisonment for anti-Soviet agitation, he is now a member of the Academy of Natural Sciences, and the Writers' Union.

Not only the guerrillas in Sarajevo need to be morally re-armed, but also the citizens of the affluent world.
Novove Vremva (New Times) *

ABOUT three years ago the interpreter Andrei Mironov telephoned and asked if he could bring two Scandinavians to see me. They were concerned about how it was possible for Shafarevich, the author of a good book about

*No 45, Moscow, November 1994, pp.36-38

socialism, to have written *Russophobia*. They had gone to ask Pavel Litvinov this question and he had sent them to me. I don't remember what I said, but that was the beginning of my friendship with Leif Hovelsen. I am obliged to Shafarevich for that. I don't know whether he wished me well, but fate so decided.

Forgiving your executioner

Leif was a member of the Resistance in Norway. A friend betrayed him. He was arrested and suffered cruel torture, but refused to be an informer and was expecting his death sentence to be carried out. Suddenly everything changed. There was an uprising of Soviet prisoners of war who joined with the forces of the Resistance to free the country. (The remarkable story of Lieutenant Colonel Novobranets, the leader of the uprising, can be read in General Grigorenko's book *In the Underground you only meet rats*, but this is not our subject now). The SS were taken prisoner and those who had been prisoners were made their guards. The new guards forced the former ones to do the things that they had had to do as prisoners: to squat and jump, squat and jump. One of the SS became exhausted and asked for water. Leif brought it – and saw the hated face of his torturer. In a fit of passion he poured the water over the man's head. Then he felt ashamed. When he had endured the torture it had been his victory. But now they had won – he had acted like them.

Leif applied for leave, went into the mountains and tried to collect his thoughts, to withdraw into silence. At one moment an inner voice – perhaps prompted by the way his mother brought him up – said to him that he must forgive his torturer. Leif went home and told everything to his mother. She supported him: 'Tell him that as your mother I will pray for him.' Leif was allowed to visit the SS man, who had damaged his eardrums when beating him, and told him all this. The SS man was staggered. Others did not withdraw their testimony, and the torturer was executed, but before his death he asked for a priest for the first time in many years. Since that time Leif has given his whole life for the reconciliation of former enemies.

For ten years or so, Leif worked with other members of the Society for Moral Re-Armament trying to bring together French and Germans. He helped dissidents and worked for the award of the Nobel Prize to Sakharov and Walesa. After making friends with Leif I twice accepted an invitation to go to Mountain House, Caux, where the annual MRA conferences take place – 700 metres above Lake Geneva, at the place where the prisoner of Chillon once languished and where later Vladimir Nabokov and Charlie Chaplin ended their days in peace.

The special spirit of Mountain House

The first impression is of the overwhelming beauty of Mountain House. The second is of the people who in no way ruin the beauty. In the Caucasus or in the Crimea there are mountains, valleys and lakes that yield nothing to Switzerland, but the people spoil the beauty with noise and dirt. Here, beside the auto route that skirts the forested slopes, you see no scrap of litter. I saw a car parked (new as if straight from the production line: I never saw any dirty ones; there are fines for dirt) – the radio was not switched on, nobody was intruding on the quietness. They drive quietly and do not interfere with the pedestrians. I never saw a drunk. Bonjour Monsieur,

Bonjour Madame. Maybe it's only custom; but a very good custom. In it is the age-old respect for another person, the sense of responsibility to others.

And supported by these customs the special spirit of Mountain House has been created, infusing customary politeness with sincere goodwill... I don't see how to avoid using this old-fashioned word. White, black, coloured come together and all live like one big family. There are no staff. Everyone chooses a team to join: preparing vegetables, cooking the meals, cleaning rooms and so on. The teams meet together; people from different parts of the world come closer to each other. Another way of coming closer is more personal: somehow somebody likes you and invites you to have lunch or supper together. The host lays the table and a conversation ensues – right here in the dining hall, or we cross into the next room for an hour, or two, or three.

There were some encounters similar to Ivan and Alyosha's talk in the tavern. Evidently this does not only happen in Russia! We spent such an evening with an American Presbyterian minister, Robert MacLennan, telling each other about the turning points of life that formed his view of the world, my view of the world and my wife Zinaida Mirkina's view of the world. Sometimes the presence of the interpreter seemed a little strange, but Andrei Mironov was not just an interpreter. There were some perestroika characters that he simply could not bring himself to translate for, whereas he joined in this conversation heart and soul. MacLennan caught our attention when he conducted a meeting of Israeli rabbis with Palestinian mullahs at a plenary session, and said that the deeper you go into the essence of your own religion the more you understand other religions. Somehow my wife and I hit it off well with him; from the very beginning our conversation went like the one with Leif in Moscow. I remember that Robert had a psychotherapist friend who had helped him greatly at a difficult moment, but upset him by going rarely to church. When asked why, he said, 'I don't have to.' At first MacLennan was offended, but a few years later he understood that this might have been the most profound thing he had heard.

Whatever you do, don't over-repent!

Another remarkable meeting was between my wife Zinaida and Djurdjica from Croatia. A passionately devout Catholic, Djurdjica, despite the difference of spiritual paths, sensed a direct spiritual experience and was drawn to it. In the conversations of the two women I stepped aside into the role of interpreter (from German into Russian and from Russian into German). Then sometimes it was the other way round and the whole conversation was with me. After my presentation in a seminar, two intellectuals, Professor Pierre Spoerri and Ambassador Mackenzie, invited us to supper and showered me with questions about the theory of sub-ecumenism. I passed the examination fairly well and even tried to answer in the same language in which they were posing their questions (Mackenzie belongs to that minority of British who pronounce words distinctly, and scholarly terminology in all European languages is more or less the same). I only flopped on one question: what form might a world government take? I have never fantasised about that and so answered honestly: I don't know.

Out of the group discussions and seminars I would particularly mention the meeting of Russian speakers. In the local understanding this did not mean an ethnic group, but all who speak Russian. Professor Landsbergis and his wife came as well. Dmitri Nikulin, the author of a good little book *Metaphysical Reflections*, in his philosophical distraction called the Lithuanian leader 'Brazauskas'. Landsbergis continued the comedy of errors by addressing Nikulin as 'Brezhnev'. However, not everything was so funny. There was a provocative intervention by Dr Ernst, a German physician who had treated Belorussians at the time of the war and kept his links with Belarus. He started to speak about the guilt of the West (and particularly Germany) concerning all the woes of the East. This stirred my wife Zina and she hotly supported him. Then Landsbergis took the floor and cautioned that under no circumstances should we over-repent. Of course, he admitted, the Nazis had done a lot of terrible things to the Jews, but stressed that this distracts our attention from the threat of Russia's imperial claims, which have still not receded into the past. In his words, Russia must prove its sincerity by liberating Chechnya.

I tried to switch the focus to the personal feeling of guilt; in my experience it doesn't follow any rules, whereas repentance by a whole state can become just a symbolic gesture. Still, one of the Russians added, repentance, even as a symbolic gesture is a good symbolic gesture. No fear of over-repentance emerged amongst the others present. Mrs Landsbergis sensed this and decided to support her husband. 'This is all words,' she said, 'We need action' (apparently granting independence to Chechnya). She spoke as 'the only one here of those who suffered'. It is true that she grew up in Siberian exile, probably a very hard one. But amongst those present were others who had gone through Stalinist and post-

Stalinist repressions; there was a Russian woman who had been born in Sevastopol harbour in 1920 (her mother gave birth having just boarded the ship, and the new-born girl was almost thrown out as a bundle of rags when the ship was being unloaded). Mrs Landsbergis brushed all this aside: 'You belong to the ruling nation.' In the general atmosphere of openness to the sufferings of others this imperviousness to others' concerns (such as is customary on Earth) appeared strange. On the planet MRA the spirit of reconciliation reigned: northern Sudanese with southern Sudanese, Israelis with Arabs, Khmer Rouge with Khmer of royal blood, and so on.

The opposite of Babel

After Switzerland I went to Latvia to give lectures and again found myself on planet Earth; everywhere one could feel the mood of two national communities gripped by anxiety and mistrust. The Russian Cultural Society in Latvia is trying to start a dialogue, a conversation in which both sides listen to each other and are ready to understand the arguments of their opponents. However, the extremists on both sides are not yet ready for that. Meanwhile, a Russian in the audience came up to me and said that the situation in Russia alarmed him even more than the situation in Latvia. The reconciliation of the communities in the Baltic states is primarily a matter of time. Disaster is not breathing down their necks. Perhaps MRA will help to start the process that succeeded on the Rhine in these former Soviet republics.

Speaking at the last plenary session, Zinaida said that in Mountain House the exact opposite is happening to the building of the Tower of Babel: then a single language broke up into many languages, whereas here people are taught to speak a common divine parent language and we, like children, are learning to understand this silent language which opens the soul.

The spirit of the founder of the society, Frank Buchman (1878-1961), lives in the people who gather in Caux. He has been compared with the son of Mr Pickwick transported to America, and to St Francis of Assisi. Buchman was a descendant of Swiss Germans who left Europe in 1740, but in him there really was something from Pickwick and from Francis; a spiritual energy coming from a feeling of inner calling, a kind of charisma, and the enlightened optimism of Mr Pickwick, and something else uniquely American, a kind of inspired practicality. The idea of the society came to Buchman at a conference on disarmament at the start of the 1930s (he attended it as an expert); if the spirit of the nations does not change profoundly, nothing will come out of the negotiations; war is inevitable. The source of energy for the transformation must be sought in silence, in a place where nature itself bears the imprint of God's thought and evokes in the mind evangelical callings.

Hardly anyone would listen to Buchman on the eve of the war. In Russia, in Germany, in Japan, the cult of force was growing headlong. Fear of communism made western politicians seek understanding with Hitler. Then fear of Hitler caused the building of the atom bomb. In the war years Buchman went into seclusion with a few friends at Island House (on one of the American Great Lakes) and contemplated what would need to be done following the destruction in Europe. In 1946, he came to Switzerland. With the money of ninety families the dilapidated hotel in Caux was bought. Here the first post-war conference was to take place.

Buchman's order

There were no Germans amongst the arrivals. They did not yet have the right to leave their country without the special permission of the occupying powers. Buchman knew a few Germans about whose convictions he had no doubts. At his request the American Command gave them permission to go to Switzerland. One of these Germans was Adenauer. Soon Buchman introduced Adenauer to the French foreign minister Robert Schuman. And at the 'grassroots' the society worked for about ten years trying to erase the traces of national hatred and to encourage the French to believe in the sincerity of German repentance (our friend Leif worked on this with others). At the same time, a major work began in Asia and Africa. Buchman did not doubt that the end of the colonial system was near, and the society did everything in its power to make the transition to independence peaceful and bloodless. Many statesmen of the new countries became friends of Buchman and members of the society. Last year one of the leaders of MRA, Rajmohan Gandhi, a grandson of Mohandas Gandhi, visited us in Moscow.

Buchman remained a passionate Christian, but the search for universal community caused the accent to be moved onto the spirit of love common to all great religions, and today MRA has become a kind of universal order where Muslims and Jews, Buddhists and Hindus have joined with Christians. The movement has its own unsolved problems which have accumulated since the death of Buchman. However, the spirit of Buchman comes to life at the meetings when the openness of faith traverses the boundaries of the religions.

Poisons and antidotes

Today, we are talking not about regions in crisis but about a global crisis, the impulse for which comes from the West. Development is not a simple movement towards better things. It creates poisons which must be counteracted. When development is too fast (in countries catching up with the West) there is no time to produce the antidote, and the illnesses which are tolerable in Europe become murderous in other parts. The West has accumulated good habits – of inner discipline, responsibility and respect for the law – and these habits allow it to hold firm despite amusing itself with destructive ideas and passions. However, after a few decades the good habits can disappear, or almost disappear; that is the experience of our country. And that is why Moral Re-Armament is not only necessary for regions in crisis. It is necessary for the whole world.

Translated by O. Tatishcheva and P. Thwaites.

15

Industry's Forgotten Factor

by Alec Porter, with Jens Wilhelmsen, Maarten de Pous and Miles Paine

Alec Porter was born and grew up in Ireland. He studied agriculture and worked for Peter Howard on his farm in Suffolk for five years. He then took part in MRA's programme for industry in Britain, Holland, France, America and India.

IN 1936, Frank Buchman, faced with the consequences of the world economic depression, was concerned how to reach the workers and industry more effectively in Britain. He invited Bill Jaeger to work with him and to start in East London, an area of much poverty, hardship and unrest, where three million workers struggled to make a living.

Jaeger came from a worker's family and while a student in London had already made many friends in East London. Now, with his studies completed, he felt the invitation was a confirmation of his own sense of calling to take the ideas of the Oxford Group (the first name given to Buchman's work) to the workers of the world and to the industrial life of nations. East London was the cradle of the British Labour Movement. Labour pioneers like Ben Tillett and Tod Sloan were friends of Buchman and strongly supported his work. It is hard to imagine it now, but East London then had 7,000 factory chimneys as well as the main docks for the Port of London.

Within two years, the Oxford Group was almost a household word as Jaeger and the team he enlisted had a series of public meetings of 700 to 1,000 all over the area. So it was a natural venue for Buchman to launch his world-wide campaign for Moral Re-Armament there in 1938. 3,000 overflowed the East Ham Town Hall. Twenty-six mayors and chairmen of local councils attended.

Jaeger chaired the meeting. Buchman in the course of this launching meeting said, 'Only a new spirit in men can bring a new spirit in industry. Industry can be the pioneer of a new order. When Labour, Management and Capital become partners under God's guidance, then industry takes its true place in national life. New men, new homes, new industry, new nations, a new world.' Frank Buchman always based his work on the premise that if people can be changed, situations in the world can be changed also. He spoke of making the wealth and work of the world available for all and the exploitation of none. And the first play dramatising his ideas, *The Forgotten Factor*, was also on industry – and used around the world.

In the 1920s and 1930s, Buchman spent much time in Britain, so it followed that the first evidence of applying his ideas was in British industry – as the reader will see from certain people's experiences. And as his message spread, so did the applications in industry; in Norway, Denmark, France, Germany, and Italy; in USA, Canada, Latin America and Australia. Those who read other chapters in this book will find yet more references to changes in industrial situations.

In the 1930s, through the Oxford Group, a number of employers whose lives and attitudes were changed had a significant impact on British and world industry in the following decades.

What is morally right can be economically viable

Farrar Vickers was managing director of Vickers Oils in Leeds, a family business which manufactured specialist oils for the textile and marine industries. In 1933, the change in his student son, John, challenged him to change his whole life; he had a clear thought to go into the factory as if for the first time with his eyes open. What he saw shocked him. There were no washing facilities although the workers were working with dirty greases all day. There was no canteen. There was no sick pay and little or no pension. Such conditions in industry were the norm in those days.

In an experiment of faith he began to change these things. He persuaded the shareholders to give some of their capital to set up a fund to benefit the employees and their dependants. During the depression he took in extra staff to implement these changes.

Five years later, the leader of one of the hunger marches, a Marxist economics lecturer, spent a day visiting the company. He said to Vickers, 'You have done more voluntarily than extreme governments could have compelled you to do.' From then on over the next sixty years Farrar and his son John, who succeeded him, proved that what was morally right could be economically viable.

In the Borders of Scotland, where wool was the main industry, Stuart Sanderson ran a family owned woollen mill. When the market for the cloth they manufactured collapsed he and his wife decided to stock the cloth and keep their employees at work. To be able to do this they sold their big house and moved into a cottage on the mill property. Years later when World War 2 started, the cloth was needed.

'Try being honest with the men like you have been with me'

John Nowell was the managing director of the Camden Tannery in the north of England and President of his national association; when a strike situation occurred he talked it over with his wife, with whom he was building a new family life. His wife said to him 'Why don't you try being honest with the men like you have been with me?' He did so putting all his cards on the table and inviting the union shop stewards to do the same and find together what was right. This led to setting up a works council which became the mainstay of discipline in the plant and a forum where ideas could be discussed. The trade union district organiser said, 'Here is a clear example for the rest of industry. Every one of my 4,000 members has benefited from what I learned at the Tannery.'

When those employers, Vickers, Sanderson and Nowell, took part in an industrial session in Scotland workers from the Clydeside shipyards and other industries came to meet them. This was the first time they met capitalists and management with new motives and new ideas. It gave them a new vision for industry and their part in changing it away from the old class attitudes. In 1939 Buchman invited some of them to join him in launching MRA in New York, Washington and California. These included Duncan Corcoran and Adam McLean, whose mother contributed the money she had saved for his father's gravestone to help with the cost; other families sacrificed too by letting their wage earners go.

In America after the launching of MRA in the Hollywood Bowl, California where 30,000 were present McLean and Blyth Ramsay were making their way to Canada when war was declared. They were advised by consular officials to continue their work in the US as their best contribution to the allied war effort. They took the chance to meet union leaders at the Boeing aircraft factory in Seattle, who then introduced them to Dale Reed, the President of the union at the Lockheed plant in California.

Lockheed were building the P38 fighter plane. The workforce there during the war grew from 6,000 to 80,000 as they took on manufacturing the Flying Fortress. Reed studied the MRA handbook *You can defend America*. He put it to senior management to give a copy to each worker. They distributed 40,000 copies through the plant. Following this meeting with Reed, Lockheed recognised the union for the first time.

Sustaining a nation's war production

Later Reed sent a message to Washington DC. 'There are planes on fighting fronts today that would not have been there but for the enthusiasm and unselfish leadership the MRA workers have brought into the ranks of labour.'

Also during World War 2 a new play, *The Forgotten Factor,* based on recent experiences in industry, written by Alan Thornhill formerly an Oxford don, was so dynamic and real that it had a profound effect on those who saw it. Bill Schaffer, the leader of the 17,000 workers at Cramps shipyard in Philadelphia and his wife nicknamed 'Dynamite', had agreed to divorce. Schaffer told Bill Jaeger, who had become a close friend, that his problems were 'slow horses and fast women'. He then admitted this to his wife. Her first reaction was to hit him but then she smiled and accepted his apology. Their marriage was completely remade. Schaffer then followed Jaeger's example and built a team to work with him and a new spirit came into the shipyard. Birch Taylor, vice-president of the company, said, 'I regard the work of these Britishers and their American colleagues as a mainstay of the nation's war production drive.'

When *The Forgotten Factor* was shown in Philadelphia about a year before he became president, Harry Truman made this statement, 'We need this spirit in industry, we need it in the nation. For if America doesn't catch this spirit, we will be lucky to win the war and certain to lose the peace. With it there is no limit to what we can do for America and America for the rest of the world.'

Duncan Corcoran and Bill Jaeger met Philip Murray, the President of the Congress of Industrial Organisations, the main industrial trade union confederation in America, a craggy Scot and pioneer of the CIO. When the revue *You can defend America* was shown at the steelworkers' national convention, he spoke after the performance, 'It exemplifies the spirit and the kind of unity for which America is looking.'

* * * * *

'Give me coal . . . and I will give you a foreign policy'

In April 1946, Buchman with 110 of those who worked with him in America set sail for Europe arriving first in Britain. Britain had many problems – one third of the dwellings had been destroyed or damaged, industrial plant run down, in debt to the tune of billions and as the Soviet Union's stance became clear, the need to maintain one and a half million in the armed services. Foreign

Secretary Ernest Bevin was saying to the miners, 'Give me 30 million tons of coal for export and I will give you a foreign policy.' But the Minister of Fuel and Power, Manny Shinwell, warned Parliament, 'The existing position contains the element of industrial disaster.'

Buchman consulted two full-time workers who had worked in the mines during the war years. It was clear that *The Forgotten Factor* would be ideal. The play was staged in London. Miners came to see it from several coalfields. The four miners from Doncaster area convinced their fellow miners to invite the play to Yorkshire. Two thousand connected with the coal industry saw it.

The very next week, one of the largest pits reported production had risen from 10,000 to 16,000 tons. The manager known as the 'the pocket battleship' and regarded as a dictator by the men had apologised to the miners. He said that the play had made him look at his work quite differently. Five years later – without extra men or new machinery – production was running at 21,000 tons a week.

Over the next two years, the play toured the coalfields and industrial areas, with the cast and those travelling with the play invited to stay in the homes of the local people. Invitations were received from 150 collieries and over 70,000 saw the play in the mining areas.

Ending acrimony and bitterness

By 1948, the mines in Britain had been nationalised. This certainly made a great difference but often the management and union leaders remained the same with the same attitudes of bitterness and mistrust. Disillusion often set in. Hugh Gaitskell, the new Minister of Fuel and Power, said that the National Coal Board had two tasks, a technical one and a psychological one: 'They had to achieve immense changes in the pits and they had to change completely the spirit of those working in the industry.' It was in the second sphere that Moral Re-Armament made its impact on the coal industry. In the valleys of South Wales in six weeks 35,000 saw the play. Tom Beecham was the National Coal Board Production Officer in the area, which included the Rhondda Valley, the scene of some of the bitterest memories of coal mining. He wrote, '*The Forgotten Factor* has had a great effect on our relationships, which is showing itself in the negotiations between the Board and the Union. The great problem is to get co-operation at pit level and this is doing it. There is not the acrimony and bitterness there was.'

Horace Holmes MP, Parliamentary Private Secretary to the Minister of Fuel and Power, speaking at the MRA Assembly at Caux said, 'It is more than 47 years since I went into the pits as a boy. Over thirty years I spent underground. For many years I took a great part in the trade union movement, and from 1902 to 1945 I helped shape the materialistic, Marxist approach to industry. I helped shape the hatred that sprang up between management and men ... Now I am in a position where I can see things in a different light. It has been a great joy for me to help spread MRA into the hearts and lives of people. I have seen great changes take place in the Midlands, in my own Yorkshire, in Scotland and Wales. I have seen management approach their problems with a different attitude, and because of that I have seen better production as far as coal is concerned.'

On a personal note, I was in South Wales for some weeks with the company of *The Forgotten Factor.* At the end of the run Frank Buchman came to Cardiff on his way to Caux, Switzerland for the MRA World Conference. Many from the coal industry came to meet him. He invited them to come to Caux. 'Come and see,' he said. Over sixty miners and steel workers with their wives made the journey to Caux. I stayed on in the valleys with others for the next months getting to know the miners and their families and staying in their homes. I then went to Caux for the 1949 conference.

I did a bunk!

However, after a month at Caux I did a bunk! I caught the night train to London without telling anyone I was leaving – not even my brother, Bill. The truth was I was not prepared to give my life to the total revolution I saw at Caux and to find my part in it. I did not take the opportunity to tell Bill, nor any friends, of the inner struggle I was experiencing. However during a sleepless night on the train I realised I could not give up the new life I had found through MRA and I could not run away from God and his calling. So I was glad to meet up with friends in London and give God a chance to sort out my life and make a new start. As I have found many times through my life when I am prepared to get honest and make a new start with God, a whole new life opens up.

It was in London I met up again with Eric Turpin whom I knew as a fellow student in Dublin, where we had met MRA. After university he worked as an industrial chemist in Belfast. While attending a performance of the MRA musical *The Good Road* he had the clear thought, 'You are not doing the maximum to remake the world. And you are not in the place you can do it.' Now in London, Eric was setting out to see what could be done to bring a new spirit to the docks. He invited me to work with him.

Strike followed strike through the years

When the European Recovery Programme, or Marshall Plan, was initiated by America to underpin the economic recovery of Western Europe, it was rejected by the Soviet Union; its regime also compelling the countries of Eastern Europe to reject it. Czechoslovakia had wanted to accept American aid. A rash of strikes across Western Europe was an attempt to negate its recovery. A strike in France was estimated to have cost half the aid for France that year.

Perhaps the most damaging was the *Beaverbrae* strike in the Port of London, which spread to other ports and tied them up for weeks in the summer of 1949. It was said to have cost Britain £217 million, the equivalent of Marshall Aid for that year. The communist-led Canadian Seaman's Union was in dispute with their Canadian employers but they waited until the ship, the *Beaverbrae*, tied up in London to call the strike. The seamen walked off. The ship was declared 'black' by the smaller dockers' union. The dockers stopped work and were suspended. Fellow dockers then struck supporting them. An unofficial strike committee was formed to spread the strike nationally. Even when the strike was over, this committee continued meeting for the next decade or more to foment grievances into strikes in the ports. The union and the government tried to control them but to no avail. Even a court action did not succeed; strike followed strike through the years.

In the following months, with the help of others including Bill Jaeger and Duncan Corcoran, we got to know the official and unofficial leaders of the dockers. They came to the public meetings where they heard and met speakers like the employers Farrar Vickers, John

Nowell and Stuart Sanderson, as well as Bert Allen, chairman of the engineering union in Birmingham, and miners from Britain and from the Ruhr. Some went to Caux. Dockers also came from ports in Holland and Germany. In this global setting the dockers appreciated that they were entrusted with economic lifelines of nations.

Dan Hurley, the union official, who declared the *Beaverbrae* 'black' wrote Buchman after getting home from Caux: 'My outlook has certainly adapted an entirely new aspect, and how much easier it has become to see the other fellow's point of view and not to be forever prepared to ram home the very aggressive doctrine which has been part of my policy for such a long time. I shall always recall you in your room resting after a very hard day's work. What a strain it must be teaching mankind an ideology, which by a great many like myself is approached with a good deal of suspicion, and yet with all that amount of strain that we fools impose upon you, you are able to look the most serene person I ever met.'

The longest war ever fought – the class war

Tom Keep was president of the National Amalgamated Dockers and Stevedores Union and for more than twenty years a communist. He worked on a coal wharf in the Port of London. He noticed quite a change in his manager, who invited him to attend a MRA meeting of employers and businessmen at The Royal Empire Society in the centre of London – not a venue normally attended by London dockers! The following week, Keep spoke at a meeting with miners in the Rhondda Valley: 'I have seen employers change and workers change. This can bring to an end the longest war that has ever been fought – the class war.'

In 1959, Joe Hancock, a well known Trotskyite militant in the Port of Liverpool, was writing and selling the Trotskyite paper of that time. However these militant activities concealed an intense search for a deeper meaning to life. Through some other workers in the Port he came to know Moral Re-Armament. As he and his wife tried it out together they found a new family life. Previously at times of disagreement and tension a number of alarm clocks suffered from being hurled across the bedroom!

'The Industrial Pioneer'

Hancock and his friends decided to produce a new monthly paper, *The Waterfront Pioneer* to give everyone in the port a constructive angle on the news and the issues affecting them. It was sold at the dock gates not only in the Port of Liverpool but in London and Glasgow too. Workers then in other industries asked Hancock to broaden its coverage to include their industries and to carry international news. It became *The Industrial Pioneer*. It continued for over forty years, produced by volunteers. It went to hundreds of workers in the major industries, to their union officials and management and to Parliament. There were readers in over fifty countries.

In the Port of Bristol, the dockers had formed an unofficial strike committee after the visit of some of the London committee. Jack Carroll was chairman. Another docker, Albert McGrath's life had been radically changed through meeting MRA and going to Caux. At his invitation Carroll with two other committee members saw a play *William Wilberforce MP*, written by Alan Thornhill, the author of *The Forgotten Factor*. Carroll was fascinated to see what one dedicated man could achieve in his lifetime.

The following weekend I drove him to London for a MRA industrial meeting where he met Les Dennison, chairman of the building workers in Coventry. Dennison had been an active communist for 22 years. His story of change convinced Carroll to make an experiment himself. Next morning he got up early, made a pot of tea, poured some for himself and the dog as well! He then sat down and wrote down the thoughts that came to him, 'See employers and union officials today.' He obeyed his thought and established a working relationship with the employers and union officials in the Port of Bristol. The strike committee ceased to function.

His fellow dockers noticed the change in Carroll and to provoke him one day when he walked into the port canteen they stood and sang, *When the saints come marching in*. This did not stop him – he took news of his new revolution to ports in India and Australia.

For years the dockers of Australia were led by communists. Jim Beggs, an ordinary wharfie was fed up with all the disputes, strikes and lost hours of work. Meeting MRA through conversations with his next-door neighbour, like Jack Carroll he made the experiment of listening. He had the thought to take back the clock, which he had stolen, from a car he had been loading. The employer was astounded and his fellow wharfies nicknamed him 'Daylight saving' because 'he turned the clock back'. Jim then decided to take responsibility in the union. In the course of time he was elected president of the union for the Port of Melbourne and later National President. Exporters testified the difference his leadership made.

Historic changes in the French textile industry

Maurice Mercier, a veteran communist, was leader of the French textile workers and a leader in the French Resistance. After the war he left the communist party when he saw the Resistance degenerate into petty squabbles for personal advancement whereas he longed that the spirit of self-sacrifice of the Resistance could be maintained to rebuild France. He broke with the communist led Confédération Générale du Travail (CGT) Union and formed the free trade union, Force Ouvrière (FO). He had the vision and conviction to speak for all the French textile workers even though they were not members of his union. At Caux in 1949 he observed that 'employers of most countries transported into this atmosphere, were reconsidering their original outdated points of view and were more easily becoming conscious of their responsibilities as men and as employers.'

Mercier said this conference at Caux and a subsequent meeting with Buchman brought a new perspective: 'Class war today means one half of humanity against the other half and possessing a powerful arsenal of destruction... not one cry of hatred, not one hour of work lost, not one drop of blood shed-that is the revolution to which Moral Re-Armament calls bosses and workers.'

His concern now was to prepare the workers in the textile industry – probably nearly a million at that time – for this new approach. Throughout the north of France, in the textile towns around Lille, he organised mass meetings with MRA speakers including management and union representatives from other countries.

On February 1, 1951, textile managers and workers signed a national agreement. 600,000 workers were immediately given wage increases and guaranteed a share in the benefits of increased productivity. It was the first such agreement in France. On Mercier's initiative that year, eighty textile factory delegations made up of employers, workers and staff attended the conference at Caux.

In 1955, textile employers and unions – except the CGT – signed an agreement, which was the foundation stone of a policy of co-operation for the next twenty years. It guaranteed textile workers a retirement pension and partial unemployment benefit. It was not until 1968 that employers at national level in other industries were obliged to grant the same level of benefits as textile workers had been given voluntarily.

Robert Carmichael, president of the European Jute Employers' Federation was one of the employers who worked closely with Mercier in those years. He won the confidence of the jute growers in India and Bangladesh and succeeded in negotiating fairer prices for them.

'If capitalists can change we do not need to eliminate them'

In the early 1930's, the president of the American Federation of Labour was Samuel Gompers. When asked what was his philosophy for the trade unions he replied with one word, 'more.' Politicians often adopt the same idea when campaigning for votes in elections. Then we wonder why there is so little idealism or self-sacrifice in today's society. Now national leaders in the West are saying that military measures are not enough to meet the threat of terrorism. We need ideas, ideals and values that we live by. We need an ideology that cures the causes of hate to answer the one based on hate, which fires the terrorist. In the years of the Cold War this is what sincere committed communists found in Moral Re-Armament. They found a positive alternative to class war – 'If capitalists can change we do not need to eliminate them,' they said and added, 'Greed and selfishness are not a monopoly of employers and the rich.'

William Penn expressed the heart of this ideology that the world must find if we are to survive the impact of materialism, globalisation and terrorism, 'Men must choose to be governed by God or they condemn themselves to be ruled by tyrants.'

Speaking of economic change Buchman talked of the full dimension of change – 'economic, social, national and international change all issuing from personal change'. He also put it in these words, 'There is enough in the world for everyone's need, but not enough for everyone's greed. If everyone cares enough and everyone shares enough, then everyone will have enough.'

Frank Buchman in the Ruhr

In post-war Germany, Hans Boeckler, a Marxist socialist was head of the newly formed trade union federation. Some historians consider his part in creating the new Germany second only to Adenauer's. At Caux he met Buchman. They became friends. Boeckler made a carefully weighed statement for Buchman to use, which contains these sentences:

'If men are to be free from the old and outmoded, it can only happen as they set themselves new goals and place humanity and moral values in the forefront. When men change, the structure of society changes, and when the structure of society changes, men change. Both go together and both are necessary. The goal for which Moral Re-Armament strives to reach is the same as that for which I am fighting as a trade unionist.'

In 1950 Moral Re-Armament was asked to hold a conference by Chancellor Adenauer and a number of prominent Germans. Frank Buchman, in a speech that was broadcast to East Germany as well as the west said, 'Marxists are finding a new thinking in a day of crisis. The class struggle is being superseded. Management and labour are beginning to live the positive alternative to class war. Is change for all the one basis of unity for all? Can Marxists be changed? Can they have this new thinking? Can Marxists pave the way for a greater ideology? Why not? They have always been open to new things. They have been forerunners. They will go to prison for their belief. They will die for their belief. Why should they not be the ones to live for this superior thinking?'

Seated on the platform with Buchman were industrialists and miners' leaders who exemplified what he was saying.

* * * * *

Now follows an extract from the autobiography of Jens Wilhelmsen, a Norwegian, who was one of a number of young people from former occupied countries who dedicated years of their lives to building a new Germany.

Jens Wilhelmsen narrates:

'The January sky was as black as the coal a few thousand metres below me. It was raining buckets. I was making my way towards Königsberger Strasse 13, narrowly missing puddles the size of lakes, as the street lights were out. I had a suitcase containing most of my worldly possessions, and in my head a mixture of anxiety and expectancy at the thought of spending the coming week in the home of one of the Ruhr's veteran communists.

'The location was the mining town of Moers in 1949. I felt poorly prepared for the introduction to a well-trained Marxist, despite my recent philosophy course at Oslo University. I was told that my host had been a communist for 26 years, three years longer than my lifespan so far. He had managed to live by his convictions under Hitler's dictatorship, when non-conformists risked being sent to concentration camps and likely death. Now he had been elected Works Council Chairman for Pit No 4 of the Rheinpreussen Company, and a member of the Executive Committee of the Communist Party of North-Rhine Westphalia.

'I finally reached my destination and hit the bicycle bell mounted on the front door. The silhouette of a large shape became visible against the interior light, apparently my hostess. She seemed none too pleased to see me. I found out later on that her daughter had insisted on me staying there, as she was keen to improve her English.

'I was in Moers as part of a theatrical group of some fifty people, performing the MRA play *The Forgotten Factor*. We had been invited by Rheinpreussen, but since guest houses and bed-and-breakfast establishments largely were in ruins, the company had asked their employees to put up the performers in their private homes. This is how I came to lodge with Max and Grethe Bladeck and their daughter Isolde.

'Their simple dwelling consisted of three rooms, and the sole source of heating was the coal stove in the kitchen. The stove was Grethe's pride and joy and she kept it gleaming from constant polishing. I was given the sofa in the front parlour to sleep on. Unfortunately, the heat from the kitchen stove never penetrated into this room. The family spent most of their free time in the kitchen. This is where Max would greet me with a cup of tea on my return late at night after each performance.

'Like most Germans, he appreciated a good discussion. I tried to sow a few seeds of doubt in his Marxist garden. Why are workers not allowed to strike in East Germany, I would ask him, and how could he justify the increasing build-up of nuclear armament in the Soviet Union? Would not fighting the class war inevitably end up as a nuclear war between a communist East and a capitalist West?

You must stop preaching

'After several evenings' discussion I resigned myself to defeat; I was talking to deaf ears. If anything my questioning seemed to strengthen Max's determination to defend what he already believed. I learned a lesson about the impotence of being just anti something. One morning I had a very clear thought, "You must stop preaching to Max about all that is wrong with the cause he has given his life to. Instead be honest how difficult you find it to live true to your ideology." I gave Max two simple examples: I would strongly condemn dishonesty in politics, but I would lie to my own family when convenient; I was passionate about maintaining world peace, but found it difficult to overcome my bitterness against the Germans as a nation.

'For the first time Max did not argue back. Hesitatingly at first, he started telling me about his own doubts and difficulties, on a personal level and concerning relations within the party ranks; that evening formed the base for a long lasting friendship. Our ideological views were still poles apart, but a mutual respect and trust had begun to grow.

'The play caused an outrage. The communists accused MRA of supporting capitalism. A meeting was called at a pub called Heier. About fifty of Moers' union leaders and political activists attended. MRA was also invited to send representation. Max should lead the meeting.

'The cigarette smoke made it difficult to distinguish the features of people present, and the beer did not make the discussion any less passionate. After a couple of hours, Max stood up to conclude the meeting. "Comrades," he shouted, "If we consider capitalism the thesis and communism the anti-thesis, could MRA possibly be the synthesis?" A bomb exploding could not have shaken the gathering more.

'From that moment the Communist Party had it in for Max, but his standing among the miners was strong. His one weakness (his Achilles' heel) was over-indulgence of alcohol, and he was again the worse for wear at a party for retired miners. The next day the communist newspaper *Neue Volkszeitung* ran the following headline, "Union leader offends female colleague". The article claimed that Max had made a suggestion of a sexual nature to the woman on the homeward bus journey.

'Max was heart-broken. He immediately penned a letter to Buchman asking for all links to be severed, as he had betrayed the MRA cause. Some days later Max received a telegram with the following message: "Man-like it is to fall in sin; Fiend-like it is to dwell therein; Christ-like it is from sin to rise. The blood of Jesus Christ His Son cleanses us from all sin. I have faith in the New Max – Frank Buchman."

'Max did not have a religious faith but thanks to the

telegram he had received he decided not to give up. In 1950, he visited Sweden, Norway and Denmark together with five fellow Germans. One of them was a Christian-Democratic member of Parliament, one a director of a mining company, one a Social-Democratic government official and two were miners like Max and previous members of the Communist Party. They freely admitted to Germany's guilt and on several occasions asked forgiveness on behalf of their nation, including when they met with Norwegian Prime Minister Gerhardsen, who had survived a German concentration camp.

'Max became a builder of bridges between nations. In the years following he travelled widely in Europe, America and Asia, putting his experience and change to good use. One night on a sleeper in India he woke up abruptly to see a vision of his mother, appearing as if still alive. This experience opened the dimension of faith and eternity for him.'

By 1950, the percentage of communist representation in the works committees in the Ruhr had dropped from 72% to 25% and it kept falling. The *Neue Zürcher Zeitung* wrote in 1959, 'The Ruhr, instead of being the apple of discord in Europe, has become the growing point of international agreement... without the Ruhr, there can be no Common Market and no far reaching plan for European integration.'

* * * * *

Frits Philips and the Caux Round Table

Maarten de Pous from Holland has been closely involved with a move which stemmed from Holland. He recounts an initiative for world industry:

'Frits Philips, who was president of world-wide Philips Electronics from 1961-1971, and later chairman of the Supervisory Council, had been associated with Frank Buchman's work since 1934 through to his death. It clearly was a source of inspiration in his life. He had been actively involved in the Caux Industrial Conferences since 1974.

'Philips took great pride in the fact that he was related to Karl Marx. The mother of Karl Marx was the sister-in-law of Frits Philips's great-grandfather. Marx had worked on *Das Kapital* in the home of Frits' grandfather in Zalt-bommel, a town not far from Eindhoven. Frits Philips believed that the sense of social concern of his father and his uncle – the founders of the firm – was developed out of their discussions with Karl Marx. Philips also made a remarkable stand during World War 2 when Holland was occupied by German forces. He managed to balance keeping the factories open while keeping production to a minimum so as not to help the German war effort. It ended in his being detained in prison for some time in 1943. He was awarded the *Yad Vashem* medal by Israel in 1995 for his work in saving Jews in Holland during the war years.

'In 1985 there appeared an article in the leading news-paper of the Netherlands, *NRC-Handelsblad*, with the headline, "Japan's false smile". It was about the danger that Japanese trade practices might ruin and destroy the

European electronics industry, by selling products below the market value.

'Frits Philips, already 80 years old and holding no official position in the company, was really concerned about this development. He feared it could lead to trade wars and possibly worse. Believing something should be done, he wrote to some friends in Japan, jointly signed by Olivier Giscard d'Estaing, then vice-president of Insead, the French management school in Fontainebleau. They proposed a meeting in the summer of 1986 of a small group of senior industrial leaders from Japan, Europe and the US at Mountain House in Caux, Switzerland, where he knew they would find an atmosphere of spirit of trust and understanding, allowing honest and open discussions.

'Among the people coming from Japan were Ryuzaburo Kaku, president of Canon, Toshihiko Yamashita, former president of Matsushita Electronics and Toshiaki Ogasawara, publisher of the *Japan Times*. Other senior people came from America and different European countries, about thirty in total.

Japanese felt unfairly blamed – and changed

'The Japanese had been told about the beauty of Caux and the friendly and peaceful atmosphere, but already during the first meeting things did not go as planned. The Americans and Europeans began to accuse the Japanese of unfair trade practices. The Japanese were getting more and more annoyed. By the end of the first session the Japanese were ready to go home. A few people from the three groups agreed that during the following sessions the Japanese would have the first chance to speak. The atmosphere changed, the Europeans and Americans began to admit that there were areas where they could begin changing some of their economic policies. At the end of the two days they had decided to continue the discussions during the coming years, and search for ways of bringing about changes in policies and practices. Thus the Caux Round Table was born. The CRT began to meet once a year in Caux and in between in different other parts of the world.

'During the following years the Japanese CRT participants made some suggestions to Prime Minister Nakasone as to how Japan could enlarge its internal market, reduce the national debt and open the Japanese market to foreign products. And in 1990 they published an article entitled, *Proposals for the Renewal of Japan*, the core of which was that Japan should change from trying to catch up with the West (which it had done anyway) to participating in a global effort of wealth creation for everyone.

'American CRT-members arranged meetings with economic policy makers in the US, like David Rockefeller and Martin Feldstein. And in Brussels meetings took place with the vice-president of the European Commission, Martin Bangemann, and others. The American Minnesota Principles were expanded for global application, creating the Caux Round Table Principles for Business. The introduction to the CRT Principles says that business is uniquely placed to contribute to bettering the social and economic condition of people with business leaders putting their own house in order first.'

* * * * *

Initiatives in Indian industry since 1970

Miles Paine, who was a factory manager in India for many years, writes after revisiting India in 2007:

'Asia Plateau, the Indian centre for IofC/MRA in Panchgani, was completed in the early 1970s, when certain areas in India were experiencing a massive expansion of industry. Pune, the nearest large town to Panchgani, was one of the fastest growing.

'Yet industrial unrest was also growing. Skilled labour was in short supply and union leaders were quick to demand increased wages and improved working conditions generally. Some managements rejected negotiation and industrial conflict resulted.

'In 1973 a request arrived from the chairman of a textile firm asking if his 5,000 employees could be trained in Moral Re-Armament at the Centre. It was decided at Asia Plateau to prepare a six day course and a programme entitled, *Creative Leadership for Industry and National Development* was offered with a charge of Rs.500 per delegate (about £10), which company managements were quite prepared to pay, more than covering the running costs of the course at that time. Included in the course were subjects such as: *Motivation and leadership in industry*; *Productivity with participation and without exploitation*; *Confrontation or co-operation*; and *Sound homes, teamwork in industry, a united nation.*

'A faculty for each course was drawn from those with experience in helping people to find change and included trade union leaders, senior executives, company directors and shop floor workers, who used their own practical experience of real situations.

'Panchgani was already well known as a pleasant

holiday resort, about two hours by road from Pune. Management found no difficulty in selecting workers and managerial staff willing to participate, including some of the most difficult union members. Word soon spread in industrial circles as to the effectiveness in changing attitudes of those attending the courses. By the mid-1970s, over twenty well-known companies were listed as participating in the programme. And it was not just management and labour relationships that were transformed. One manager spoke of his surprise that in the ambience created in these seminars, shop floor workers came out with creative ideas for running of the factory, which they never expected from them.

Open honesty is contagious

'It was unusual at that time for wives to attend courses with their husbands but encouragement for such joint participation was given. The course was broadly centred around human relationships and with this in mind a certain amount of practical help at the Centre was included – washing up after meals and laying tables beforehand, for example. Many workers were not accustomed to engage in domestic help in their own homes but because of the general spirit at the Centre gladly joined in such activity and were surprised to find management doing likewise.

'Those who had come with their wives found the open honesty among those running the courses contagious and a number reported on their return that the whole atmosphere in their own homes had been transformed. And the companies benefited also. The industrial climate in Pune began to change and those wishing to establish new enterprises were keen to select Pune as preferred location.

'Over time the courses were adapted for a much wider range of participants – even the armed forces now regularly send groups of army chaplains of all denominations. At the heart of all these programmes remains the message of the need for a transforming experience in the life of each individual. One of the colleges of Pune University now regularly sends its students taking their Business Management courses.'

* * * * *

In conclusion

Today, we still live in a world where industry is not meeting the needs of all. The divisions caused by greed, hate and fear are preventing that happening. Frank Buchman has pointed the way for humanity to overcome these obstacles. The forgotten factor is that God has a plan and we can all have a part in it. God at work in the human heart is the most powerful force for change in the world today – change for all is the one basis of unity for all. 'Before a God-led unity empty hands can be filled with work, empty stomachs with food and empty hearts with ideas that really satisfy.'

Bill Jordan, then general secretary of the International Confederation of Free Trade Unions (ICFTU) representing 125 million workers in 143 countries and territories, concluded a speech in Caux by saying, 'Whatever ideology or direction the world chooses to take, it must not lose its values, its standards. Although there is a difficult road ahead, not even the colossal forces of globalisation are a match for the collective power of individuals to defend social values and justice. That power, that strength, is in the heart and hand of every person we meet. Let's use it. Let's change the world!'

16

The Economics of Unselfishness

by Pat Evans

Patrick Evans spent three years as an assistant technical officer with the Essex War Agricultural Committee. He took an agricultural degree at Cambridge University from 1945. From 1953 until he retired in 1988 he farmed in Herefordshire in partnership with his brother Edward.

DOUGLAS ADAMS, author of *The Hitch-hiker's Guide to the Galaxy*, was both a comic and creative writer. In reflecting the omnivorous artistic tastes of the second half of the twentieth century he seemed puzzled by religion. 'The fact that I think Bach was mistaken doesn't alter the fact that I think the B-minor Mass is one of the great pinnacles of human achievement. It still absolutely moves me to tears to hear it. I find the whole business of religion profoundly interesting. But it does mystify me that otherwise intelligent people take it seriously.' Yet as Albert Einstein put it – 'The presence of a superior reasoning power, revealed in the incomprehensible universe, forms my idea of God.'

So when Frank Buchman declared that 'Spiritual leadership must have a content of positive action far greater than the world now associates with that term', he was addressing a visible need. And it was particularly poignant in the years immediately before the Second World War, when so many could see war coming. Some pondered the challenges while others sought to shut them out. As someone born to a privileged life in the countryside, I had a foot in both camps. Yet it happened that in May 1938 I was off school through illness, and had the chance to attend the launching of Moral Re-Armament in East Ham Town Hall.

'We, the Re-makers of the World – is that not the thinking and willing of the ordinary man? .... Moral recovery is essentially the forerunner of economic recovery. We might find in this new spirit an answer to the problems which are paralysing economic recovery. Suppose everybody cared enough, and everybody shared enough, wouldn't everybody have enough?' – such was the vision which entered into my soul, whatever might be the pitfalls, failures or disappointments to come. It suggested that the decisions we make as individuals play an essential part in the spiritual evolution of humanity, and the commitment we make will determine the inner strength and outreach of our lives on earth.

Farming crucial to future world development

A year earlier, my form master at school had written in his report – 'There still seems to be a lack of ambition. Is he to be a farmer?' Although probably the most perceptive of those who taught me, he had still not understood the sense of vocation which was stirring. Nor had he evidently imagined that farming might be so crucial in the war and to future world development. He could certainly be forgiven for that, because its significance is only just beginning to be recognised to-day, as we grapple with questions of climate change, biodiversity and the overall life of our planet.

The programme of MRA initiated by Frank Buchman was a huge liberation to the spirit. Being of an introspective nature, I was often more concerned with the struggle to change myself than focusing on developing a vision of God's purposes in the world. It was a big shift to move from rules of conduct to a daily time of quiet in which to write down the promptings of the spirit. It meant accepting a responsibility I had never sought, and seeking practical expression for a passion to 'remake the world'. That was the phrase of the day and whatever words are used, it still represents the aspirations of those who want to change the course of history whether in politics, economics or science. Human imagination will always leap ahead of history, but though a long life may measure our limitations, it doesn't dim the conviction that increased potential can still match the problems.

In the post-war world, coal and steel were still the drivers of economic development. They became through Jean Monnet the practical foundation for Franco-German reconciliation. Both Konrad Adenauer and Robert Schuman paid tribute to Moral Re-Armament as the catalyst in the process. But it was also in the time before money entirely took over from people at the heart of economic thinking, and Frank Buchman always understood that men with a new motivation had to pave the way for new structures. He never put the cart before the horse, and always expected personal change to lead people to take on situations far beyond their expectation.

The story of George Light, a leader of the unemployed, illustrates this. I remember him as a burly but gentle man, but if it had not been for Buchman he would never have entered our home. Garth Lean, Buchman's biographer, records how George came to an Oxford gathering in 1933, full of bitterness at his own unemployment and that of the men he represented. At the end of a conversation together, Buchman asked him how he was placed for getting home. Buchman then turned out his pockets and gave him the £9 he found, saying 'That's half of all the money I have. So we each have the same amount. That makes us both socialists now.'

When Christianity is put into practice

George Light wrote later – 'This was the second talk I ever had with Frank. He did not know me. I might have been a twister or anything. I went home and told my wife and family. That £9 was very useful, but it was not a fortune. Yet my family was so overjoyed at anyone taking such an interest in us that they just wept. Frank never postponed an act of unselfishness on his own part, because a far greater one was needed on the part of society. What he did and what he fought for, had in it elements of true revolutionary action.'

The very next year (1934) George joined Buchman's party on a journey through Canada. They arrived in Vancouver to find a shipping strike paralysing the Pacific Coast ports. Complete deadlock had been reached, but mainly through the intervention of Light and Walter Horne, a Californian shipbuilder, a fair settlement was reached. 'It took them seventy-two hours of continuous effort moving between the men, who had longstanding and justified grievances, the strike committee, union leaders and employers.' The *Ottawa Evening Citizen* commented: 'When Christianity is put into practice, it is spiritual dynamite. There is no greater force for enduring reform known to mankind.'

Many of Frank Buchman's insights have had an enduring quality in the sense that they were a challenge to action and had universal appeal. Bill Wake, a Canadian farmer, describes his first meeting with Buchman in Bill's home town of Saskatoon. 'It was a time when the drought and wind were at their worst, and the skies were filled with the drifting soil. 'Is this,' asked Buchman, 'one of the dust storms I've read about?' 'Yes,' I replied, 'it comes from drifting farmlands.' He walked on a few steps further, and said quietly, 'It is bad, very bad,' then added, 'But our real problem is moral drift.' Bill felt a challenge to his farming world in that moment, which led him ten years later at the age of 46 to work full time with the force of people who, inspired by Buchman, set out to tackle the needs of the post-war world. It took him into situations he had never dreamed of in a variety of countries, but he also left his mark among the farmers of North America and New Zealand.

It was in New Zealand that Bill Wake was invited to the farm of Alpheus Hayes. Alpheus had been impressed by a performance of the play *The Forgotten Factor*, and as a result had been invited to give a report on MRA to his church's annual meeting. But he felt the need to know much more about it, so he invited Bill to visit. Bill was impressed with the farm, but it was immediately clear that the urgent need was the breakdown of Alpheus' marriage with his wife Myrtle. Bill became the catalyst for a new relationship which grew out of honesty and the rebirth of love.

Later Bill was able to greet both the Hayes in the United States, where the new life they had found together broadened out into reaching many others including US farm leaders. At one point Frank Buchman had the conviction that they should be present at the signing of the Japanese Peace Treaty in San Francisco (1951). Despite being only two days before the event, this was duly achieved and the Hayes were the only New Zealanders present, apart from officials.

The most secure, satisfying and stimulating advice

A generation later Alpheus' son Garfield, at the Caux Conference in Switzerland in 2005, told how the farm was progressing on the same foundations. 'I was on the National Council of the New Zealand Farmers Federation when the Labour government decided to drastically change the economy. A 10% goods and services tax was introduced. The New Zealand dollar was floated, the reduction of tariffs was started, and overnight all farm subsidies were terminated. We were receiving 20% of our income from the New Zealand taxpayer. Our farmers marched in the streets, but as one of their leaders I knew in my heart that New Zealand had no alternative. We exported 90% of our agricultural production and our trading partners had threatened us to either remove subsidies or face tariffs.

'The next years were difficult. Some farmers, big and small, lost their farms. Some committed suicide. I worked so hard my hips gave out. We survived by selling a city property we had been led to purchase when we were receiving subsidies. But the fact was we were over-producing a product which was hard to sell.

'During the past twenty years there has been an enormous turnaround. New Zealand's sheep population has fallen from 70 to 40 million. Farmers have become very innovative and, where possible, have successfully diversified into producing trees, venison or dairying. Sheep farmers and our meat processing industry have substantially improved efficiency and quality. We now cannot meet demand, and product prices are the best they have been. During this time I could purchase farm advice from specialists, but by far the most secure, satisfying and stimulating advice came from my early morning times of silent reflection. If God could steer us through such changes, I am convinced that he can supply the answer to the problems and challenges of world agriculture, if we choose to listen to him.

'For instance, for twenty years we baled our wool in jute packs instead of synthetic packs to give trade to the jute growers of Bangladesh. To keep things transparent all our farm sales go through the company books. Historically there has been division between farmers and trade union leaders in our meat processing industry. My wife Helen and I have met these leaders, had them to stay in our home and arranged meetings with local farmers.

'Alcoholism is a big problem among our sheep shearers. Although contravening custom we ran an alcohol-free wool shed. But with Helen giving excellent meals, the shearers were always keen to return. In a global world where the need for change and innovation is always constant, there has definitely been a good life for New Zealand agriculture after the removal of subsidies.'

Trusted for the moral battle against corruption

The post-war years were a time when many committed their lives to make a difference, and fifty or sixty years later their impact can be appreciated, and not only in their own countries or on the farms where their experience was honed. Roly Kingwill, in the dry Karoo of South Africa, tackled soil erosion, education and the provision of training and jobs for unskilled workers. It opened his eyes to a new vision for all the races in Africa. Reducing the number of sheep on his land by one third meant tightening his belt, but it paid in the long run.*

In the struggle for an independent Kenya, Alan Knight, a white farmer, apologised for his attitude of white superiority to hard core Mau Mau prisoners in Athi River Camp, of which he was the commandant. He was trusted to his dying day for the moral battle he sustained against corruption and all that threatened to derail the new Kenya.

Stanley Barnes, a dairy expert trained in Aberystwyth, established the first pasteurisation scheme for the goats' milk in Malta. After service there with the RAF, he worked for many years in Australia for Paul's Ice Cream and Milk, and then the Australian Dairy Board in Asia. Even in retirement after a heart attack, he wrote the book, *200 Million Hungry Children*† and worked single-mindedly for the proper nutrition of children world-wide through the better functioning of the dairy industry and its milk producers He took a special interest in the National Dairy Board of India, and was a friend of Dr V Kurien who inspired and led its progress.

Meanwhile, in the post-war years when a host of new policies were being sought, Buchman and his party were guests at a Sri Lankan government rice transplanting demonstration in 1952. It was an official attempt to re-

---

*see video: *The Promise of the Veld*, obtainable from FLT Films, 24 Greencoat Place, London SW1P 1RD

† published by Grosvenor Books

popularise rice growing after excessive emphasis on export crops had reduced the country to importing rice. At that occasion he declared, 'Empty hands will be filled with work, empty stomachs with food, and empty hearts with an idea which really satisfies.' It is the outline of a comprehensive programme which puts people's needs first, and assumes everyone will have a part in doing what needs to be done to make things work properly.

Fifty years on it could be said that the truth is beginning to dawn that the food market needs regulation. Growing inequality reflects a lack of care, so it is not just regulation but a fresh motivation which is required. Only a change of culture can meet the varied needs of society. Life is meant to be creative for everyone, and agriculture could be the sector which illustrates this on a global scale.

Lifeblood for the European Union

Frank Buchman foresaw the vacuum which would be left by the collapse of Communism. In the event, it came so suddenly that nobody was prepared. Yet my friend Stanislaw Choma in Poland was one of those whose branch of Rural Solidarity did not collapse with the sudden removal of opposition. In many cases former Communist officials still had their hands on the levers of power, and were looking to profit from the new situation. Stanislaw himself had suffered from unprovoked aggression from the police, which landed him in hospital. But, lying in a hospital bed, he had time to reflect and was freed from the bitterness that could have taken hold and colour his subsequent attitude. At a time when the membership of Rural Solidarity had fallen dramatically, Stanislaw's local branch boasted 5,000 members.

This can be mainly ascribed to the care and service he

provided both officially and unofficially. From a strong family base he offered contract services with his machinery at a reasonable price, which helped him keep in touch with local families.

One friend who had fallen on hard times turned to drink, and very soon his marriage was breaking up. Stanislaw, who like many of his countrymen is a devout Catholic, had the thought to visit him and see if he could help. When he knocked on the door, husband and wife were locked in a fierce shouting match and didn't hear him. Standing there, he felt he had come too late and, getting cold feet, was tempted to turn away. But he persisted and crossed the threshold to find himself warmly welcomed by both antagonists.

To cut a long story short, his friend found freedom from alcohol, his marriage was remade, and, with a loan from Stanislaw, he was able to get a viable business going. Such care beyond the call of duty is the lifeblood of village communities. In all essentials it could also be the lifeblood of the European Union, if we focused on such values, and committed ourselves to making it people-friendly.

More recently Stanislaw has met the Ukrainian farmer, Mikhail Marinichenko, usually known as Misha, and they have found much common ground. Both Poland and Ukraine have had a chequered history, with wars moving frontiers or even obliterating them altogether. In such circumstances people become toughened to blows they cannot effectively resist, and resourceful in making the best of a bad job.

The settlement after the Second World War saw Stanislaw moved from eastern Poland (which became part of Ukraine) to Silesia in the west, which Germany had ceded to Poland. Misha meanwhile grew up as a Soviet citizen and a loyal young communist. He rose to responsibility on a collective farm in the Dnepropetrovsk region, and has been one of the few to lead a successful transformation to a private company. Part of the land has gone to independent farmers, whose rugged character has brought them individual success. But Misha has succeeded in welding 18 partners into a profitable enterprise farming some 2,500 hectares, which includes a number of smallholders who trust him to deal fairly with their land.

Misha has always been a man of the people, and has ignored the perks he might have acquired as a leader. But it has not been easy to see the ideals of his youth crumble, though he did not shrink from showing us the vandalised farm buildings in the neighbourhood, and the terrible state into which some livestock enterprises had descended. Yet he has stuck to the work of transformation, and has faith in Ukraine's future. I was present for the opening of the new village church, which replaced that destroyed by Stalin in the Thirties. His effort in support of it was evidently inspired by his mother, and a memory of values which have stood the test of time.

So the historic paths of Poland and Ukraine meet again in a new chapter symbolised by these two farmers, both struggling with large areas of land and slender resources. The dialogue which they have begun is growing across their nations. So the fact that they trust each other will enable a new spirit to shape the next developments.

The electronics of the spirit

Frank Buchman spoke of 'the electronics of the spirit' as a way in which technology could serve the development of humanity. As he put it, 'Electronics is a new science. Spirit has been known for a long time. It's an old science. But linked with electronics, it hitches the world to a new dimension of life and thought.' Frank Buchman, himself, was always reaching out for what each individual could do with a new aim and a readiness to take responsibility. He didn't think in terms of blueprints for a new society, but of the millions of ordinary people whose individual decisions would shape a new direction. He was always questing in his spirit, and when questioned about his own life, would say 'I have been wonderfully led.'

Neither military nor economic power can shape the world most of us want to see. Power may buy time, but it is an idea which must win the world - an idea which can grow and to which all can contribute. That is the soil for consensus. From the earliest days of Moral Re-Armament, Buchman believed that ordinary people could take responsibility not only for families but for nations. In fact it was the integrity and creativity of family life which would bring a new dimension to democracy. 'A world philosophy will be brought to power through the cumulative effort of millions of people beginning the experience of listening to God. True it may be only an initial experience. Enlistment does not immediately make the trained soldier, but we can all begin.'

Something of where this has led me personally I have tried to express in my book *A Hand to the Plough* as a vision for the 21st century. Buchman's Moral Re-Armament is still spreading into the far corners of the world under the name of Initiatives of Change. Such initiatives and programmes may multiply and reflect a variety of cultures, but the original concept remains at the core of them. The whole adds up to a growing unity of the spirit.

The Farmers Dialogue

The international Farmers Dialogue is one of a number of programmes seeking to weave the positive influences at work into a coherent pattern. The dialogues of a farmers' world network may not yet have progressed very far, but they are already clarifying the need to keep family farming at the heart of the engine power, even if the design of the new model is changing. Specialist development makes it more important to ensure that it addresses the fulfilment of human nature. The adventure lies in the vision of an overarching purpose shaping millions of personal dreams. It is in one sense the difference between a partnership and a collective. The whole is only possible through popular participation, and will never be static. It will always be shaped by those who commit their lives.

It is interesting that one of the first labels attached to Buchman's work was coined by a journalist, Harold Begbie, who dubbed it a 'First Century Christian Fellowship'. This was accurate in the sense that it was founded on the following of Christ himself, before added doctrine and the human failings of succeeding centuries. Christ came with a message for the world, and was making a universal appeal. In today's climate of constant change, we need a spiritual anchor more than anything else, and we may be destined to find a unity of spirit against all the odds. It will not be attributable to a single source, but there can be no doubt that it will be seen unmistakably as a turning point in the modern world.

Such a change of culture involves something which can turn the huge growth in knowledge into a blessing rather than a threat: the fruits of peace rather than war, of change rather than of conflict. It needs to be a banner borne by mankind rather than any kind of elite. That may be the task which democracy is meant to shoulder. It is not a perfect mechanism for enforcing our will which is required, but a clear reflection of overwhelming public opinion.

Cultivate the inner voice rather than human power

That perhaps is the secret of a change which begins in people: so many diverse characters, not only finding a new purpose in life, but also the daily application to develop it. Money plays an important part in everyone's life, and the way we handle it may be more significant than researching new economic laws. Some writers on the 'post-capitalist economy' talk of the 'knowledge economy' defining the future. Peter Drucker of the United States says in his book *Post Capitalist Society* that we need to understand knowledge as an economic resource: 'We have not had enough experience to formulate a theory and test it. We need an economic theory which puts knowledge at the centre of the wealth-making process.' He foresees that this will be quite different from any existing view of economics. But it is also quite possible that the growth of unselfishness will create something even more unrecognisable in today's terms.

Economics is increasingly dominant among those forces which shape our present. It is not a science, but it is bound up with the development of human society. Hopefully public opinion is moving to support a culture of caring rather than the celebrating of successful tycoons. So it is significant to find that Bill Gates intends to lessen his money-making role in favour of finding the most effective ways to spend it. He is a fresh and formidable recruit to an honourable tradition, which expresses the need to give disenfranchised people opportunities rather than simply encourage economic growth wherever it may be. In a sense it is seeking a strategy to put right some of our most glaring failures.

Yet even spending money to produce a desired result can raise complex issues, which depend on the vagaries of human nature. It seems more likely that in the long run a complete change of culture is needed. Only such a change could produce the economics of unselfishness. But the growing obligation to meet the challenge of climate change points in that direction. It will increase the awareness that the most effective steps may be in the evolution of the human spirit, and this is something which is not sure to command. We live in an age of transformation when the exact shape of the future is uncertain and eludes definition. But for all who seek it, there is evidence that a clear road ahead will come from those who cultivate the inner voice rather than human power.

17

The Media – Heralds of Hope

by Bill Porter

Following six years of Army service in World War 2 in North Africa, Italy, Austria and India, William Porter took up journalism as a career. As a reporter, press officer and foreign correspondent he travelled widely in Europe, Asia, Australia, North America and South Africa. On returning to London he became the chief executive of the British publishing division of the Wolters Kluwer multinational group, vice-chairman of Publishers Databases Ltd, chairman of the Law Panel of the British Publishers Association and a national committee member of the Periodical Publishers Association. Shortly before retirement he became the founder president of the International Communications Forum, whose objective is to give to the media a positive and trusted role in society. His autobiography, Do something about it! was published in 2006.

THERE are press and radio mentions and quotations at least 36 times in Frank Buchman's published speeches before World War 2. He clearly understood the importance of mass-media communication and that it could be a positive force in the life of humanity. He also realised that it had a darker side and that light would come from enlightened media practitioners.

These he began to enlist and we read of names like Arthur Baker, leader of the British Parliamentary Press Gallery; Fredrik Ramm, editor of Norway's national daily; Jean Martin, editor of *Le Journal de Genève*; and, in the forties, Peter Howard, one of Britain's outstanding journalists of the time, who later took over the mantle of Buchman's leadership following his death in 1961. Sadly, Howard himself died in 1965 having contributed many articles, several books and a number of plays to promote the ideas of Moral Re-Armament, as the movement was then called.

In the following period of the seventies and eighties decades, Garth Lean, writer, and Alan Thornhill, playwright, continued to take Buchman's challenge that we, the journalists, should be 'heralds of a new world order'. That key thought merits much attention. I found it first used in a speech made by Buchman at a luncheon given by Edouard Benes, president of the Assembly of the League of Nations, at Geneva in 1935. In my Chambers Dictionary the word 'herald' is defined as 'a person who announces important news' and 'someone or something that is a sign of what is to come'. Now to me it also means the presentation of totally accurate information that will help and inspire the people who receive it to build a world of peace and justice, where their physical and spiritual needs will be fully met. It means that they will choose the right persons to lead them in community and political life; live a personal life based on the highest values, and be responsible and contributory citizens. They, the heralds, will also be exposers of evil, corruption and incompetence, and warn us of violent, unfair and dead-end courses of action. So a simple phrase, 'heralds of a new world order' becomes a challenge for the highest standards in our professional lives, as communicators to the millions on our Earth.

In 1955 Frank Buchman made a speech of remarkable foresight and prescience in a world broadcast from America entitled 'The Electronics of the Spirit'.

> *'Now electronics is a new science. Spirit has been known for a long time. It's an old science. But linked with electronics it hitches the world to a new dimension of life and thought. We can scarcely grasp what the Electronics of the Spirit means. Think of the veritable instantaneous reaction whereby a thought can travel across America in less than one-fiftieth of a second. It works with an Infinite Mind. It circles the globe instantly. It taps resources hitherto unexplored and forces hitherto unknown. Take the whole question of God's Mind and my mind. The thought that slips in any time of the day or night can be the thought of the Author of mind. We are dealing here with facts that no one can measure. These truths are readily perceived and speedily acceptable to the far-flung Moslem world, which can be a girder of unity for all civilisation.'*

In the 1980s my company and our competitors were spending millions in developing electronic publishing and databases that were to widen out into the Internet, whereby everyone in the world could communicate with everyone else and all of the information and knowledge in the world could be made available to us all. In the early days it was a hard sell when even lawyers, doctors and businesses had no computers. At this beginning of the 21st century their possession is widespread and to the utmost corners of the globe.

A hard interview with myself

Here I must introduce my personal contact with Frank Buchman and its eventual influence on my life as a media professional. As a demobilised young officer after six years of war service during the Second World War, I was preparing to complete a university career and to join the *Birmingham Post* as a reporter. Due to the influence of some fellow soldiers whom I had met during my time with the Eighth Army in Italy and the Eighth Indian Infantry Division in Asia, I was persuaded to devote my journalistic ambitions to becoming a press officer with Moral Re-Armament (MRA), as it was then known, by editing their Information Service and writing up their activities in the British coalfields and post-war France.

I was also affiliated to the Press Corps at the United Nations in Geneva. In that latter capacity, along with a colleague, David Hind, later to be a director of a leading printing company, we persuaded many journalists and diplomats taking part in UN Conferences, to travel up to Caux-sur-Montreux, at the other end of Lake Geneva, to attend the MRA Conferences at Mountain House under the chairmanship of Dr Frank Buchman. As a consequence I came to meet him and earned from him the compliment of being 'ubiquitous' – a word which sent me to consult the Oxford Dictionary.

Eventually my personal ambitions and quest for fortune led me to pursue my own path and to become a successful publisher and a leader in media associations.

In 1989 sheer chance led me to visit Caux again and, at the same time, to read in the *Financial Times* that 'the communications industry in all its forms including the mass media had become the largest industry in the world.' In the ambiance of Caux, which was a vital part of the legacy of Buchman, I then asked myself the question, 'If we are the largest industry, are we the most responsible?' The answer had to be NO and this led me to some introspection, being the chief executive of the British publishing activities of a multi-national, as to my personal acceptance of responsibility.

I had what might be described as a hard interview with myself. I realised that my principal motivations were to make money and to become important for myself and my companies. I am not saying that these are entirely bad motives, but they lacked that of taking responsibility for the effect of our products on those who read, listened to and watched them. I realised that if we did something that had a good social effect I was happy to take the praise. But if we had a bad effect, I washed my hands of it saying that it became a matter for politicians, religious leaders and sociologists, but not for me. So freedom of information becomes freedom from its consequences, particularly when they are bad! I decided that we in the media had to stand up and be counted for our impact.

When I told my wife, a Yugoslav heroine of Tito's wartime resistance – three years in a German concentration camp, lawyer and linguist – of my change of thinking, she listened carefully and looked me in the eyes and said, 'If you're thinking that way, why don't you do something about it?' That was a second major trigger for me and I decided to talk to some of my media peers. Four of them responded and shared my conviction that the media had been dragging people down instead of lifting them up, and that we could become a positive force in society. We decided to try to build a world-wide network of men and women in the media who believed in moral values, applied them in their own lives, and so naturally transmitted them to their audiences.

ICF has put the issue of the media on the world's agenda

Our first conference was at Caux, the scene of Frank Buchman's work for reconciliation between France and Germany and between all sides in industry, an appropriate venue to launch a positive force. This was 1991 and was followed during the next seventeen years by 26 conferences across the world from Russia to the USA, from Australia to Canada, from Poland to South Africa, from France to Jamaica; and many journeys to meet and inform our media colleagues at all levels. We now have some 3,000 professionals on our mailing lists. A recent president of the World Association of Newspapers said that 'the ICF has put the issue of the effect of the media on society on the world's agenda'. It is surely fair to ascribe this global outreach into the press, radio, television and website providers to the legacy of Buchman and his vision that we should be heralds of a new world order.

In addition to the journalists and writers mentioned earlier, others who were certainly influenced by Buchman or his close colleagues, were John Farquharson, deputy editor of Australia's *Canberra Times*; Graham Turner, one of Britain's highest paid investigative journalists; Sanjoy Hazarika, for many years correspondent of the *New York Times* in India; Rajmohan Gandhi, the Mahatma's grandson, who was trained as a journalist with Edinburgh's *The Scotsman*, and was later editor of the Madras edition of the *Indian Express*; Geoffrey Lean, dean of British environmental correspondents; Mary Lean, author and editor of *For A Change* magazine; and

Mike Smith, contributor to many British and overseas newspapers. In the Arts world one could count Sven Stolpe, the Swedish author; Victor Sparre, Norwegian artist and friend of the Russian dissidents; Lennart Segerstråle, the Finnish painter; Heaton Cooper, the British Lakelands artist and Henry Cass, the London West End theatre producer.

Edouard Rosental, a foreign correspondent of Soviet Russia's *Novosti* press agency, who had written their ideological attack on Moral Re-Armament following a visit to the Caux Centre, responded to his own attack by writing a strong defence of MRA's ideas.

Robert Webb, a lifetime working journalist and, currently chairman of the Washington Chapter of the US Society of Professional Journalists, wrote, 'As a Southern journalist I had been a stout defender of racial segregation in my editorials and columns, but, as I began to change through my contact with MRA, I wrote to heal rather than to hurt, to unite rather than to divide, to write not to stimulate or exploit conflict but to avert or ease it. I also tried to project a vision of white and black working together for the good of their community, state and nation. I began to reach out to African-Americans in a different way, forging new friendships, and to people of all races, colours and creeds.'

In today's world the public is longing for media voices who will lift them up instead of dragging them down, for role models who will help them to become remakers of society instead of drug-addicted morons. It was a central part of Buchman's vision that journalists, writers, film producers, musicians and artists could play a major part in bringing that about.

Many scurrilous attacks

There is often a negative side to a legacy and, in the case of Frank Buchman some determined efforts were made to give it one by some sources in the media, particularly in Great Britain and Scandinavia. Tom Driberg through his regular column in the *Daily Express* and other channels was at the heart of many scurrilous attacks on Buchman and the work of Moral Re-Armament, particularly during the Second World War and the years after it.

I quote from Chapman Pincher's book, *Traitors*: 'The apparently devout Anglo-Catholicism of Tom Driberg is as mysterious as much else about him. He was a member of the Central Board of Finance of the Church of England. Yet he seemed to be without scruple of any kind, and betrayed anything and anybody if it suited him. Possibly he used his religion as part of his cover; as he used his Labour politics. He certainly used it to mount a sustained attack on a major target of the KGB – the Moral Re-Armament movement – claiming that it was pro-German (i.e. pro-Hitler) which was untrue. MRA, which embraces all religions, seeks to promote moral values in all societies. When the MRA founder, Dr Frank Buchman died and was buried in Allentown, Pennsylvania, many world figures attended the funeral and signed their names in the church book. A week later Driberg appeared and tore out the relevant pages.'

Driberg's views were supported by the British writer, A P Herbert, who was also an MP, and by some journalists in the Scandinavian countries who appeared to be stung by the moral challenge of MRA.

These and other attacks added up to a serious hostile prejudice on the part of mainly London writers and publishers which was still in evidence in the sixties and seventies, when I can recall being told to keep quiet on my sympathies for the subject if I wished to keep my job and make progress with my career.

However, at the beginning of the 21st century it can be said that this negativity is now a non-legacy, as most journalists of the day are either uninformed about MRA (Initiatives of Change) or have an open-minded attitude towards it. In fact the time is due for it to become a subject of widespread interest and a rallying challenge for a fearful and distressed world.

Inspire and enlighten

Journalists in the main do not like to be labelled with an affiliation to any particular activity of an evangelical nature whether religious or secular. This is not to say that they escape certain mindsets of a negative or revelatory nature. As a consequence our media give the impression that they are mainly interested in things going wrong, in problem situations, in the foibles of pseudo-celebrities and the multitude of dangers to our health and well-being. The alternative to this bad news syndrome seems to be to stop reading, listening, viewing and looking up the Internet, hardly a recipe for an effective and flourishing democracy. The International Communications Forum now led by Bernard Margueritte, a leading journalist, along with other initiatives like *Reporters D'espoir* in France, the Committee for Concerned Journalism in the USA, the *Sorry* movement in Australia and other activities, are working to end this negative hold on the minds of our media professionals and give them a sense of ethical and social purpose. One result is that in recent years many of our leading journalists and editors and producers have become vastly more self-critical and more open to receive criticism than during most of my working lifetime of the last century. This is an indication of better days to come and I believe that the influence which the life and philosophy of Frank Buchman had on many of my and later generations in this direction is indicative of his legacy to the world of today.

I have written of Peter Howard, certainly one of the great journalists of the 20th century, and one who paid with the sinews and brain cells of his life to help build a fair and just world. He was only 54 years old when he died of a sudden illness and I have lived 33 years more than that. He was a short-lived part of the legacy of Buchman, and his wife Doë, who died recently, told me that she felt that the ICF had taken over the torch which he carried to inspire and enlighten the people of the creative word whom he loved and served. I know myself too well to believe that I have come anywhere near that aspiration, but I will keep trying and hope that I will be doing it with you.

18

Youth Looks Back – and Forward

Confidence in a strength beyond my own

by Rob Lancaster

Rob Lancaster graduated from the Australian National University with a BA (International Relations/French) and a LLB (Hons). His passions are for cricket, Australian rules football, and for debating – formally as well as with friends. His hobbies are drinking coffee with friends, playing the piano (not very well!) and watching BBC dramas.

ACADEMIA has for centuries grappled with theories of political, moral, economic and legal philosophy in an attempt to rationalise the world around us. As a student of law and international relations, I am regularly reminded of the disconnect between the normative and the empirical, the utopian and the realist, the way we would like the world to be and the way the world is. Many hefty tomes have developed myriad explanations of today's global environment and it would be impossible in such a short space properly to address even one of these issues, without over-simplifying or misrepresenting in an unhelpful way. Suffice it to say, however, that whatever else may be the case, we live in a world of division and yet we also live in a world of harmony. What IofC has endeavoured to do since its inception as Moral Re-Armament is to encourage individuals at all levels to be guided by principles that overcome the former and foster the latter – which, for me, boils down to being guided by God.

This idea is far from popular. In 1887, Nietzsche declared the death of God. Since the Enlightenment, any attempt to incorporate the divine into an outlook on the world has met with fierce intellectual resistance. And yet so often experience seems to indicate that this is exactly what the world needs – not a wholesale rejection of God, but a renewed commitment from all people, not only Christians, to live out their faith fully. Conflict and insecurity are not an unalterable inevitability, but rather the result of decisions made by the world's actors. The work of Moral Re-Armament after the Second World War demonstrated the need for individuals of moral conviction at all levels – everyone, from the likes of Robert Schuman and Konrad Adenauer to those such as Irène Laure, had a role to play in laying the foundations for a peaceful Europe. Today, the European Union stands as a testament to the possibility of human cooperation.

The work of Initiatives of Change is as relevant today as it ever has been and I hope it will continue with the boldness to respond to the need for moral leadership. That leadership, if is it to be sustainable, needs to be grounded in integrity, which I believe can only be attained through a strength beyond ourselves. At its origin, this movement was committed at its heart to connecting people with a higher authority and realising the potential that comes from that encounter. How can we continue to challenge people to explore this possibility, not with indifference or insensitivity to the way in which that challenge is received, but with an inner conviction that changing the world is a task beyond our own means? I hope this challenge can remain at the core of IofC. It is a challenge that is neither exclusive nor inclusive *per se*, but rather a question of having something at the core worth including people in.

For us to engender a sense of unity in the world around us, we need equally to be fostering a unity of purpose within the IofC network and, perhaps most importantly, we need individually to be attentive to the divisions in our own lives that can so often undermine our capacity to be effective agents of God's work in the world. What I often find most difficult is not the articulation of my grand visions, but the more immediate concerns of the here and now – how to respond to the daily needs of those around me, and to do so from a position of integrity. In this regard, I hope the future of IofC will continue to give as much emphasis as possible to accompanying people in their personal journeys. For whilst the training programmes and international conferences provide an invaluable foundation, the ongoing personal touch is their indispensable concomitant.

We are all raised in one cultural tradition or another, and in my case it was a Christian tradition. But there comes a point where we have to question the underlying assumptions of our childhood and determine whether our beliefs are grounded in an enduring truth, or simply assertions of those around us that we have accepted as fact. For many years, despite being an avid thinker (too much so, according to many of my friends), there were still a number of my beliefs that I had not genuinely questioned. It was only a few years ago that I clearly perceived the two roads diverging, one which would rely on my own wit, the other which would involve searching for and trusting in God's plan, and it was at this point I had to decide where I actually stood on the most fundamental questions. Choosing to pursue the second path has not meant an abandonment of my searching and critical disposition, but rather built my confidence in the reliability of a strength beyond my own. And whilst I regularly deviate from the path, the more faith I place in God's guidance, the more irresistible the life entirely guided by God becomes.

* * * * * * *

A Perspective on Frank Buchman
by Chris James

HAVING never met the man, I have been curious and surprised at how one individual can have so much impact on the world, including personally on me. This is my perspective on how he did it through my own experiences with what I know now as Initiatives of Change.

Growing up in a Christian family, I often struggled to understand the abstractions of religion and found it difficult to relate to it. It was in 2003 that John Bond asked me if I would like to travel to the Initiatives of Change Centre at Armagh in Melbourne to attend a Life Matters course. Going through ten days of community and personal development, I came to realise that being a Christian is not so much about what I do but about who I 'be' in every moment, in every day.

It was at this course that I first met a Muslim and was surprised that he was just like me, yet much more dedicated to his prayer than I ever was. For the first time I saw that it is more enjoyable to celebrate our differences than it is to segregate ourselves using labels such as old, young, black, white, fat, thin, Christian, Muslim. Although this seed of love for others began to grow, I still did not want to compromise my reckless fun life in any way, so became a hypocrite.

For instance, while I was speaking on the phone and emailing to my new-found international friends about building peace by being honest and starting with yourself, I still told a lot of lies in many areas of my life – about being sick to get out of work, the size of the waves to look cool, and even that I am working hard to look busy to my parents. It wasn't until a year later when I was invited to attend an Australian-Pacific Youth Conference in Cambodia that I saw the impact of *change yourself and the world changes*. This was demonstrated when at the beginning of the conference the Cambodians said, 'We have tension towards the Vietnamese at this conference,' and by the end they realised that they are just the same as other young people and don't need to carry the hate from their ancestors. I was excited by this and decided to make it my life-long goal to reach out and open closed hearts.

The journey *beyond* for me

After I completed university in 2005 I attended the Action for Life Journey which represented the journey *Beyond* for me. *Beyond* everything I could have ever imagined, *beyond* my understanding of religions, *beyond* my knowledge of the world, *beyond* my own sense of self, just *beyond* the paradox of life. Through all the pain and suffering I saw and felt in the people I met, I always saw a light of hope that they held onto. I realised that our purpose as humans was to struggle in this space of the globe to grow in the spirit.

Frank Buchman spoke of it as 'Living for the eternal'. It was the sunrise over the mountains of Panchgani, in India, that gave me a sight of the eternity – which is another word for now. To truly live in the now was Frank Buchman's greatest secret. He saw people as being part of God, no matter whom they were, and treated them like that in every moment he had with them.

After tracing his steps to Caux in 2006 I then proceeded to work with Howard Grace, Roshan Gul and Vlad Oleatovski in England with a schools programme which we wrote called 'Beyond Satisfaction'. This was an attempt to express Buchman's message of 'The choices we take directly influence how satisfied/fulfilled we become'. On that journey into over fifty schools I confronted the need for these values in the western world, and how rare they really were. After every presentation a few students came up and expressed how much the presentation meant to them and asked how they could be more involved and supported by us. I was sad that we had no follow up. It was here that I perceived that follow up is Initiatives of Change's greatest need if it wants to survive.

On my travels to Ukraine, Poland, Norway, Scotland, Taiwan, China and Hong Kong I learned about Initiatives of Change teams around the world. Were they becoming less motivated, and were less people involved than ever before? The constant struggle is how to clearly express the message of forgiveness and inner-listening. Frank Buchman had a clear vision and found a clear expression for it. A good part of what has deeply moved me has been the community development through the Life Matters Programme and the Action for Life training courses. If we run more programmes like these, then more people will be involved.

Throughout the past four years I have grappled with the question of *What is Initiatives of Change?* I have been through many stages in telling different people different concepts of what it is. To my Christian friends I have often said it is a Christian organisation, and to my non-Christian performing friends I have said it is a theatre development organisation, and to my normal friends I have said it is a global peace-building organisation. But if I was to be really honest with myself and others, I would have to say it is a global family that supports people to listen to their deeper voice – whatever they may call it – and act upon it to create a better world.

Currently I work full time with Initiatives of Change as a creative programmes co-coordinator in Armagh, Melbourne, Australia. I feel that I have received so much inner-peace and freedom from what I have learned, not so much from the organisation of Initiatives of Change, but through the people who carry the original spiritual energy of daily living for others.

One of the greatest space creators known to man

What I love about this organisation that Frank experienced, and will always remain unique about it, is the focus of committing to people in such a way that you 'stand up for their spirits', to *inspire* them (to breathe life into another) to be better than they know themselves to be. It is about seeing people's potential and giving them the space to express it. Frank was one of the greatest space creators known to man. He did not have all the skills and abilities to lead, but he knew how to touch people in such a way that they felt confident to take up leadership. From what I have read about him, I greatly respect him. However, I feel that we often do exactly what he spoke out against and hoped people would never do, and that was to idolise him. As long as we keep saying to each other how great he was and quoting him, we disempower the people who are alive today by not giving them the space, or resources, to fully take on this life lived for others.

I am not committed to the organisation *Initiatives of Change*; I am committed to every person I meet finding an inner-freedom and peace with their creator, feeling that they are fully self-expressed, living to their full potential every moment of every day in alignment with who they were created to be. I am using Initiatives of Change to do that. Every now and again I get a glimpse of what it is really about. I have received so much and have lived a very rich and happy life so far, but the quote that haunts me when I wake is 'From whom much has been given, much is expected'. It is this that keeps me working for this organisation and keeps me passionate about serving and giving as much as I can to others.

As I journey day to day I struggle over keeping to the four moral standards and quiet time as much as anyone else, but now I have the power to discuss it openly and share my thoughts with a global family. Learning more about who Frank Buchman was inspires me to know that there is an alternative way to live, other than the materialistic realm of loneliness I had lived in so much of the time. He makes me want to become a person of true integrity and leadership, qualities which I have so often lacked. And more importantly he gives me the courage to share my darkest secrets with the people I love most, helping me to experience true vulnerability in community. However, I know that Buchman did not do this just for me; it was what he stood for in his life that gave me all this – that is, the love for God and the authenticity of people.

This was his true power and that will remain in this world always even though it may change form and will continue no doubt to change name. I have no interest in getting people involved in Initiatives of Change; rather my interest is to get them involved in living life to the full, being mentored by someone and mentoring someone else. That is what Frank Buchman lived for, and it is what I live for as well.

* * * * *

Buchman's Unseen Impact
by Bhavesh S Patel

Bhavesh Patel graduated from Leicester University, and works in the area of people and organisational development, with a special interest in coaching and Open Space technology

I BELIEVE that MRA – the idea, the movement, the organisation – had one of the greatest effects on the thinking and living of the last century. A big statement to make, and I will not attempt to justify why I think that here. I met MRA in 1997 and wanted to know more about its roots and so read a lot of the early books and spoke to a lot of older people. MRA shows the huge impact that one person's life can have on other lives, and the world around them. Multiply that by the number of people who were deeply touched by MRA in the last century in all sectors of society, politics, and industry, and you start to get an idea of the unseen impact of Buchman's life work. Meaningful plays travelled the world, often hosted by governments, and the casts were usually from many countries, well before 'intercultural dialogue' had even been coined!

However my interest is not in looking back, but as a young person looking forward. I believe MRA, now IofC, could have a crucial role to play in this century, too. Buchman always tried to use the language of the day to get his ideas to the masses. His speech entitled 'The Electronics of the Spirit' given at Mackinac Island in May 1955 is a clear example of this. In America, transistor radios and the first pocket tape recorder were the topics of the *Popular Electronics* magazine (April 1955). Buchman, a friend of Thomas Edison, was using this language to communicate ideas about the spiritual life – wow!

Presently IofC's greatest challenge is to find the language of today, so that Buchman's crucial ideas can have a voice in this century. The world is already full of lots of excellent approaches to Remaking the World (Buchman's vision, and the title of his collection of speeches). Some of these methods have deep spiritual roots and, I imagine, would have inspired Buchman to use them now. However, IofC finds it difficult to recognise these methods because we are still trying to 'remake the world' with the ways of the last century. The biggest challenge is fear, fear of letting go of the old and trying the new. The fundamental ideas do not change, but everything else needs to. T S Eliot wrote: 'For last year's words belong to last year's language, and next year's words await another voice.'

I am finding that Buchman's ideas are alive and active in many of the new methods and thinking of how we effect change in this century. I believe many of these methods may even have roots in the work Buchman pioneered almost 100 years ago. My hope is that IofC can find its way out of its fears to fulfil its mission in this century. The simple idea of a change of heart through listening to that voice inside is as powerful today as it was then. Our direction can come from inner leading as well as outer events. Buchman's firm belief was that the person who has just had a change of heart probably knew more about MRA than him. Buchman believed the next generation had more to offer than the previous one, that MRA wasn't a fixed idea, or something you were 'in'. I leave the final word to Buchman: 'Conferences on the current pattern will never solve the problems and needs of people and nations. That can only come from heart speaking to heart.' – from 'For All Men Everywhere' speech, 1954.

* * * * *

What's your Story?
by Joanna Margueritte

A first-year MBA student, Joanna Margueritte is also a passionate portrait photographer. Originally from Poland, she lives in Paris, and travels the world as often as possible with her camera.

THE Persian King Shahryar decides, once his wife's infidelity has been brought to light, to declare all women unfaithful as a rule. Every other day, he takes a new wife and kills her. Finally, there aren't any virgins left to serve as one-day brides for the king except Scheherazade, the vizier's daughter. She herself suggests becoming the next wife; and against her father's will does take on this perilous role.

In order not to be executed the morning after her wedding night, Scheherazade leaves the King desperately needing her to keep on living at least a couple more hours: she tells him stories and interrupts them at the most crucial moments, thus buying time for herself. She proceeds to tell stories within stories, and still more…

The art of telling stories is as old as humanity; it stems from the need to explain natural phenomena, to communicate experiences to others, the desire for sustaining continuity and tradition across generations within a given community. There is no culture devoid of stories: founding stories and stories of heroes, anecdotes and fables shared are listened to decade after decade. It isn't difficult to see how stories, radically different from the novel which is associated to a written form, tend to create appropriate conditions for bonding, through the sharing of personal experience, in order to create a sense of community.

Hannah Arendt remarks in her *Men in Dark Times* (1968) that storytelling 'reveals meaning without committing the error of defining it'. This is what allows for the sharing of 'a sense of meaning' apart from the actual 'moral' of the story; the meaning remains in the minds of the listeners and transforms them in a certain way, so that they too may want to tell the same story to others. A story is thus an essentially intangible object destined to be shared by members of a given community; be it a family, a township, or an entire world.

Unfortunately, something had happened to storytelling in the First World War which, it seemed, could not be reversed: all of a sudden trying to build community through speech was perceived as utterly absurd. One need only read such works as *Voyage au bout de la nuit* (1932) by Céline to understand this situation. Throughout the novel, stories are told without any logical conclusion, certainly with no wisdom whatsoever for younger generations to learn. In the opening sentence, Bardamu, the main character and narrator, tells us: 'It began like this. Me, I never said anything. Nothing. It was Arthur

Ganate who made me talk.' [1] Not only does this sentence indicate that the storyteller himself fulfills his role half-heartedly at the least, but also it introduces a character, Arthur, who isn't mentioned even once in any of the subsequent five hundred pages.

Only a few years after the publication of the *Voyage* by Céline, Walter Benjamin explains this downfall of storytelling in his essay entitled 'The Storyteller'. Unsurprisingly, he blames the sudden decline in storytelling practice on the collective experience of World War 1:

> *'With the [First] World War a process began to become apparent which has not halted since then. Was it not noticeable at the end of the war that men returned from the battlefield grown silent—not richer, but poorer in communicable experience?*[2] *If we accept the notion that storytelling draws from the basic human need to explain reality, no wonder there was less enthusiasm about it in 1919. How could one hope to explain anything in a world where human technology driven by human greed changed everything except the clouds in the sky?'*

With the horror of the Second World War, storytelling received yet another, stronger blow, and was utterly discredited as a means of communicating wisdom or experience, of creating community, not because its method was disavowed, but because no one any longer believed in the possibility of sharing values. The era of relativism

1. French : Ça a débuté comme ça. Moi, j'avais jamais rien dit. Rien. C'est Arthur Ganate qui m'a fait parler.

2. Walter Benjamin, 'The Storyteller: Reflections on the Works of Nikolai Leskov', II, 1936

had begun. Benjamin, still in his 1936 essay, prophesies the death of storytelling in the twentieth century: '... the communicability of experience is decreasing. In consequence we have no counsel either for ourselves or for others. After all, counsel is less an answer to a question than a proposal concerning the continuation of a story which is just unfolding ... Counsel woven into the fabric of real life is wisdom. The art of storytelling is reaching its end because the epic side of truth, wisdom, is dying out'.[3]

Wisdom was dying out because relativity was settling in. As Paul Johnson remarks in his *History of the Modern World*, 'At the beginning of the 1920s, the belief began to circulate, for the first time at a popular level, that there were no longer any absolutes: of time and space, of good and evil, of knowledge, above all of value'.[4]

Thus, in 1962, when Hannah Arendt recounted listening to Isak Dinesen (Karen Blixen) in New York City, although the fascination with remarkable storytelling talent and 'sense of meaning' conveyed is still present, there is no longer any question of meaning or moral experience. The pleasure received by listeners is of a purely aesthetic nature. Arendt remarks about an aging Dinesen: 'She came, very very old, terribly fragile, beautifully dressed; she was led to a kind of Renaissance chair, given some wine, and then, without a shred of paper, she began to tell stories [from Out of Africa], almost word for word as they exist in print. The audience, all very young people, was overwhelmed.... She was like an

3. op. *cit.*, IV

4. Quoted by Garth Lean in *Frank Buchman: A Life*; Paul Johnson, *A History of the Modern World from 1917 to the 1980s* (Weidenfeld and Nicolson, 1983), p. 4.

apparition from god knows where or when. And even more convincing than in print. Also: a great lady'.[5]

And yet, one person more than any other in the twentieth century did revive the tradition of storytelling in its original form and purpose: communicating transformed lives in order to transform the lives of the listeners. Frank Buchman mastered it throughout his long involvement in the work of Moral Re-Armament. Even before founding the movement in 1938, Buchman used storytelling in his everyday work, in Pennsylvania State College where he worked as YMCA Secretary, as well as in all his travels.

As Garth Lean points out through the words of one of Buchman's students, Edward Perry: 'His [Buchman's] lectures were totally unlike any others in that sedate institution [Hartford]. Mostly they consisted of stories of people whose lives had been changed by God's power working through him. It was fascinating, up-to-date, real...His picture of a real ministry was not a matter of eloquent sermons and well-organized parish activities, but of meeting people's deepest needs one by one . . .'[6]

In 1924, when invited to a house-party at Baron van Heeckeren's home, Buchman was expected to make a speech. Instead, here's what happened: 'Actually, Buchman gave no formal address. Sitting down in the drawing room, 'among many question marks, some exclamation marks, many curious, others prepared to be bored,' records Albertina, he said, 'I think I'll tell you a story . . . ', which he proceeded to do. Other stories of changed lives followed, and as the evening wore on he remarked cheer-

5. Lynn Wilkinson, 'Hannah Arendt on Isak Dinesen: Between Storytelling and Theory', *Comparative Literature*, Winter 2004

6. Garth Lean, op. *cit.*, Chapter 9 'Resign, Resign!'

fully, "I can see the walls coming down."'

When Buchman met with Iranian prime minister Mossadegh, the latter was impressed by the simplicity with which he was capable of making an impact on people's moral actions. Buchman replied that he was only doing 'simple things', but that was exactly what the world needed.[7] Indeed, perhaps the efficiency of Buchman's life-changing stories, some taken from his own life, some from the lives of others, some from the Bible, stemmed from his humble capacity of performing a simple art which relied on moral determination rather than relativity.

The art of storytelling as a means of changing lives was and is preserved thanks to Buchman and his teaching of a simple truth: everybody has a story to tell, one which does contain definite meaning, and perhaps even a little bit of wisdom. In recent years, Initiatives of Change programmes such as the Hope in the Cities programme have relied heavily on storytelling as a means of healing unspoken divides between people of different races, cultures, or historical traumas.

Dr David Campt, former adviser to President Clinton on race issues and architect of the Connecting Communities Fellowship Program, spoke about the intrinsic connection between storytelling and trust: 'It's easy to talk about lack of trust out in society. Analysis is important. But we need to ask among those who are change agents, how much do we trust each other? Where do we as change agents need to do intentional work? ... We tell our stories to invite others into a circle of trust where barriers can be broken down and real change can occur.'[8] At the

7. Garth Lean, op. *cit*., Chapter 36 'Buchman Ki Jai!'

8. Hope in the Cities News, 06/28/2007

conference centre in Caux, Dr Campt led several workshops on the techniques of good personal storytelling, which were strikingly popular, because they made participants feel empowered to share what was already waiting within them.

We could simply end here and thank Fate for having given us Buchman, who amongst all the other good brought us this gift of preserving and cultivating the art of personal storytelling, which anyone will tell you is the main advantage of staying at Caux. However, remember that storytelling is a tool, a certain method, a rhetorical procedure, and like any rhetorical means it can be, and is, used towards very different goals. In the last few years, sharp criticism of storytelling has developed. For example, the new book by Christian Salmon, *Storytelling: The soul-formatting and story-fabricating machine*[9], denounces the widespread use of storytelling in marketing as well as politics. According to him, this method enables decision-makers to blind listeners with stories which engage their emotional comprehension, give them the now famous 'sense of meaning' and obstruct actual thinking. Listeners forget that they have not heard what they have come to demand, i.e. clear and honest opinions or information about a given subject pertaining to daily life or social organisation, and delight in a well-told story.

In particular, Salmon quotes Ira Chernus' article[10] describing Karl Rove's 'Scheherazade's strategy': 'Rove is telling Republican candidates to follow Scheherazade's

9. Christian Salmon, *Storytelling : la machine a fabriquer des histoires et à formater les esprits*, 2007

10. Ira Chernus, 'Karl Rove's Scheherezade Strategy', in Tom Dispatch, 07/08/2006

rule: When policy dooms you, start telling stories – stories so fabulous, so gripping, so spellbinding that the king (or, in this case, the American citizen who theoretically rules our country) forgets all about a lethal policy.' Stories are seen and denounced as a means of diverting listeners from the heart of the matter by luring them into an emotionally engaging narrative. How's that for spin?

We must not allow Frank Buchman's legacy to go to waste because of a surge in this cynical usage of storytelling as a means of simply captivating the imagination and the emotions so as to freeze the action of the brain. What is at stake is a complete disqualification of storytelling as such, simply because it can potentially be used for purely selfish ends. We cannot continue changing lives if we don't commit to building stories well, and listening to those of others, in complete awareness of the beauty as well as the responsibility and importance of this age-old human pastime.

* * * * *

My vision for Korea and my generation
by Yeon Yuk Jeong

Yeon Yuk Jeong and his wife, Joung-Suk, from South Korea have been working full-time with IofC since 1996. He is a civil engineer by profession and committed to building bridges between people, nations and cultures. They with their friends are running the 'Hurb Community Centre' in Seoul for training others and together providing a force for changing their nation.

KOREA has been divided into North and South for the last sixty years. We still share a common language and culture even though fundamental differences have arisen since the division. The division on the peninsula came soon after the end of the Japanese colonisation of 36 years. During the Japanese occupation Korea and the Korean people suffered along with the land since the Japanese used Korea as a base for their war preparations. I believe however that the Korean peninsula one day will become reunified politically and economically. There may be some roles that Initiatives of Change can take in this. But the real task of IofC is in aiding and opening the way for a true unification between people of the North and the South. It may take another sixty or more years to really become one.

There is a saying that the people who have suffered the most have the most to give. Korea should become a bridge-builder in Asia, overcoming her own bitterness and sorrow of the past.

Meeting and sharing with friends helps me find some common insight into their lives. Most are very busy and exhausted by long working hours. And they are all worried about buying houses and/or cars, or paying off their mortgages. South Korea has developed rapidly since the Korean War in the 1950s and Koreans as a people are quite well-to-do. But her people feel empty inside and lost. Materialism has stretched across society and we are suffering from 'poverty of the spirit', as Mother Teresa once said. IofC has an answer to this through listening to the still, small voice in our hearts, changing our lives in a positive response to absolute moral standards and following the directions or leadings which come in a time of quiet. I want to see Korea governed by people who are governed by God or by their conscience. Conscience needs to be in action!

* * * * *

Buchman's challenge – can I handle it?

by Ann Njeri

Ann Njeri, from Kenya, holds a diploma in Information Technology. She took part in a six-month internship programme at the IofC Asia Plateau centre in India last year. She is currently working full time with IofC Kenya.

'I WILL not turn back, even if you all do...' This commitment by Frank Buchman (made 70 years ago at Visby, Sweden) is a great challenge in my life – and to everyone who wants to be a change activist. As we celebrate his life and the movement he started, I can't avoid asking myself the question: Do I have what it takes to make a commitment, a decision, to stand and fight for what's right in my society, my country – no matter what challenges I face?

Living in a society that every other minute asks for a compromise in one way or another, can I stand strong and overcome the power of the 'compromise corner' which to me is the beginning of failure; leading to selfish ambitions which have seen my country and the world fall into the thorny situations they are in? My answer to my question is that it is possible... but, the commitment has a price-tag attached – getting out of my comfort zone and learning how to think and act beyond myself!

I think of the post-election violence in my country which has left lives of millions turned upside down... all in the name of power and tribal hate which, if not solved, will continue to re-surface whenever an opportunity arises. At this point my fingers all point at our leaders for failing us, for being selfish and using hate to achieve their goals. But when I face reality, the leaders never fought; we the ordinary people dehumanized and victimized ourselves by demanding to know 'which tribe do you come from?'!

On this, just like Buchman did, I see the importance of realising that we the common people have been wrong. We must stop blaming it all on our leaders, because we accepted to be actors in their disgusting scripts. I am a victim of tribal hate, and part of a very big population of young people swimming in the same ocean of tribalism. I was personally taught to feel superior over the other tribes and specifically to hate one in particular. I know what tribalism can do; I have seen what it has done to dear Kenyan friends. I dream of a Kenya free of tribalism. This can only be built through developing trust. In my opinion, trust will be realised when individuals at the grassroots, as well as diplomats, accept their wrongs and failures and take the not very easy, but very crucial, step of apologising and forgiving.

I know that it has to start with me; fighting my own tribal monster. I have taken the first step; I have been asking my friends from the rival tribe to forgive me for my resentments and prejudices towards them and for being a perpetrator of hate. This has now given me a sense of inner freedom. I am also requesting people from my tribe to forgive, to ask for forgiveness and to respect the other tribes equally. Young people are the greatest target, they hold the future of our country – their decisions will determine what shape the next generation will take. My plea to them is 'Can we break the chains of hatred passed to us by our parents and people close to us?' After all, who chooses to be born in what tribe or region?

I have consciously taken on Buchman's challenge and have made a decision that 'no matter what, I will not turn back, even if everyone else does! I will be part of the healing and solution in my country and the world . . . I will let God guide my life: not my will . . . but His.'

19

Reconciliation comes from Change

by Pierre Spoerri

FRANK Buchman never wrote an essay or a study on reconciliation or conflict resolution. The one and only book written in his name never made the bestseller list or earned him scientific awards. Neither Buchman's speeches, published under the title *Remaking the World*,[1] nor the films of him, nor even the books about him, ever quite encompassed his whole personality.

My father, Theophil Spoerri,[2] who accompanied him to many countries, worked for twenty years on a biography of Buchman which he called *Dynamic out of Silence*.[3] He re-wrote it seven times. I remember him saying in the evenings after having been writing all day: 'This is the best thing I have ever written'. And next morning, after re-reading his manuscript he would just shake his head and start all over again, as he found it so difficult to capture the essence of Buchman's life and thinking. In his speeches, the word reconciliation seldom appears. Yet he was one of the great reconcilers of the 20th century. And it was he who the down-to-earth French foreign minister Robert Schuman asked to go to North Africa when some of the former French colonies were going through their fight for independence. And for his bridge-building and reconciliation work Buchman was decorated by the German, French, Japanese and Philippine governments.

So what was his secret, his basic philosophy, his method, especially in the field of reconciliation? How did this philosophy evolve in the course of his life?

There is no doubt that during his early years Buchman was more interested in personal salvation than in political issues. His first and foremost aim then was to help the individual to face his past, make restitution where needed and be reconciled with God. After working in North America and Europe he was sent to Asia and visited India, China, Japan and Korea. It was during this time that his interest grew beyond the strictly personal to the national and international. These nations became then for him a 'proving ground of the power to turn nations Godwards.'[4]

In the thirties, the challenge of a re-arming and aggressive Germany brought him face to face with the need of the democracies surrounding Germany to be united inside and reconciled with each other. At the time of his first visit to Norway, a dispute over Greenland fishing rights was poisoning relations between Denmark and Norway and had just come before the Permanent Court of International Justice in The Hague. The Court decided in favour of Denmark. This decision angered one of Norway's leading journalists, Fredrik Ramm, whose intense hatred of the Danes was daily reflected in his columns. Ramm went to Buchman's first conference in Norway in 1934. Buchman's concept of personal change leading to national change caused him to review his whole life.

A few days after the end of the conference he said: 'The ice melted in my heart, and a new unknown feeling began to grow, a love of people unfettered by what they could give me.' Shortly afterwards he was addressing a mass meeting in Odense in Denmark. He simply described what had happened to him and ended by asking the audience to stand and join him in singing the Danish national anthem. The audience rose and spontaneously started singing the Norwegian national anthem. Hearing this story, one can ask the question: Did Buchman know of the conflict between Denmark and Norway and did he encourage Ramm to do what he did? Or was he just deeply convinced that men and women who put their life in order would become natural reconcilers between individuals and nations? We shall never know the answer to this question.[5]

A little later a similar experience, what I would call miracle of reconciliation, happened a bit further south of Scandinavia between the Netherlands and Belgium. In this case, there had been a seventy-year-old river conflict between the ports of Antwerp in Belgium and Rotterdam in Holland. The World Court decided in favour of Belgium. The delight of Belgian leaders and the Belgian press got understandably on the nerves of the Dutch, not least of the Dutch ambassador to Brussels, J A E Patijn. He was due to speak at a banquet in Brussels and had prepared some bitter retort to the statements in the press. As he was dressing for dinner, some inner conviction grew in him saying: 'Forget your pride. This is your chance. Seize it'. To everyone's astonishment he complimented his host country on the court decision, which, he said, paved the way for better friendship in the future. The next day, the Belgian press had changed its tune, and the Dutch press followed suit.[6] The following year, Patijn was made foreign minister.

When Buchman tells this story in one of his speeches,

he does not mention Patijn's name and of course does not speak about the various touches he had had with the man during his many visits to Holland. Again, one can ask oneself whether Buchman knew of the conflict and actively helped the Dutch statesman to follow the road of reconciliation, or whether he just encouraged him to listen to his inner voice. And in a way, that does not matter. To a Swiss professor who encouraged him to be more – what we would say today – pro-active in trying to bring change to the German leadership, he wrote: 'Our aim is never to mediate, but to change lives and unite them by making them life-changers . . . '[7] I shall return to this fundamental element of Buchman's thinking when I try to formulate his principles for reconciliation. In the speeches of these years, Buchman did not often use the word reconciliation, even if the preservation of peace was never far from his mind. When he visited Switzerland in 1935, he said: 'I can see Switzerland a prophet among the nations and a peacemaker in the international family. . . . Nationalism can unite a country. Supernationalism can unite a world. God-controlled supernationalism is the only sure foundation for world peace.'[8]

And then, after World War II, when the doors to Mountain House were opened and representatives of the nations who had fought against each other met at the first meetings of this kind after the end of hostilities, the need for reconciliation was obvious to everybody. So during the years 1946 to 1950, the emphasis was clearly on the material and spiritual reconstruction of Europe and especially on German-French reconciliation. In one of his speeches of that period, Buchman said: 'Ideas quick and powerful to reconcile nations, to conquer all hearts and wills, to inspire a world-wide renaissance, are instantly available, immediately applicable.'[9] During that period, Robert Schuman, the French Foreign Minister and initiator of the Schuman Plan which led to the European Union, wrote in his foreword for the French edition of Buchman's speeches: 'To provide teams of trained men, ready for the service of the state, apostles of reconciliation and builders of a new world, that is the beginning of a far-reaching transformation of society in which, during fifteen war-ravaged years, the first steps have already been made.'[10]

Then, at the beginning of the fifties, Asia became the centre of Buchman's attention. And what had happened between Germany and her neighbours started to happen in the relationship between Japan and her former enemies.

Now we need to come back to Buchman's thinking, motivation and vision: If we want to get the essence of his philosophy of reconciliation, what were his basic principles?

The first, without any doubt, was the **centrality of the individual**. Buchman was convinced that in every situation there was one person holding the key. Sometimes it was a leading politician, sometimes an ordinary person with extraordinary ideas. He said once, looking from Caux to Geneva at the other end of the lake: 'Some of the real problems at the conferences down there are not on the table; they are sitting right around the table.' The President of the Norwegian Parliament in the thirties, the Hon C J Hambro, when he introduced Buchman and his team to delegates of the League of Nations on 15 September 1938, said: 'Where we have failed in changing politics, they have succeeded in changing lives, and giving men and women a new way of living.'[11] For Buchman, the material to work with, if peace was to be achieved, was human nature and the forces of hate, greed and fear which were dominating. And where human nature was concerned, he was the greatest realist I ever met.

The second principle – possibly a bit more controversial than the first – was that the peace-maker or reconciler had to **start the process of peace-making and reconciliation with him or her self**. In Geneva, in the middle of the crisis of 1938, he again addressed delegates to the League of Nations and said to them: 'The great people of history are those who can articulate and translate into action the answer to war, the people who will confess their own shortcomings instead of spotlighting those of others.'[12]

His own deeply-held conviction was that one's own experience was an essential element in helping people loaded down with hatred, resentment or traditional enmity to become free men and women. All his life he looked back to his own formative experience. At the beginning of the century, in his first job as head of a home for underprivileged boys, he had come up against the men on the Board of his institution who had tried to save money at the expense of food for the boys. Buchman's experience of being freed of his bitterness made him feel that this was something that could happen to every person everywhere. So in a way he preferred the word change to the word reconciliation. For him, reconciliation was more the fruit than the root.

The third principle is that **those who have suffered most may have most to give**. In the immediate post-war years, when Buchman was invited to send his first teams to Germany, two Frenchmen were often asked to speak. Both were French of Jewish origin who had lost a great number of their relatives in Nazi extermination-camps. The fact that they had been able to free themselves of all hatred and that they had come especially to Germany to share their experience had a profound effect on the traumatised post-war Germans.

In contrast, as a Swiss I sometimes felt in the time after the second World War, and still feel today, that prosperity and our having lived in peace for so long are certainly a gift but also a definite handicap when it comes to peace-making. The capacity for compassion does not grow easily in soil like ours. Also the fear of losing what one has – especially if one has acquired it by hard work – can make one hard and self-centred. So we Swiss, who as a small neutral people have been considered by many as 'natural peace-makers', seem to have handicaps which are not always realised – by ourselves or by others.

The fourth principle was the one that sometimes got Buchman into trouble. He believed, and believed it deeply, that **no person should ever be written off.** The most hopeless case could be the biggest miracle; you must hate the sin but love the sinner. For him, even dictators, terrorists or extremists of the left or the right had to be given the chance to change. In the thirties Buchman got into difficulties when he applied this principle to the German situation and tried to bring an experience of change to some of the leadership of the Nazi Party. It is easy to say sixty years later: he failed. It is even easy to say that Buchman might have been naive. But he did make the attempt while so many others stood on the side-lines and did nothing.

An interesting test of the same principle came when the conference centre of Caux was opened after the Second World War. Friends of Buchman suggested he invite a leading but somewhat controversial personality from a country which had been involved in the war to take part in one of the first international conferences organised in the new centre. The government in Berne refused to give this person a visa. Buchman turned to the legal adviser to the Swiss government, Professor Max Huber, who had been head of the International Red Cross and of the International Court of The Hague. Huber, who happened to be on holiday, wrote by hand a four-page memorandum describing it as a constitutional duty for Switzerland to receive people who might be capable of going through an experience of change in their lives and through it helping in the process of reconstruction of their countries. As a result of this move, the Swiss government reversed its decision and has ever since granted visas to the people suggested for the Caux conferences. Until recently, all those going to Caux also received their Swiss visa free of charge.

The fifth point may not be so much a principle but a question of faith. Buchman saw in peace-making **not just a humanistic work** that could be planned with human intelligence and organisation. He believed deeply that God could and did intervene in the affairs of man and that all human planning could be superseded by extraordinary events. A person who was recognised later by many leaders in Europe as having been a decisive factor in French-German reconciliation was a French woman called Irène Laure. Her going to Caux as a former resistance-leader and as a person with a deep hatred for Germany and the Germans was not planned by Buchman, as he probably did not know of her existence until she arrived in Mountain House. Buchman's genius may have been that he recognised in this woman what she could become if she were able to face her hatred and let it go. This is not the place to go into the details of her story, but I want to use it as an example to show how often Buchman, who believed in good and detailed human planning, put this aside when a new person through a deep experience of change in his or her life opened new doors and suggested new initiatives.

The *sixth* of Buchman's principles was his belief in the **centrality of the experience of forgiveness.** He saw in the process of repentance, apology, asking for forgiveness and accepting forgiveness a universal truth available to everybody everywhere. Of course as a Christian he could – and often did – draw his inspiration from his study of Christ's life, but he knew from his friends of other faiths that for instance in the Muslim or Jewish faith the way to forgiveness was also something experienced and clearly defined. He also expressed gratitude for what he had learnt at various moments of his life from Hindu and Buddhist tradition.[13]

An integral step on the way to forgiveness was to face the past. If one did not face the past it would run you all your life. Often the door to a new future would open when a person would tell you something he or she had never told anybody before. So discretion was an essential element in such – what Buchman called – life-changing work. The aim was not just personal repentance, but for many there was a need for national repentance as well. At the same time Buchman often warned against being obsessed by the past. His experience was that those who had been in the wrong were often more helped by being given a vision of what they could become rather than by emphasising their sins time and time again. One of his greatest qualities was his sense of expectancy. He expected the best from everyone and was often rewarded with a positive response. Of course sometimes he was also disappointed but he never let reverses stop him.

Finally, as a seventh principle I would mention **commu-**

nication. It is often rather easy to see who in a conflict situation ought to change and where he or she could become part of a reconciliation process. But how do you transmit the ability to recognise yourself and the will to change? If there is one single issue Buchman grappled with all his life it was this: how do you transmit a vision or an experience to another person and then to another country?

I had the privilege of being one of two hundred people who were invited to travel with Buchman when he accepted the invitation of a prominent group of Indian leaders to visit the Indian sub-continent not very long after India and Pakistan had become independent. The wounds of partition were still fresh, as were the wounds left by colonialism. So it was obvious that a group of people coming from the West would not be received kindly if they just preached what the Indians and the Pakistanis were meant to do. One contentious issue dividing the two countries was the question of water. Was it a conscious decision or did it just happen that Buchman took with him a musical play dealing with two brothers in the western United States who were quarrelling over water? In any case, the message came through to the leaders of the two countries and to thousands of ordinary people as well, and it came through in a way that newly independent nations could accept.

* * * * *

I would like to end with a quote in which the essence of Buchman's philosophy is best summarised. In a speech with the title 'The answer to any Ism – even Materialism' he said:

> *Division is the mark of our age. Division in the heart. Division in the home. Division in industry. Division*

in the nation. Division between nations.

Union is our instant need.

Division is the work of human pride, hate, lust, fear, greed.

Division is the trademark of materialism.

Union is the grace of rebirth. We have lost the art of uniting because we have forgotten the secret of change and rebirth.[14]

Buchman would have been the last person to say that his experience and his principles were the final truth. If he were still living today, he would encourage all to continue their search to discover new truths about reconciliation and to walk on this road with courage and hope.

* * * * *

Notes:

1) Frank Buchman, *Remaking the World* (Blandford Press, London 1947, 1958)

2) Theophil Spoerri, professor of French and Italian Literature at Zurich University, Rector of the University from 1948 to 1950.

3) Theophil Spoerri, *Dynamic out of Silence* (published first in German: *Dynamik aus der Stille*, Caux Verlag, Luzern 1971)

4) see Michael Henderson, *The Forgiveness Factor – Stories of Hope in a World of Conflict*, (Grosvenor Books, USA and London 1996), p. 260.

5) Garth Lean, *Frank Buchman – a Life* (Collins Fount Paperbacks, London 1988) pp.224/5.

6) ibid, pp. 274/5.

7) Letter from Frank Buchman to Emil Brunner, 23.12.33.

8) Frank Buchman, *Remaking the World* p.18.

9) ibid, p. 241.

10) Robert Schuman, Foreword for the French edition of *Remaking the World.*

11) ibid, p. 68.

12) Frank Buchman, in his speech 'One thing can swing the balance', 15.9.38, p.69.

13) ibid, pp. 166/7.

14) ibid, p. 166.

Index